MAN
RAISES
BOY

ROB STURROCK

MAN RAISES BOY

A revolutionary approach for fathers who
want to raise kind, confident and happy sons

ALLEN&UNWIN
SYDNEY•MELBOURNE•AUCKLAND•LONDON

First published in 2020

Allen & Unwin
83 Alexander Street
Crows Nest NSW 2065
Australia
Phone: (61 2) 8425 0100
Email: info@allenandunwin.com
Web: www.allenandunwin.com

A catalogue record for this
book is available from the
National Library of Australia

ISBN 978 1 76087 521 3

Internal design by Kate Barraclough
Index by Puddingburn Publishing Services Pty Ltd
Set in 12.5/17.5 pt Adobe Garamond Pro by Midland Typesetters, Australia
Printed and bound in Australia by Griffin Press, part of Ovato

10 9 8 7 6 5 4 3 2 1

The paper in this book is FSC® certified.
FSC® promotes environmentally responsible,
socially beneficial and economically viable
management of the world's forests.

This book is dedicated to Julia, Aila and Luke,
the three loves of my life.

CONTENTS

PROLOGUE

This book was forged in the fires of early fatherhood. Honestly, I'm still not quite sure how it came to be.

My wife, Julia, and I had our daughter, Aila, in 2016. Like a lot of dads, as I got immersed in our new life of being parents I started reading about the experience of other parents. Except I couldn't really find the voices of dads. The more I read, the more I felt that parental blogging and journalism was designed predominately for an audience of mums. What was also obvious was that they targeted mums because they, overwhelmingly, were the main carers for young children. In all this literature, dads were considered the support act, working hard during the week but largely absent from home and caring responsibilities. The fact that respected parenting books still had sections about why dads matter in parenting was a demonstration of this reality.

Not only was there so little written *about* dads, there was even less written *by* dads. I thought adding my own voice, and my experiences in the very early days of fatherhood, might be valuable. Julia and I had both taken extensive leave from work during the first year of Aila's life to take care of her. And I had consciously decided to switch from full-time to part-time work so I could also take care of her midweek. I thought relaying my experiences might be a signal, however faint, to other fathers that a different work/life approach for dads was possible.

I began writing short pieces about what it was like to expect a child, to take time off work to care for a baby, what I had learnt so far as a dad, and my views on what men are truly capable of in fatherhood. Sites like *Mamamia* and *Women's Agenda* published them, and while they didn't go viral, there was a decent amount of interest in what I was saying. Writing these pieces gradually led to the opportunity to do some media to talk about them. Within the space of a year I was asked to go on the ABC's *Weekend Breakfast*, Channel Nine's *The Today Show*, *Weekend Sunrise*, *The Project* and ABC Radio National to talk about my experiences of fatherhood, plus I attended a couple of forums about parents taking leave from work to care for their kids. Occasionally someone would even offer to pay for me to write a piece, but mostly I wrote because I loved the subject and thought it was important to expand the public discussion on the role of fathers in raising kids. Just what the world needed, right? Another person's opinions on universal experiences!

Somewhere during all this I had a meeting with a publisher, courtesy of a lovely friend of mine, an accomplished author and fine editor in her own right. Over a coffee and a sandwich in a bustling and noisy Sydney CBD cafe, we started by discussing how there had been an explosion in literature that aimed to empower and embolden young girls. Books of all shapes and sizes were being pumped out to a hungry audience of parents who wanted their young girls to know that the world and its future belonged as much to them as to the other sex. I certainly had my copy of *Good Night Stories for Rebel Girls* well before Aila was born, and tried reading her the profiles of heroines throughout the ages before she could even focus on pop-ups. Movies like *Frozen* and *Brave* and TV shows like *Dot* and *Nella the Princess Knight* were worldwide hits. There was a core message at the heart of these stories: young girls can be as capable, heroic, strong, courageous, intelligent, intrepid and entrepreneurial as any boy, and they can be anything they want when they grow up. This was music to my ears.

But what were we telling our young boys? Were we encouraging them in the same way to be truly free to be whatever they wanted to be? Or were we reaffirming the same old notions of manhood, based on a narrow set of character traits and career choices? How could beautiful young boys grow into confident, happy men if they weren't just as free to blaze their own unique trail?

If boys were to be set free, I came to see, there was one player required who had been missing for too long: dad. Dads are the first person through whom boys understand masculinity. If the attitudes of boys to their future were to be transformed, dads would have an enormously influential role in how successful and positive that transformation would be. Even if they themselves had been trapped by social or family pressure into a typecast male breadwinner role, dads could break the mould with their sons. But the stats showed that fathers did little direct caring for children during the week, and often didn't back themselves to do it as well as mum. Dads' work behaviours barely shift once they have kids, and a lot of men still think their best contribution to parenting is providing financial security. As critical as that is, it's far from the only thing dads are capable of.

With that, I suddenly had my first book deal. Excitement, nerves and terror followed quickly. The idea of writing a book was a dream in my life, but at that stage only a dream. But opportunity comes knocking when it wants, not when it's convenient. As incredible as this book deal was, it had come at a profoundly challenging time in my life. There were a hundred reasons why it was the wrong time to write it. I had a two-and-a-half-year-old daughter, my wife was about seven months pregnant with our son, and was fighting a hard, horrible, draining battle with perinatal depression. I was doing whatever I could at home to share that awful burden with her, to support and care for her and to get her to see the light at the end of what had been a long, dark tunnel. It was exhausting both of us. I had a relatively new job working part-time in the community sector, and we had only recently moved into a new house and started Aila at a new daycare. On top of that, Julia had family from America staying with us for several months during summer. I didn't really know how this writing journey would play out, but I knew it would be incredibly hard.

I talked to some friends in publishing for advice on how to best write my book, given the pressure-cooker environment I was in. The key messages were: have a clear plan, have a weekly or monthly word target, have a consistent routine and schedule time to write regularly. In the end, I followed next to none of this advice. It wasn't that I didn't want to. I simply couldn't. Perhaps a more A-type personality would have willed the unpredictable nature of my life into order, and forged a fixed, clear space in which to write. Just like with those troublesome sex-changing dinosaurs in *Jurassic Park*, life kept getting in the way for me.

In the months available before our boy was born, I made a frantic and frenetic start on the book. Whenever I could, I got up at 4.30 a.m. to work for a couple of hours before Aila woke up. The fear I felt looking at a blank page, at the start of my first book, lit a fire under my arse. I took the laptop to bed to write at night when I could, no matter how shattered and mentally weary I was after a day of everything-else-in-life. I scrambled a decent start, and slowly my self-belief that I might actually pull this off started to rise. Then, on 16 October 2018, Julia was induced at the hospital to have our son, Luke. It was a hard and scary labour, which included an epidural that was incorrectly applied; Julia lost consciousness at one stage, and spent all day fighting very low blood pressure. I never want to see her go through that again. With some turbulence, our gorgeous little boy was born that evening. He came out looking like a tired, cranky, red-faced smurf who had been rudely woken from a long sleep.

Within days, our lives collapsed. It was a glorious Sunday morning in spring. Some close friends had just visited to meet Luke, and share coffee and croissants with us. Aila was merrily dancing around the lounge room, living her best life. I was happily cuddling my boy on the couch, when I looked down and saw that he was completely blue. I held him up—he seemed lifeless. He was only four days old. He'd been home for just 24 hours. That moment, and that feeling of dread, panic and sickness, is something I will never forget.

I passed Luke to Julia and rushed outside to call triple zero. I had to hold on to a deck chair because my legs were so weak. My lungs and stomach were tight and airless as I gasped into the phone. An ambulance came and checked him. He was alive, breathing very shallowly, but not in a good way. Luke and Julia were taken to the emergency ward at Sydney's Royal North Shore Hospital. And the most stressful 36 hours of our lives began.

My mum arrived to take care of Aila, and I raced away to join Julia and Luke. All I could feel as I drove to the hospital was guilt. Guilt that I had started writing a book on fathers raising sons before my own son was even born. At that moment, it felt like all that early writing I had done was a brazen act of hubris, daring the universe to intervene. It was irrational, I know, but it was my attempt to feel some of the pain Luke was going through and to take the burden of his crisis.

I arrived at the emergency ward, and saw Luke lying meekly on a table, naked and exposed, with a dozen patches and cords hanging off him, strapped to a dozen machines and monitors. There were several doctors attending to him, and Julia was by his side, hollow and numb, trying to hold it together and remain calm so she could make decisions as they arose. He had stopped breathing several more times since leaving home. This was incredibly serious, about as serious as it gets with a newborn.

Within moments I had to go to the nearest toilet so I could burst into tears. This little boy, who I barely knew, was now fighting for his life. He didn't yet have a favourite blanket, favourite toy or favourite song. He had no preferred way of being soothed or cuddled, and we didn't yet understand his looks and movements. I wondered whether we would get that chance at all.

He was administered every test deemed necessary by the doctors. That included a lumbar spinal test, where they extract fluid from the spinal cord—one of the more painful things someone can have done. The worst part of an already horrible day was holding his tiny hand, crying, watching him groan and moan as a massive needle was pushed into his back. He was defenseless, and I was helpless.

It was all gut-wrenching. Until those tests came back, we would not know whether he had a congenital defect, a major life-threatening virus or something else yet undiagnosed, rare and sinister. Julia was numb. She spent the next four days by his side, experiencing every aching moment with him, unable to retreat to home like me. I had to leave them so I could maintain some semblance of normalcy for Aila. But she already knew something was off, and was sad too.

Broken and despairing, I waited for updates all through that first night away from Julia. Luke was in clear agony, she said. With tubes and cords everywhere, he was unable to even suckle his own hand for comfort. He was naked but for a nappy, and was lying on a table with heat lamps above him. He wasn't allowed to be cuddled or soothed. He couldn't get the love he desperately needed because survival came first. All Julia could do was to sing to him. In her sweet southern American drawl, she serenaded him. It was the lowest I've ever felt in life, surpassing the lowest points of anxiety and depression I've experienced.

With each passing hour, things slowly improved. Test result after test result gave us positive news. I zigzagged back and forth between hospital, home and daycare to take care of Aila. Cognitive deficiencies were gradually ruled out, as were certain other viruses. In the end, Luke was diagnosed with viral meningitis, most likely caught from his sister. In fact, we probably have a photo of the very moment Aila gave it to him, when she first met him and kissed him on the head. For a toddler, this virus is a nasty bug but doesn't do much damage. For a tiny newborn, it is deadly serious.

With huge relief, the whole family was back together by Wednesday. We were beyond grateful for the extraordinary care Luke received from the Neonatal Intensive Care Unit. But our relief at being reunited was mixed with a feeling of being permanently scarred by the trauma of almost watching our boy die in our arms. It sucked the confidence out of our parenting. This incident defined our experience with Luke for the next several months. We took family life carefully, one day at a time, treading on eggshells every day. My irrational guilt about having started the book subsided, but doing any work on it was the furthest thing from my mind. I could barely write short emails updating family and friends on Luke's condition, let alone substantive prose on fatherhood. Our experience had left me raw and without words.

He recovered from his virus, but he remained an unhappy baby for months. We were all miserable as a result. He slept terribly, even by newborn standards. He was constantly in pain, arching his back in discomfort and bursting red in the face, tears streaming down his cheeks. He often seemed to be saying, 'Do something—for fuck's sake!' He spent long hours screaming loudly, day and night. We called all the usual advice hotlines— Tresillian, the Australian Breastfeeding Association, Health Direct Australia—begging for any insights that might help us. The advice, mostly, was to 'ride it out'. There were days when we didn't put Luke down *once* because it was the only way to get him to stay quiet and sleep.

I felt a creeping urgency to get back to the book, but during those first few months of our son's life, I had scarcely a morsel of time to write anything. One day, though, we all woke up and our wailing little boy had become a calm, quiet angel. It was like someone had flicked a switch. Suddenly he was sleeping superbly, and spending most of the day smiling and watching people. And with that change in behaviour, space started to open up for me to write. I started forming something resembling a writing schedule. Then he turned four months old and had the mother of all sleep regressions. He went from being a reliable and low-maintenance sleeper to an anxious, whiny, clingy, unsettled mess, all night long, no matter what we did. Already tired, we became shattered.

Working through the immense fatigue, my challenge for the next several months was to build momentum with my writing, and then keep it from week to week. At first I would get up at 5 a.m. and quietly sneak down to our spare room to write while everyone else slept. But as the kids woke up and came downstairs, my seclusion would end: either they'd tiptoe in to see me or I'd get distracted and go out to see them. Julia then came up with the idea that I should head out the door early to go work somewhere where I couldn't be distracted. I started getting up at 4.15 a.m., dressing quietly in the bathroom, where I'd put all my clothes the night before, and catching the 5 a.m. bus into the city, a black coffee in my hand to get me going. I stumbled across a hotel in the CBD that was quiet and open in the wee hours, and I would huddle at a desk in the corner and write for a couple of hours. It was the closest I came to having a set work pattern for the book.

I'd have a couple of good early mornings, or half-days, and be feeling good about the pace and direction of the book, then some new obstacle would get tossed up—typically another daycare bug lovingly brought home by Aila. Before I knew it, a fortnight or more would drift by without the chance to write, and momentum was lost. This battle was fought back and forth through most of 2019. At points I would feel a surge of confidence, almost glimpsing what the finished product would look like, and on other occasions I was convinced I would be writing this book for the term of my natural life.

This undulating period of immense frustration, across many months, points to something else important about this book— that it is the manifestation of the very thing it explores, the insane juggle of being a working father holding down a job and desperately trying to be as involved at home as possible. I had no nannies or au pairs to take the kids while I wrote. I didn't have a sabbatical from my paid job. I didn't abscond to a cute little beach hut for weeks on end to stare at the ocean and busily type away. I had to fit writing around my family and work life, not the other way around.

When he was painted by Anh Do on *Anh's Brush with Fame*, Tim Minchin described how, while he was writing the musical *Matilda*, a producer told him that all art is an artefact of the time available to create it. Now, this book is not art, but it is certainly a reflection of the time I found to pen it. I stole time where I could, and created it out of thin air if none was available. If there is any value in the issues explored and advice given in the pages that follow, it is largely because it comes from a place of real-world practice. The book is a product of my devotion to my family, and its virtues or shortcomings are a consequence of my family-first, everything-else-second approach, and the scrapping for time that ensued.

Imposter syndrome was rife throughout my writing process. There were many times I worried that I was not contributing anything new or meaningful to the public conversation. There were much-heralded parental experts pumping out child science and psychology, giving parents a manual to follow for raising children. Their works come with the authority that clinical certifications impart, or years in the public eye. I had a lot of regard, too, for others who'd written about their experience of fatherhood. At my more doubtful moments I came back to the hard numbers being produced by the researchers—that although men held overwhelmingly positive, public attitudes to sharing the caring, and taking on more domestic responsibilities, they weren't really shifting their work patterns at all. The number of hours that men directly cared for their kids had increased, but not by much. Their working hours remained very long, and the time spent on domestics was still a limited portion of what working mums were doing. Something is stuck in this country about getting fathers to believe they can be amazing carers.

There's evidence that a younger generation of fathers are bringing a new mindset to balancing work and parenting. However, it is not inevitable that men will end up doing as much caring for children as mums. Such a future will not simply unfold with time and more open attitudes. Instead it must be forged by each of us that want to see it realised. We almost need to go one household, one suburb, one workplace at a time to build a critical mass for major social change.

On top of this, men still seem so unsatisfied with our masculinity and with our relationships with each other. On both sides of my family there are men estranged from one another: grandfathers, fathers, sons, grandsons, uncles and nephews. These relationships often crumble on the road from boyhood to manhood. That road is so poorly lit and poorly signed, and our boys can so easily get waylaid. Suicide is the leading cause of death in men aged fifteen to 44,[1] and men are overwhelmingly the main contributors in domestic violence. I know sad men in my life, old and young. Men who regret the state of their relationships with their children, men who are lonely, men who feel trapped in a life which they feel they can't change. With every year that passes, the laughter shared among my male friends softens and the sorrow strengthens, as the pressures of life mount into our late thirties and forties. Additionally, our boys can easily get the wrong messages about what it means to be a man—and the internet is a whopping great big place to start getting bad information. Boys need active and continuous love, compassion and guidance from the men in their lives, and who better to provide this than dad?

If you went into a bookstore and swung a cat by its tail, you'd soon hit a massive section on parenting that is replete with books by experts and celebrities. There is a book for almost every style of parenting, and every parental problem imaginable. Yet I believe there is value in a book written by a dad who's still in the trenches, who's looking for advice and help, who's reading the same literature, who's struggling with kid-induced sleep deprivation, who's dealing with family dynamics, who's grappling with the same problems as the next guy. This is a book from the front lines of fatherhood, shaped by the daily struggles common to all mums and dads.

I also hope that what is contained in these pages is compelling and relatable to all fathers, because all fathers matter equally. Indeed, modern fatherhood is more incredible, inclusive and beautiful than we really appreciate. The boys in our community are raised by married fathers, single fathers, stepfathers, divorced fathers, fathers who adopted, and men who act as father figures and are cherished just the same. Australian dads encompass all races, sexualities, religions, creeds and classes. If we are to pass on a richer form of masculinity to our sons, then acknowledging that fathers come in a variety of shapes and sizes is a good start. We're only beginning to discover the full story of contemporary

Aussie dads. In coming years I'd really like to see our media tell that story more often. I'd also like to see a greater investment in research that explores the diversity of fatherhood and the unique challenges that different fathers face, rather than simply more examination of the experiences of straight, married guys in the suburbs.

In many ways it would have been easier to write a book that pivoted on my relationship with Aila. I have known her for longer, for one thing. And I have a guilty confession: when Julia and I decided to try for a second child, I really wanted another girl. Parents aren't meant to admit that, but it's true. It took me a long while to get my head around the fact that I'd be raising a daughter and a son, and not two girls.

As I put together the following pages, I was getting to know my son for the first time. Luke has since gone from being a scrunched-up, sick newborn to a small child. The glimmers of his personality are starting to shine through, and they are indeed radiant. He is markedly different from his sister. She is vivacious, unstoppable, loud, adventurous and cheeky to her core. She courts mischief as a way to explore the world and make others laugh. Our little boy has a big, sweet heart and the most magnificent smile. He is gentle, calm, loving and happy. He interacts with the world in a more subdued but more focused way. He adores his sister as the powerhouse of the family, and everything she does is amazing and hilarious all in one, even her tantrums. He is happier to explore things on his own and let the world flow around him, so long as he can show you what he's discovered. He is never happier than when he is close to your beating heart. I'll do everything I can to nurture his sweetness, for as long as I can.

In the end, if the world passes this book by, it will always stand as my love letter to Luke. My hope is that, one day, when he's older and ready, he will pick it up and read it. I hope he will understand the toil that was poured into each page, as I tried to more perfectly love and care for him. If he's proud of me for what I sought to achieve, then what else really matters?

1

A LITTLE HELP?

———

I'm a dad, and I'm looking for answers on how to raise my son, Luke. He's still just a little guy, born in October 2018. It hasn't been the easiest of starts with him. My wife, Julia, experienced some stressful complications during the labour. When he was only four days old he was rushed back to hospital in an ambulance because he'd stopped breathing. His first year was filled with digestive problems, lots of illness and horrendously bad sleep, even by baby standards. But we made it. Julia and I are still here, and our boy is a sweet, happy fella in toddler territory, with his unstoppable four-year-old big sister towering over him.

To the number crunchers at the Australian Bureau of Statistics: we've done our part and had our two kids. No more pregnancies, no third child to outflank and outnumber us at every turn. Nope, we're done. For us, it's just the long and winding road of parenting ahead. I want a roadmap to help us as we go, so the journey is as rewarding as it can be. I want help building a happy, close, affectionate family, whose members enjoy each other's company and, even 30 years later, still share more than just strands of DNA. I want us to end up at Disneyland, not that chaotic, post-apocalyptic desert town from *Mad Max: Fury Road*.

It's certainly not the future I imagined for myself as a young man. If I got in the Doc's DeLorean and went back to 2009 to talk to younger me, loitering at some big, soulless beer barn in the city, he'd be shocked at how my life has unfolded in the ensuing decade. After I got him to actually look at me instead of trying to make eye contact with all the women around us, he would quickly become speechless when I tell him I'm married. ('But I thought we had a pact!') He would break out in a cold sweat when I tell him kids are one of the best things that have happened in my life. At this stage, he'd either run for the door after pouring a beer on my head and hurling a string of insults at me, or I'd be consoling him as he slumped on the nearest couch and started crying.

I come from a small family. My father worked all the time and travelled a lot. I had no siblings, did no babysitting as a teenager and showed zero interest in anyone's kids if they attempted to talk to me about them. In my twenties, the thought of having a baby terrified me more than almost anything. As a junior worker in various corporate settings, I was the guy burying his head in his desk, or skulking in his office, when the mums on maternity leave brought in their babies for a visit. In my early thirties, I grimaced as babies cried in my local cafe while I tried to enjoy a chilled-out brunch with Julia to kickstart a Saturday morning. (She was always far more accommodating than me.) Don't even get me started about babies on planes. So how the hell did I end up becoming not only a father to two children, but a strong advocate for more men to join the club?

How does a man deliberately turn his life upside down and shake it about until it resembles something entirely different and extraordinary? It started with a massive kick up the arse from Julia, who told me words to the effect of 'we're having kids or I'm outta here'. I had to get backed into a corner before I decided to have a family.

Well, I'm a few years into this chaotic, balls-to-the-wall adventure called parenting. I've never exercised less, slept less and comfort eaten more than I do right now. But I've never felt more like a man than I do right now. It's all down to crazy, awesome fatherhood. American educator Elizabeth Stone once said that having children is like having your heart walk around outside your body.[1] Julia and I love that description. It aptly explains why I've never felt this hypersensitive, emotionally vulnerable or plain scared. I wouldn't want it any other way.

I want to do a good job of being a dad. I want to help Luke and Aila to put their stamp on the world. I'm not talking the Steve Jobs–style 'put a dent in the universe' impact, although free smart devices for life would be nice. I want them to be able to face a world that's changing so damn quickly it's making our heads spin, and stare it down with confidence. I want them to be resilient to whatever gets up in their grille. I want them to have a positive impact on those around them, to respect people and be kind, compassionate, empathetic souls.

My two children are my light. If I'm Luke Skywalker, they're my binary suns on Tattooine. My daughter also happens to have as much energy as both those suns. When Aila wakes up, which is 6 a.m. if we're lucky, she turns it up to eleven. My toddler-sized She-Ra sits bolt upright, throws the covers off, arches her back, tosses her long, lioness mane back out of her face, and announces simply, 'AWAKE!' She does not give Julia or me the chance to ease into the day. No warm and cuddly snuggles under the doona. No morning smooches. No chat about what the day might bring. No checking the news (i.e. has Trump started World War III yet?). No admiring the gorgeous palm trees glistening outside our bedroom window. Certainly no time to exercise. It is simply Go Time. This daily ritual is repeated in homes across Australia, our suburban reveille.

I'm madly in love with Aila and have been since the moment I met her. She blows me away. This girl seizes the day. The sparkle in her eye and the effervescent cheekiness in her smile shows me the world is one gigantic Adventureland to her. Long may it continue.

She's also growing up in probably the best era for women ever. That's crazy. EVER. Humans have been around for a long time, and Aila has won the equivalent of the Golden Ticket. She lives in one of the most prosperous countries at the most prosperous point in human history. The world tells her, confidently (but not yet unanimously), that she can do, and be, *anything*. She has strong female role models all around her, from her brilliant mum, to her grandmas, to daycare teachers, to our close friends who act as her urban aunties. She's hit the ground running. Every day she grows in self-belief, declaring to us that she is 'strong, brave and smart' to our cheers and applause. The track she's running on is getting smoother all the time. Hundreds of thousands of women ahead of her continue to sprint ahead, trampling its rough spots, smoothing the way for the generation of girls charging behind them. I can hear the stampede of feet, and the roar of destiny— *the future is female*. Goodbye to the notion that girls have to be shrinking violets, quiet and polite, and hello to an age of powerful lionesses leading the pride. We're increasingly accepting that girls can choose their best self and grow to fill that role as they wish. As the dad of a girl doing just that, I'm profoundly grateful we live in this brave new world.

But what for my son? My gorgeous, beautiful baby boy. The little fel. Ben to my Han Solo (yes, I realise Han got murdered by him). The world is also his for the taking. But a big change from previous eras is that he's being asked to share the future with the girls in his life. This wasn't something asked of me as a young man, nor of my dad before me, nor of my grandpas. We were told to take our rightful place in a man's world, not help create a more equal world for men and women alike.

What does the world expect of a boy growing up at the moment? Can Luke truly be *anything* he wants without judgement or scorn? Is he getting the same messages about exercising his free will and living his best life that we are telling our daughters? Are all options open to him in life, or is he expected to behave in a certain, narrow way? Our community is pulling against itself to answer these questions. On one hand, our boys are getting more encouragement than ever to be whoever they want to be, but on the other there is still a lot of old-school noise about 'what it takes to be a real man', with the strong suggestion that any deviations against this prototype are abnormal or unacceptable.

As a boy growing up in the 1980s and '90s, I was told that I could be whatever I wanted, so long as I closely followed the directions. While women were working to forge a better path for themselves, I was on a flat, hard, smooth road, rolling along from school to uni to work. The road didn't deviate, and it was gun-barrel straight, stretching towards the horizon. On my journey I was expected to find full-time work that was well-paid and secure, get married and eventually have children. At that point I was to be awarded the exalted title of Male Breadwinner. Becoming a male breadwinner was the end of the line: there was nothing more to do but work to provide for my family.

That was the way it was supposed to be for young men across the country. With kids staying at home until they're older, and the cost of living being insane everywhere, we were simply expected to work and be the breadwinner for the rest of our lives. We may get a little time with our kids in between being a corporate baron, litigating the hell out of some legal case, or building the nation's roads, bridges and houses. We may even have a really nice chat with them when they're adults. But *raising* the kids was women's business. Boys in this era weren't just being pushed towards particular futures, we were being pushed towards particular personalities: physically strong, emotionally stoic, always in control, never doubtful.

For two generations, the men in my family did what they were told. My dad slogged his guts out for over 40 years in the car industry. He did not have a deep-seated passion for cars. As a kid, he never dreamed of being a Formula 1 driver. He did what all young working men were expected to do in the late 1960s: find a profession, learn it and stick to it. He went from being the nice young man in the mailroom to eventually becoming the CEO, taking the board of directors through the company's latest corporate strategy. Dad made an incredible career for himself, and climbed higher than he'd ever imagined he would when he walked out of school for the final time after Year 12. He was the model breadwinner, working dutifully, tirelessly, for decades, dealing with long hours, stressful responsibilities and constant travel to reach the pinnacle: captain of industry. He even dealt with a late-career redundancy, something all men dread when they still need to provide for a family—especially when you've got to feed a teenage son who ate like Makybe Diva (without the corresponding prize money).

For the final ten years of his career, Dad liaised with federal ministers and prime ministers on the future of the auto industry in Australia, and hosted a major international auto conference in the year he retired—the final feather in an already stuffed cap. Despite the rigours of his job and the frequent trips away, he did his absolute best to be there to support me, no matter how exhausted or stressed he was. His presence at my weekend sport, school concerts and speech days was the way he showed his love. But raising me fell almost exclusively to his wife, my mum. Dad is a soft, decent man, whose general warmth, honesty and integrity is acutely lacking nowadays in the nation's boardrooms. As I became a graduate worker, I looked at his career, and his efforts as breadwinner, with awe. If that was what it took to be a father, and to be a man, how on earth could I ever match up?

My father didn't have a great role model for fatherhood. His father, my grandfather, was in every sense the 'real man' we still hear so much admiration for today. He was a tough, strong, stern, stoic, intimidating guy. He did his duty by fighting a global war before returning to the suburbs and folding away his uniform, to carry on as if nothing traumatic had happened to him or his comrades in arms. He created businesses in metro and regional Australia. He had children, although, to put it mildly, they weren't really his thing. My dad and his siblings grew up around the edges of their father, who sat above them like a fortress atop a steep cliff, imposing and impenetrable. To my grandpa, his kids were simply free weekend labourers in his expansive backyard, with schoolteachers and their mother taking care of their daily demands. In time, perhaps one of them could take over the family business and prove their manhood to him, finally winning his approval.

Then there's me. I started down that same road, but then bailed on my well-paid and secure job as a lawyer at a big commercial firm to do a belated gap year at the age of 27, and then on to a master's degree in London, with no firm plan in mind for how to use it afterwards. I met Julia over there as well, and we came back to Sydney to nest. But from there I went off-road.

I've changed careers more in the first decade of my working life than my father and grandfather combined. I have no desire to wear the mantle of male breadwinner because my wife is extremely talented and has a terrific career. We split our domestic responsibilities evenly. I work part-time, four days a week, so I can look after my children and spend as much time with them as I can while they're young and radiate love on to them. I've taken extended time off to be the 'primary carer' for both our kids in the first year of their lives. Those have been some of the best months of my life. I can feel my grandfather reaching an arm out from his grave to try and throttle his weird grandson, who is more interested in caring for kids than commercial conquest.

This intergenerational experience shows how masculinity is evolving. It's slow, but as a community we're expanding what we expect from boys, young men and fathers. What we consider a good father is changing too. We expect dads to be more involved at home while also still working. And dads have an increasing desire to *be* different—they want to be more involved in the lives of their children and to do more at home. They want the chance to prove themselves as carers, rather than just being stuck forever as the breadwinner. Our partners want this for us too, as they know how incredible it is to raise kids—and how fucking hard. They want us to do more of the heavy lifting. They want to see dads immersed in raising kids, doing more domestics *and* shouldering the mental burden of running a home more equally. If dads want to do more, and partners are encouraging us to do more, maybe we of this latest generation really can change fatherhood forever.

However, there are major barriers to progress. Fatherhood remains a fragmented fraternity. Our bond with each other is fractured. There are approximately 5.4 million dads in this country—that's about one in five people.[2] Over 300,000 babies are born each year.[3] Yet we tend to be fathers in isolation from one another. As a community, we don't support fathers the same way we support mothers. Health services pay far less attention to the wellbeing of fathers. Dads are less likely to ask for help when they're stressed, depressed, anxious, overwhelmed or just plain stumped about what to do. We're only just beginning to acknowledge the mental health effects on becoming a dad. The rate of postnatal depression for dads is estimated at about one in ten.[4] If there's a birth somewhere in Australia about every minute and 46 seconds, then that means every day about 80 dads suffer depression after their baby is born.[5] Research suggests that dads with postnatal depression are also at a much higher risk of suicide.[6]

Academics spend less time researching the role of fathers than mothers. Parenting literature, for what it's worth, treats fatherhood as a niche topic. One of the most popular baby books, *What to Expect the First Year*—it's sold over 11 million copies and has been described as 'the world's best-selling, best-loved guide to the instructions that babies don't come with, but should'[7]—is a 700-page tome; dads are referenced only a few times. Our work structures trap dads into being breadwinners, and our parental leave policies label them 'secondary carers' who should only have a few days off to meet their new baby before returning to work. Culturally, we tend to think 'real men' are breadwinners and not homemakers and caregivers. It's no wonder that men don't really change their work patterns once they have kids, or that they find it hard to discuss what it's really like to be a father.

If we want our dads to help raise our sons, then things have to change. Addressing this notion that men are meant to be breadwinners is a good place to start. This isn't some self-evident biological law. It is literally a Dickensian relic that emerged out of the Industrial Revolution, when men started leaving the family plot to work in city factories and storefronts. Before then, fathers were more actively involved in raising their sons. Our contemporary approach to fatherhood has more to do with eighteenth-century Great Britain than 21st-century Australia. We might as well ask dads to build supercomputers with self-learning AI systems, with a first-edition copy of *Great Expectations* as the design manual.

We need to encourage our dads to think of themselves as amazing, competent, tender, loving carers of children. A dad can do absolutely everything a mum can do when it comes to raising a boy, except breastfeed. Just as your wife or partner can work any career, so you can do any part of parenting except bust out the milk. That's my counter-argument to the male breadwinner trope. You too can provide all the necessary physical and emotional nourishment for your son.

We've also got to help dads redesign their work life so that it wraps around their family, not the other way around. Our dads deserve to have the time and the space to focus on their kids without feeling they're damaging their career prospects. They deserve as much leave from work as mum to care for babies. They deserve access to flexible work arrangements so they can manage life with school-age kids and teenagers during the week, not just on the weekends. There is too much awesome stuff that dads are missing out on, when promising new work patterns are already starting to emerge that can assist them. It's not easy—in fact, juggling work and kids during the week is bloody hard, given how scarce time is—but it is doable. If we want more for our fathers and our sons, we've got to fight for the time and space to be dads. All men have the right to find their best, fullest, most impressive version of being a father. And sons have the right to a close relationship with their dads. Most importantly, this shouldn't just be in wealthy pockets around the country, it should be fathers and sons everywhere.

At its heart, this book is about unlocking the power and potential in the relationship between fathers and their sons. So many of our public discussions touch on the character of men and how they shape the world we all inhabit. Yet we place little emphasis on strengthening this unique relationship, even though it is the first intimate male relationship our boys ever experience. We often think fathers should only teach boys how to do certain things—kick a footy, shave, put on a tie—when in fact they should be imparting character traits and an understanding of manhood. The attitudes and actions of fathers can expand or confine what masculinity means to our sons.

Just to be really clear, this book is not a comprehensive textbook on parenting. I'm not going to give you the top ten tips for settling a baby, making food for fussy toddlers, managing your teenager's social media usage or teaching your boy about sex. It explores some of the big, contemporary challenges that all fathers are grappling with, from the perspective of a dad who is just trying to do his best, get the most out of his time as a youngish father, and learn from his own mistakes. It's not meant to lecture other dads or preach to them about how to live their lives. Nobody needs that. It's meant to help men see that they have more choice in life than they might realise, and that they can rewrite the rules on masculinity. We can ensure our sons lead fulfilled, independent, free lives, grounded in the unconditional love their father gives them and, when needed, replenished by that love when they suffer setbacks.

It's also about my own experiences grappling with the challenges of raising a boy. I'm at the start of a long journey, but I have aspirations for him. I want to raise a boy who fits the times he lives in, who understands himself—his emotions, desires, ambitions, passions, strengths and weaknesses—and who can articulate these things to those close to him. A boy who gets that he is a part of a family, and part of a community, and who is conscious of how his thoughts and actions affect others. A boy who treats others with kindness and respect. Who, importantly, understands the boundaries of others, and knows that love is a two-way street littered with compassion and kindness. A boy who (mostly) thinks before he acts, considers the risks in different situations and doesn't do insane, crazy shit that will get him killed or arrested, or that will become viral to the point they make him unemployable. A boy who can filter out the worst elements of social media and online spaces, including bullying, threats of violence and, just as disturbingly, the torrent of deliberate misinformation masquerading as facts. A boy who has a deep, unwavering sense of self-belief, grounded in the boundless love he receives from his family, which gives him the confidence and resilience to live his best life. A boy who feels empowered to determine who he wants to be, unshackled by prejudice, expectation or the burdens of others. And a boy who knows (despite what I've written here) that he is not expected to be perfect, but has been raised to be a good man.

I hope a lot of what's in this book is useful for other parents raising their kids. Being a father is more than having offspring. It's a role someone performs to raise a child. We also have a more inclusive understanding these days of what's considered a family, and a father, that better reflects who we are as a community. About 4.5 per cent of gay couples have children, and one in four lesbian couples.[7] There are just under one million single-parent families in Australia, just about the hardest job there is, of which 18 per cent are single fathers.[8] Just under half of all divorces in this country involve children under eighteen years old.[9] This book does not prioritise one relationship, or one type of family, over another. All parenting is bloody hard and should be respected and valued the same. I'm one perspective on this experience that is common to most of us.

In time I hope we will stop separating parents into mums and dads, and instead support each other as equals on the same crazy journey. Maybe one day parents' groups will comprise mums and dads in equal number, meeting for coffee and croissants in a sunny suburban playground with their chubby bubs and cheeky toddlers. I'd love such a scene to be so normal that it's completely uninteresting. For now, though, it's a daydream.

2

BEYOND THE BREADWINNER

It was in deciding to take time off work to be a full-time carer for my kids that I came to better understand what men were up against when they try to do fatherhood differently. In 2016, I took three months' extended leave to look after Aila when she was about nine months old. In 2019, I did the same with Luke when he was a similar age.

I was lucky to take over both kids when I did: they were moving from being adorable, drooling little blobs to showing sparks of personality and wanting more interaction and playtime. Aila was lively and chatty, and starting to be cheeky while hustling around our apartment. Luke was an independent explorer who loved to play with all the toys his sister had casually disregarded for years. After the long months Julia spent slogging it out, recovering from the brutality of labour (including a dislocated tailbone), dealing with mastitis, needing wrist braces because of the strain of breastfeeding, tending to sick kids while also suffering from the same lurgy, and battling acute sleep deprivation, I got to sweep in as Mr Fun Time with two kids eager for entertainment. While my leave was unusually long by dad standards, it was still only one-third of what Julia had already done.

Among my family and friends, there were plenty of people who were genuinely supportive. My family were encouraging, albeit bemused, and typically worried about two things: my job and the boredom I would surely suffer. I regularly got asked questions like 'What are you going to do with your time off?', 'Won't you go crazy with nothing to do?', 'Can you *really* take time off work?' and 'Is your boss happy about it?' One very close family member even said that they assumed stay-at-home dads were only there because they had failed in their careers.

Hey, where are the dads?

A lot of my male friends were already dads, and they largely saw my decision to take extended parental leave as a novelty, or a luxury they didn't think they could afford. Some were intrigued to know how I'd arranged it; others patted me on the back, said, 'Good for you,' and moved on with their lives. None of these guys took extended leave themselves, even when their partners urged them to consider it. I was a little disappointed, as I was hoping to convince at least one good friend of the benefits so we could spend time hanging out together with our kids. But it was not to be, on either occasion. The most supportive friends tended to be my female friends who were would-be mums, or mums already on mat leave. They were all getting ready to go back to work.

Invariably, when I was out and about midweek with Aila or Luke, someone would invariably refer to me as 'Mr Mum', or ask why I was 'babysitting' today or had the 'day off' and what their mother was up to. Whenever I took either kid to a park, a soft play centre, a mall or a swimming pool, I'd be surrounded by mums, who often chatted easily with each other over coffee, or sat on picnic rugs with snacks for their kids. Their solidarity with each other was great, but with no other dads around I felt like a bit of an outcast. And there were loads of dads where we lived. At the beginnings and ends of the day I'd see them dropping off and picking up their kids from the local schools and daycare centres. On the weekend they filled the cafes, parks, beaches and swimming pools. They proudly marched up and down the street with carriers and prams, looking as shattered as the next parent. But during the week I had a better chance of seeing a wookie than another stay-at-home dad.

My experiences on parental leave were a serious reminder that I was one of a tiny number of dads doing the same thing. I was an anomaly. Yet I cherish this period of my life: it was incredibly special and I'll never get it again. Even so, it did feel lonely at times. In 2018, I was invited on Deborah Knight's podcast *Honey Mums* to talk about my experience of being a stay-at-home dad. It was a great chat, in which I talked about all the positives but also mentioned my feelings of isolation during my leave. When the podcast was posted on social media, the online crowd let me have it. I was criticised for failing in my duties as a man by not working, for unfairly burdening my wife by sitting around at home all day with the kids, and for being a sap for complaining about my 'holiday'. Plus I was accused of sleeping with all the 'bored housewives' in the neighbourhood. Weirdly, I copped as much flak from women as from other men.

When I went back to my job I continued to rock the boat by working part-time, four days a week, so I could look after Aila. Scratching of heads and curious looks continued to be directed towards me, as they do right up until today. I still work part-time—although in reality it means I do a full-time workload in four days every week. For four years now I've been surrounded by men with kids who work full-time, smashing out long hours, eyeing that next big project or next promotion, and I know they look at me askance as I do my part-time juggle. Some people embrace what I'm doing, but many think I've committed career suicide. Some suspect I haven't put in the effort that other colleagues do.

So the past four years have shown me that a lot of people remain unconvinced about the merits of fathers caring for their kids. It's all thanks to that bloody notion of the male breadwinner.

What's a breadwinner to do?

Every family needs a breadwinner. Providing financial stability for your kids is one of the most important things you can do to ensure they grow up in a stable environment. And because the cost of living is so freaking high, that can be an incredibly stressful responsibility. Everything costs money—even going to the 'free' local government school can cost upwards of $1300 per year.[1] In 2013, the cost of raising two kids to Year 12 on a middle-class income was conservatively estimated at over $800,000, and in 2016 it was estimated that Aussie households with kids were spending between $1833 to $2085 per week to meet the cost of living.[2] That's why most families these days need two breadwinners: of those Aussie families with two parents, just over two-thirds of them have both parents working.[3] The gender pay gap means there are still a lot of industries in which men get paid more than women for doing the same work. Similarly, male-dominated industries tend to have higher wages than female-dominated ones. No wonder many fathers have to focus on full-time work—it's an economic imperative for their family.

But a dad is so much more than just a worker bee. He is more than a collection of paycheques, hours worked and job titles. A dad has much more to give to his family beyond security and stability. Yet my experience has taught me that we still talk about fathers almost exclusively in terms of being breadwinners. It still seems unusual if dads want to be the carers, even for a short period of time when their kids are still babies. Those who dare to care are often viewed as cute novelties, unmanly wimps or career suicides. Our dads deserve to have choice in how they want to be involved with their kids. They shouldn't simply be trapped in male breadwinner roles.

From an early age, boys have the breadwinner message drummed into them, and the din gets louder as they become young men. Think about the number of images you see, in mainstream and social media, of dad walking into the family home after a long, hard day at work, dropping down to one knee and embracing his excited kids while they're screaming, 'Daddy!' Melts your heart, right? Airlines, banks and insurance companies love using these fuzzy scenes in their advertising. In celebrating these images, we celebrate dad being away from home working. We idolise the concept of the male breadwinner, and remind men everywhere that they should aspire to that lifestyle.

I definitely drank the Kool-Aid when I was a teenager at one of those fancy, all-boy private schools overflowing with religion, wealth and entitlement. The school would bang on about how it was turning boys into 'young men ready for the real world'. The aim was to transform us into real men with big careers—white-collar corporate drones, sports stars or soldiers. Real men *fathered* children, but caring for them was not something they did. They earned big coin (and played golf).

That's exactly what my dad, an old boy of the same school, had done. He'd done what society told him to do, and he did his absolute best, no doubt; he had a stellar career. The result, though, was that my relationship with my father, as I grew up, was characterised by his absence. He walked in the door 6.30 or 7 p.m. each night, grabbed a Scotch and watched the news. Even as a kid, I could tell he was beyond exhausted. He had nothing left to give after a long commute and a pressured day running a major company. He travelled a lot as well—overseas when I was in primary school and my early teens, and then back and forth to Canberra for almost a decade when I was in high school. We know now that it's between the ages of six and fourteen that young boys are working out what manhood is all about, but my dad wasn't there for a lot of that time. He was working hard for the money.

Spoiler alert: men are not biologically predetermined to be breadwinners. It isn't some masterfully designed, carefully researched social project aimed at delivering happy, cohesive families. The male breadwinner paradigm is simply a by-product of the Industrial Revolution, the economic disruption that started in the English midlands in the mid-eighteenth century. That's also when modern notions of fatherhood were born.

With the growth of factories and cities as places of employment, men increasingly started leaving the family homestead to go elsewhere to work. The emergence of new technologies also made it easier to do domestic tasks at home.[4] Instead of working alongside the wife and kids, dad spent most of the day labouring somewhere else. Family relationships started to change, as a father's primary responsibilities were to his boss, not to his wife and children.

These major economic changes brought about profound social change, and triggered a process whereby dads started to become less involved with their kids. The art of fatherhood, which had stood strong for centuries, started to transform. On the flipside, mum stayed behind to tend to the home with the children, and so she picked up more of the domestic tasks. The Industrial Revolution spread to other countries across the world, where the pattern repeated.

Creating a better world for dads in the 21st century won't just be about finding new ways of doing things. It will also be about reviving old ways of fatherhood that almost died out during the last 300 years. Until the cusp of the Industrial Revolution, both mothers and fathers were jointly responsible for taking care of things at home. Men worked on the land and were near their families all the time. They were actually stay-at-home dads. Hell, 'husband' is an old-timey word for a man's *bond* with his *house*—it literally means a connection with home![5] Fathers in Britain and Western Europe were doing all kinds of domestic tasks, like cobbling shoes for the family, and making the cradle for the soon-to-arrive baby.[6] In the American colonies, fathers were often predominately in charge of bringing up their kids.[7]

Importantly, during this time, dads cared for their children. It wasn't all just cobbling, cradle-making and household work. They were invested in their kids and provided them with emotional nourishment. This idea of the attuned dad doesn't really fit with our assumptions about the Middle Ages. We assume the dads were stern, disciplining, emotionally distant patriarchs. And a lot of the public material we have from that time—paintings, literature and religious sermons—promoted this concept of the father.[8] The man tilled the soil and fought the enemy. Researchers in the mid-twentieth century actually wrote off any insights that suggested a different story of the medieval dad.[9] However, groundbreaking research done in the 1980s uncovered a bunch of records by fathers going back to the 1500s, including private letters, diaries and personal autobiographies. These tell a more sophisticated story of fatherhood before the Industrial Revolution.[10] In private, a lot of fathers were loving, big softies, besotted with their children and worried about their wellbeing. The words of these fathers showed that notions of the distant patriarch were exaggerated at least, if not entirely inaccurate.

What these researchers found creates an image of fathers that we can absolutely relate to today. Behind closed doors, dads helped nurture babies as much as mums, settling infants in the middle of the night while their wives rested.[11] There were the over-sharing dads, proudly nursing their kids while showing them off to visiting friends. In one letter, a visitor wrote about how annoying he found his besotted mate's new interest: 'Speak to him, he directs your attention to the form of its nose, the manner of its waking and sleeping, and feeding and digesting.' You could slide a flat white into that dad's hand at the local park tomorrow and he'd fit right in, apart from the scurvy.

This same research showed that fathers were intimately involved in their kids' lives and were happy to display physical affection. One dad wrote in the 1600s how much better he felt when he spoke to others about his children when he was apart from them: 'for when I cannot see my children it does me good to talk of them'.[12] I do that all the time when I'm away from my kids too. Many men resolved to be better fathers than their own had been; a French dad in the seventeenth century wrote that his father 'didn't like me—I don't know why, for he hardly knew me', and promised to be his son's 'loving father and loving friend'.[13]

This was an era with high rates of child mortality, and fathers were often stressed and anxious about the health of their children. When their kids got ill, dads would sit up with mums all night comforting and taking care of the kids, while worrying and hoping for their recovery. Rich dads and religious dads pitched in with the hired help, with one official writing about how he stayed up for two straight nights with his very ill son.[14] There's evidence of dads playing nurse to the whole family when they were sick: one dad in the mid-1600s wrote about how he was so exhausted from 'going to and from one sick to another'.[15]

Just as dads worried about their kids being sick, they grieved intensely when they died. Although child death was more common, this didn't dampen fathers' love for their children or the deep pain they felt at losing them. One dad in the late eighteenth century expressed his anguish at losing his fourteen-year-old daughter: 'Pardon me for allowing any earthly object thus to engross my feelings and empower my whole soul! I [have] buried her in my pew, fixing my coffin so that when I kneel it will be between her head and her dear heart . . . that when the great author of my existence may please to take me I may join my child.'[16] He grieved as any dad would these days. It shows that fatherhood has always been a greatly emotional journey for men across the ages.

As the Industrial Revolution picked up and the work behaviours of men started changing, dads still tried to hold on to their responsibilities at home. Massive kudos to William

Cobbett, who in 1830 wrote this cracking summary about the times he lived in:

> The man who is to gain a living by his labour must be drawn away from home, or at least from the cradleside, in order to perform that labour; but this will not, if he be made of good stuff, prevent him from doing his share of the duty due to his children . . . What right has he to the sole possession of a woman's person; what right to a husband's vast authority; what right to the honourable title and the boundless power of father: what right has he to all, or any of these, unless he can found his claim on the faithful performance of all the duties which these titles imply?[17]

These are the echoes of an era of fatherhood hidden from us. I feel incredibly grateful that we can glimpse the ghosts of fathers past, for they offer an invaluable record showing that fathers have always been involved with raising their children. What we are trying to revive is an ancient artform. This was the era before machines mashed man into a breadwinner and sent him off to work far away. The sentiments of these fathers tell us to be better dads, and to find a better way to fulfil our responsibilities at home, and to savour the incredible joy and amazing journey that is caring for children.

Now, I am not for one minute suggesting that fatherhood in pre–Industrial Revolution Britain and Western Europe is some paradise lost, or that men were perfect at balancing their work and family responsibilities. I sure as hell wouldn't want to be dropped into the Middle Ages, even if it was into a happy family unit all merrily working away in some green field. It was a rough world filled with hardship for most people. Life expectancy was low. Men were often conscripted to fight and leave home indefinitely.

Children from poor homes could still be sent away to work.[18] And just because men were home a lot doesn't necessarily mean they were inherently good parents. But this era can reveal a lot about who we used to be. It shows us that the current emphasis on getting dads to do more caring is not a new phenomenon, but history revisited. And it reaffirms that a father's instincts to care for his children are timeless.

When I stumbled across this information, I was palpably relieved. It showed me that my desire to care for my kids more and to be at home with them wasn't abnormal, or unmanly. It was something men had done over the course of history. I was in fact tapping into a natural instinct, if one that had been suppressed for most of the last three centuries. Yet too few dads hear these echoes from history, which are drowned out by our current societal attitudes and expectations around being breadwinners. Maybe, in this generation of dads, we can strengthen our links to the old ways of doing things.

Fatherhood's rough patch

The Industrial Revolution changed men from fathers who worked to workers with children. But the last couple of hundred years have not been kind to fatherhood either. We've had it rough thanks to the calamity and crisis-ridden timeline of modern history. It's left a fairly chequered legacy of what fatherhood, and indeed manhood, means.

The past two centuries are marked with calamities that scarred generations of Australian fathers, and badly damaged our understanding of what it means to be a dad. Dealing with so many existential crises narrowed masculinity to a limited set of traits: those for survival. Stoicism, physical strength, resilience—

these were the qualities needed to survive most of the past two and a half centuries in Australia.

Let's start with the fact that fathers from families of our First Nations have suffered more than 230 years of intergenerational trauma courtesy of the invasion, the Frontier Wars, the dispossession and the Stolen Generations. Traditional notions of kinship and family were devastated. Research suggests that incidences of significant trauma can be passed on through parenting practices, behavioural problems, violence, harmful substance use and mental health issues.[19] The latest scientific research shows it can even be passed through markings in family DNA.[20] Original trauma each time has been passed down the line to the next generation.[21] The Frontier Wars alone are likely to have killed more than 100,000 First Nations people across the nineteenth and twentieth centuries—about the same number of Australian soldiers we lost in all foreign military engagements combined.[22]

This is a trauma that has left generations of Aboriginal and Torres Strait Islander dads saddled with profound grief and facing unparalleled adversity. Today, First Nations men have a life expectancy of approximately 59 years, which is about seventeen years less than that of non-Indigenous men. Their mortality rate is three to seven times higher than for non-Indigenous men of the same age group.[23] They are fifteen times more likely to be in custody than non-Indigenous men. Indigenous children make up 7 per cent of the general youth population but 54 per cent of those in youth detention across Australia, including almost all the children in detention in the Northern Territory.[24]

And then there's all the stuff that has happened since Federation. Steve Biddulph has argued that '[t]wentieth-century fathering was something of a disaster', and that there were 'few great dads' who would cuddle, play with, talk to or teach their kids.[25]

No wonder. For the first three-quarters of the twentieth century, men were told that the best way to be a father was not just to work, but to fight. Just think of all the calamities that previous generations of Aussie dads dealt with: World War I, the Great Depression, World War II, the Korean War, the Vietnam War. In total, over 1.5 million Australians served in eight major wars or conflicts during the twentieth century. More than 100,000 were killed in action, more than 200,000 were wounded, and more than 30,000 were taken as prisoners of war.[26]

World War I set up the type of century Australian fathers would endure. From a population of less than 5 million people, some 416,809 men enlisted. More than 60,000 were killed and 156,000 wounded, gassed or taken prisoner.[27] The propaganda posters of the time needled men as fathers and protectors of their children. There were posters advocating for Australian fathers fighting the Germans that showed a mother and daughter huddled together with the caption 'God Bless Daddy'.[28] The real cracker is the poster with a father in an armchair gazing intently into the middle distance, his son on the ground nearby playing with toy soldiers, and an inquisitive, immaculately dressed daughter sitting on his knee. 'Daddy, what did *YOU* do during the Great War?' she asks.[29] How could you not feel skewered by that? Your manhood is being directly questioned. At this time, protecting your family was a noble aim, but staying home with them as a way of doing so was considered cowardly.

The Great Depression didn't let men off the hook either. For a generation of Aussie dads born and raised to be male breadwinners, the impact would have been profound when unemployment peaked at 32 per cent in 1932, the equivalent of one in three workers.[30] Men felt ashamed and humiliated as they begged or stood in queues, unable to fulfil society's expectation that they be the breadwinner. This deep crisis was the ultimate emasculation for generations of men. Suicide rates went through the roof in Australia.[31] How could you focus on playing with your kids when the whole family was starving and you've been out of work for two years with no end in sight?

On the heels of the Depression came World War II. During the war, 926,900 men served in the armed forces.[32] Almost 40,000 were killed, over 66,000 were wounded and over 30,000 taken prisoner.[33] Many returned home, but a lot didn't. And 'normal life' was meant to just resume. In 2006, *Saturday Extra* on ABC Radio asked their older listeners to write in and share their experiences of childhood during World War II. A common one was a father away at war, constant worry for his safety, relief at his return home, but shock at how he'd changed.[34] One listener, Christina, said she only met her father when she was three years old, and he seemed unhappy as he had been drafted into the Army Medical Corps: 'He was not now the caring man I knew he could be.' Phillip said his dad had flown bombers and survived, but suffered an 'untreated disorder' and dished out severe emotional and physical abuse to his children. Another listener, Robyn, shared how the war years were ones of extreme anxiety and loneliness, not knowing whether an official would come and tell her family that their father had been killed. At the end of the war, the men would go to dispersal centres in their home states, where their weapons, uniforms and equipment were taken from them. The officials would check their teeth, give them a chest X-ray and a physical, then send them home with some information about getting a job, getting a loan or getting some land.[35] They didn't bother to check the mental anguish of dealing with war, or make any suggestions about how to reconnect with family. No longer a soldier, you were suddenly a breadwinner again—so get on with it.

As the post–World War II boom kicked off, and suburban stability emerged, our fathers lugged an enormous psychological burden and untreated trauma as they tried to build a 'normal life'. How could they possibly connect with their children? How could we expect that of them? For many men, notions of being a loving, happy father didn't exist. This was what my grandfather dealt with. He fought in North Africa, came home and never spoke about his experiences to his family. His uniform lay in a box in a spare room in his house, only discovered when my father was going through his things after he died. My grandfather is one dot in this painting of anguish and struggle during the last century. And his experience is only one generation removed from mine.

We want to help men be better dads, and we talk of opening up masculinity for our gorgeous little boys, but there are ghosts lingering in our recent past. Being a loving dad wasn't a celebrated, idealised concept during this time. As a result, we further hollowed out the essence of fatherhood, beyond what the Industrial Revolution had done. Calamity stole the time and space in which men could be loving, hands-on fathers. It was impossible to wear your heart on your sleeve and talk about your emotions. Twentieth-century fathers largely became empty shells detached from nurturing children.[36] Fatherhood, something sacred and glorious, was pummelled into a misshapen rump. Because of this we almost lost a skillset that had been developed over millennia: the ability of fathers to actively raise their sons and train them in the ways of manhood.

History doesn't determine the future. But it's only when we understand the history of fatherhood, and appreciate the wreckage of the last 250 years, that we can unshackle ourselves from the past and build something better. We can liberate ourselves to create a version of fatherhood that fills the soul, not just the wallet. And we can reach further back in time, to where there really are history lessons on fatherhood worth learning.

FIGHTING FOR FATHERS

SENATOR TONY SHELDON, SYDNEY

It's all well and good for white-collar dads to talk about stepping out of the workforce to care for their kids. But what about the millions of Aussie dads in jobs that need more than a laptop, wi-fi and a mobile phone? Tony Sheldon is a father who has been fighting for these dads for his whole career.

When I spoke to Tony, he was the National Secretary of the Transport Workers' Union. The TWU's membership is about 95 per cent men, with the average age being around 47. That's a lot of dads with teenagers; Tony himself has a teenage son and daughter. He would take care of them for six days out of every fortnight. Even though he was head of the TWU and had international work commitments, Tony adjusted his travel to maximise his time with his kids. 'Fatherhood for me is about priorities,' says Tony. 'I structure my life in such a way that my kids know they are the really special people in my life.'

A lot of men in the transport sector do a lot of overtime: to make a decent living they have to work more than 60 hours a week. And that means a lot of time away from family. Because the nature of the work is rigid, it makes access to parental leave programs that much more crucial. Many moons ago, Tony and the TWU fought for paternity leave for working dads. During a consultation with members, a few younger blokes stepped forward to demand paternity leave. A lot of the older members at first argued that 'real men' didn't care for kids. According to Tony, some prominent members of the media also disparaged the union's campaign for the same reason. But ultimately the older members supported the younger ones' demand for paternity leave, and before long a genuine conversation had started within the TWU about the caring responsibilities of fathers and the importance of incorporating this into work practices. Over time, the TWU culture started to become more family-friendly.

Transport remains a tough industry for fathers. 'It used to be that during the school holidays, truckies would take their kids with them to give mum a break and so they could spend quality time catching up on what they missed,' Tony recalls. 'The boys found that their dad, typically reserved at home, would open up on the road. It was really special bonding time for them, and a simple way to overcome their continued absence from home. It is partly why so many sons went on to follow their fathers into the industry. However, they're not allowed to [do that] anymore, and those opportunities for long chunks of time together are incredibly difficult to come by.'

Tony encourages workers at the TWU to bring their kids to the office. 'They're not a distraction at all,' he says. 'They make for a lovely work culture. It's so great for kids to get some special attention from the staff, and to see what dad does all day long.' Tony himself used to bring his kids to work two days a week when they were younger. 'I once brought my son when he was a baby into a workplace negotiation. It really changed the atmosphere in the room. After a while, one of the key negotiators on the other side was helping feed my son! We were reminded about our shared humanity.'

Tony is a passionate guy, and has thrown everything into his work. At the time we spoke in mid-2019, he was about to become Senator Sheldon in the Australian parliament. He sometimes wonders whether he could have done more to put his family at the centre of his life. 'Spending time with your family is reinvigorating for work,' he says, 'and helps give you perspective on what matters in life. I wonder whether I could have done more of that when I was younger.'

Now Tony is at the stage of fatherhood where he is helping his son become a young man. Tony strongly believes that fathers have a responsibility to help create well-rounded young men who understand that masculinity is a broad spectrum. 'A big part of that is respect for women and a belief in gender equality,' he says. 'That becomes so much harder with the availability of porn and the number of mobile devices it can be accessed on. It can really impair boys' view of healthy relationships with romantic partners.'

Tony and his son recently attended a ritual for teenage boys to become young men, run through his son's school. Tony said it was a fantastic and rich experience. 'My son and I went away with a bunch of other fathers and sons from the school, and it's all about acknowledging the transition from teenager to young man,' he recalls. 'We spoke maturely to one another and explored our emotions. We had open discussions about sex, love and relationships, and what it means to be a man. We spoke about our relationship with each other. A trained psychologist was present to help guide the discussions. It was a tremendous experience, and I highly recommend doing something like that if you can.'

3

GETTING STUCK IN

Fatherhood was not something that came naturally to me. I wasn't convinced I'd be a good carer of little ones. I wasn't surrounded with lots of nieces and nephews growing up. I wasn't into dolls as a kid. I never babysat as a teenager. For most of my life I considered being a dad a terrifying nightmare, a point of failure if my life didn't work out the way I hoped it would. There's a great scene in the sitcom *30 Rock*, where Jack Donaghy (played by Alec Baldwin) is standing in line for a food cart with his gorgeous girlfriend. He's in a beautiful suit, slicked-back hair, every bit the corporate baron, and he's watching a dad order his food while bumbling around for his wallet, juggling a huge nappy bag and toys as his kid watches on. 'Look at this guy,' Jack says. 'He used to be a man once.' That's how I felt about fathers for most of my twenties.

Zero knowledge

Julia and I had no idea about kids prior to our own offspring coming along. When we got pregnant in 2015, I used every second of those nine months to psychologically prepare for the changes that I knew would come with fatherhood. Now that I was going to be a dad, I wanted to be hands-on and competent, at the very least. Naturally enough, we turned for advice to our friends who already had kids. We asked about everything—which hospital to use, which books to read and classes to attend, which prams and car seats to buy.

The fact that we genuinely had no clue where to start meant we got a lot of unsolicited advice as well. That first time around, I lost track of how many conversations included the phrases 'You know what you should do . . .', 'Have you thought about . . .', 'Surely you'll be doing . . .' and 'You know, the best thing I found was . . .' No one can deflect an irritating or invasive question quite like expectant or new parents. I made a lot of empty promises about what I would do or not do once our kid was born.

That said, the best and worst pieces of advice I got on fatherhood have stayed with me. They are cosmically opposed to one another. I'll start with the worst piece of advice, which came from a close friend. This guy has a gorgeous family. He's smart, responsible and hardworking. Julia and I were around at their place not long before the arrival of Aila. I had sought him out for 'any last tips as we enter the final straight'. I'll never forget what he said to me: 'Mate, there is nothing you can do as a dad in the first six months of a baby's life. All they want is their mum. So just wait out those first six months and then you can be more involved a little later, when the baby is more interesting.'

This was not quite the insight I was expecting to hear. As I was processing this pearl of wisdom, I noticed he was using the book *Baby on Board* as a coaster for his coffee mug. That book was the only one my wife and I read before the birth of both our kids, and in my opinion is an excellent guide.[1] Thinking we could swap notes on its contents, I asked him if he'd read it. Again, his reply was revealing: 'Nah, I don't look at that stuff. I leave that to my wife.'

My mate's intentions were good. He thought he was imparting some hard-earned wisdom that would help me be a new father. But even at that point, his advice jarred. How could I possibly start learning to be a competent and confident dad if I sat on the bench, waiting out the clock for six months, leaving everything to Julia? It also seemed manifestly unfair on her. I didn't want to leave her to grapple with new motherhood—I wanted to be alongside her in the trenches. Letting her take all the heat for half a year? That's not how we roll.

Now, I shouldn't be too harsh on my mate because he's hardly Robinson Crusoe in thinking that dads don't have much to offer newborns. In fact, what he told me is actually one of the most common myths still circulating in our community about fatherhood.[2]

The Parenting Research Centre has done extensive work mapping the attitudes of Aussies to parenting. Over the past few years they've conducted in-depth interviews with ordinary punters to ask their views about raising children. They've discovered that there are a lot of furphies still doing the rounds in our homes. The big whoppers include that dads can't take care of kids as well as mums, and that men are destined to raise their kids in the same way their fathers raised them.[3] According to this research, lots of people also think that good parenting produces good parenting, and bad parenting produces more bad parenting. Wrapped up in these views is the belief that poor parenting is more pervasive in disadvantaged communities, where families experience poverty and hardship.

There's enough fatalism about this perspective to make a gloomy French philosopher blush. If you're born into poverty, sorry, but you must have really crappy parents too. What baloney. These cultural attitudes emerged from the Industrial Revolution, and we've been repeating them so often, for so long, that they've become conventional wisdom.

We have a deeply ingrained belief that mums and dads have different skills because of their gender. In 2018, an Australian organisation, the 50/50 by 2030 Foundation, did a major survey of people's attitudes to gender, work and caring. The survey showed that 40 per cent of men, and 31 per cent of women, still thought women were better suited to being primary carers, with 56 per cent of men and 45 per cent of women agreeing that men and women have different skills and talents 'based on their gender'.[4] The assumption that parental skills are in part based on gender means lots of people don't think dad can cut it taking care of the kids.

In 2017, the Australian Institute of Family Studies (AIFS) examined what people thought about stay-at-home dads, and found that only 57 per cent of mums thought the kids would do just as well with dad at home while mum earns the coin.[5] Those least likely to agree that dad could do it just as well were from couples where the mum stayed at home to look after the kids. What's worse, only 50 per cent of dads thought they could do as well at home as mums—not exactly a huge show of self-confidence.

So when my friend told me to play second fiddle to Julia when our kid arrived, he was representing views that are widely held across the country. It seemed I might be the weirdo with the out-of-step views.

Rolling up the sleeves

The best advice I ever got on fatherhood was at the other end of the spectrum. This insight came from another friend after he and his wife had just had their first child. Julia and I went to visit them on a summer's day, eager to hear about their early experiences. In only a few weeks their stylish and tasteful home had been taken over by baby appliances, and the sleek marble floors were lined with things that were either plastic or fluffy. After I'd given my friend a congratulatory bro-hug, I asked again for any advice he had for me. He simply told me to 'get stuck in' from the moment Aila was born.

When it's offered as advice, it sounds pretty glib at first. 'Get stuck in'—how many times is that said in Australia every day? Coaches, teachers, bosses and politicians love using that phrase in all manner of situations. But in the months leading up to her birth, it was actually the most meaningful and helpful advice I received. It remains my daddy mantra to this day.

To me, 'getting stuck in' means doing all the things that come with being a father. It's not sitting on the bench for the first six months. It's not handing mum barf rags and hot coffees while she does the kid wrangling. It doesn't mean just going to work to get the next paycheque. It's about immersing yourself in fatherhood from day one, and doing *all* the things: bottle feeds in the middle of the night and at the crack of dawn, changing nappies, soothing an upset baby, settling, resettling, resettling again, resettling again after that, bathing, cleaning up vomit—whatever is required. It's about being involved in the nitty-gritty of caring for kids, and doing it with passion and enthusiasm (most of the time).

It was really daunting just 'getting stuck in'. Looking back on those first few days at the hospital, it's hilarious how gun-shy Julia and I were to do anything without the nurses standing over us and telling us what to do. Next to the bed in Julia's maternity suite was a green button to call for assistance, and this magic green button was our lifeline. We pestered many different nurses, day and night. Does she need to have her nappy changed? *Buzz*. Is she hungry? *Buzz*. Does she need a warmer top on? *Buzz*. Is it normal for newborns to cry? Errr . . . *buzz*. A lot of the time we buzzed 'just to be on the safe side', just as so many other new parents do. I'm sure the nurses appreciated walking all the way down the corridor to advise us that, yes, we should feed our baby if she was crying!

After a few intense days of buzzer dependency, we left the maternity ward and went home. Already by then life with a baby wasn't as scary or daunting as I had imagined it might be. And I remember being determined to apply my friend's advice of rolling up my sleeves and doing it all.

Unsurprisingly, each day brought a new set of challenges, whether it was our newborn or us as new parents figuring things out on the fly. There was mastering the mundane tasks that you need to do over and over again, as well as the handling of emergencies. I tried hard to ensure nothing was off-limits to me. If Julia was up breastfeeding in the middle of the night, I was up with her. (If it wasn't for those early-morning binge sessions of *Suits*, I'd have had no idea who Prince Harry married.) If she had trouble feeding the hungry little beast, I'd call the hotline run by the Australian Breastfeeding Association and explain her problem to one of the patient and friendly volunteers on the other end. I learnt by doing. My confidence grew. Within only a couple of weeks, I felt pretty confident that I could tackle whatever challenge came my way as a dad. And I'm not overly endowed with self-confidence, as I'll explain later on, so having this foundational self-belief was sensational.

It also helped Julia enormously, who was recovering from a hard labour and had to deal with complications from breast-feeding. There were many times when I just had to pick up a bunch of parenting tasks and handle them while she recuperated. In only our second week home, after the three of us had enjoyed a lovely, sunny Friday afternoon wandering the neighbourhood, I was quietly setting up on the couch for the night, dreaming of pizza, while Julia had a bath and the bub slept. Nothing could get better than this, I was thinking—and then Julia suddenly rushed out from the bathroom, barely dry, shivering and looking pale. She was suffering from mastitis, a cruel infliction for breastfeeding mums. She spent the whole night in bed feeling miserable, but it was okay, because I was there and able to do all the things that needed to be done with Aila. There was no stress about how she was going to be both mother and patient at the same time, and she didn't need to instruct me constantly on what to do next. I had her back.

I took care of our daughter through the night, took Julia to the GP the next morning, and continued to look after everything at home as she got better over the weekend. After a few more emergencies, I never doubted my ability to handle times like these, because I'd been doing the required tasks the whole time.

Every man's home might be his castle, but castles require upkeep. Getting stuck in is also about being a domestic god, doing all the necessary household tasks, not just giving the kids a cuddle at the end of the work day. It's a big part of the deal.

The endless cycles of washing, drying and folding, the grocery shopping, cooking and cleaning, the vacuuming of all manner of unidentified objects off the floor, the scrubbing of food and crayon off the walls, the clearing away of toys and related mess. Just as our dads can be amazing carers, they can also be top-notch domestic workers.

However, dads aren't exactly reaching their godly potential in this area. Men tend to strongly support gender equality . . . in surveys. Over the past ten years, there have been many credible studies on Aussies' attitudes that show strong support among men for tackling gender inequality. In that 2018 survey by the 50/50 by 2030 Foundation, 85 per cent of men thought inequality between the sexes was still a problem today.[6] Similarly, 80 per cent of men agreed that domestic work should be shared equally between partners.[7] That all sounds pretty good—men get that gender inequality is a big problem, and that they need to share domestic responsibilities.

However, as dads and as partners, we're not walking the walk on gender equality. Our families rely heavily on mums to shoulder most of the domestic responsibilities as well as the childcare, even though there are more mums than ever back in the workforce after having kids. When you combine paid and domestic work, dads are putting in, on average, about 75 hours of work in a week, but mums edge them out with about 77 hours of work.[8] According to the Australian Institute of Family Studies, dads do about sixteen hours of housework and thirteen hours of childcare per week. Mums, on the other hand, rack up about 30 hours of household work and 27 hours of childcare.[9] Put another way, dads are doing twice as much paid work as mums, and mums are doing twice as much domestic and childcare work as dads.[10]

On top of that, we also know that in households where dad is the primary carer, a full-time working mum still does more domestic work than her partner.[11] Yikes! Similar trends have been found by the Melbourne Institute, which has run the Household, Income and Labour Dynamics in Australia survey (HILDA) since 2001. HILDA tracks the lives of more than 17,000 Aussies each year, collecting information on their family, income, employment, health and education. It helps tell the story of how our families are (or aren't) changing over time. Whichever way you cut it, women still do a lot more housework and childcaring than men, whether they're at home or at the office. In 2018, HILDA data showed that the amount of childcaring and domestic work being done by dads has barely moved over the past two decades. Since 2002, dads have added about one hour *total* to the amount of domestic work they do each week; the amount of childcaring they do has remained unchanged. At the current rate, it's estimated, it will take another 30 years for men to do as much housework as women.[12] As each new child is added to a family, the gap between the amount of housework done by the mum and the dad increases. In 2019, HILDA found that female breadwinners with children still do more housework than their male partners—43.4 hours per week compared to 30.3 hours. Men do about five hours less housework every week, and eight hours less childcare where women are the primary earner.[13] A female breadwinner with kids also does more housework than a male breadwinner with kids, who only does 26.2 hours.[14]

According to the ABS, heterosexual couples across the country are lagging behind gay and lesbian couples, who tend to more evenly share the domestics work in a household.[15] Understanding how Aussie homosexual couples share childcaring responsibilities is an underexplored area of research.

Our mums are slugging it out, doing a huge amount of unpaid domestic work, doing more paid work than ever, and carrying most of the childcare load at the same time, while dads spend more time in paid work and less work at home. When fathers remain the breadwinners after kids, not only do they not do an equal share of domestics, their partner adds another responsibility to her already crowded life. Mum becomes the household manager: the person in charge of knowing what needs to be done, in what order, and by when. Given how complex all our lives are these days, that's a massive job.

In addition to the daily cooking, cleaning and caring, which is already draining enough, it adds further tasks like coordinating the kids' schedules, staying on top of daycare and school requirements, doing family budgeting, nursing sick children and arranging health appointments, and liaising with grandparents and/or babysitters. Being the household manager is an enormous mental load that mums everywhere know all too well. As the household manager becomes more overworked, the male breadwinner tends to become more passive, relying on her to tell him what to do next.

The whole saga pushes our mums' physical and mental health to breaking point. No bloody wonder that a 2019 study in Britain found working mothers are about 18 per cent more stressed than other people, and working mums with two kids (that's the dream, right?) are about 40 per cent more stressed, when biological markers like hormones and blood pressure are examined.[16]

I've seen first-hand how overwhelming this mental load can be. One of my close friends contracted a horrible virus from the stress, anxiety and exhaustion of being a young mother running a household and working part-time while her husband had a very demanding full-time career in the city. She now has permanent health problems as a result.

And then there's Julia, who is a brilliant person and an amazing mum. She is smart, self-assured and usually bullishly optimistic about our future. From the moment I met her, in a dinner line at a uni residency in London, I was entranced by her—and I remain so to this day. During my regular bouts of self-doubt and insecurity, I would turn to her to help replenish my confidence. That's why it has been so agonising to see her fall into a long, dark tunnel of perinatal depression, from which she is still trying to resurface after almost two years. Depression robbed her of her natural optimism and self-assuredness, and her symptoms were exacerbated by a complicated second labour, our son's immediate illness, and his soul-shattering inability to sleep well. Watching her grit her teeth and push through depression to still do the things that needed to be done with our kids, and remain such a wonderful mum, is something that breaks my heart over and over. I am able to be home a lot to share the housework and childcaring, but even then I have witnessed how hard it is for Julia while she is fighting her own mind.

It's why I'm a devotee of 'getting stuck in' at home and with the kids: I have seen the difference it can make to our whole family. I will never stop getting stuck in either. Honestly, it's the least I can do.

Particular set of skills

The best advice I could pass on to another expectant dad builds on my 'get stuck in' philosophy: *fathers can do absolutely everything a mum can do except breastfeed.* Apart from that one task, there is not a single thing a dad can't do as well as, or better than, a mum. To the dads reading this, regardless of whether you're a total newbie or an old hand, know that you have just as much talent, instinct and potential as a parent as any mum, and do not let anyone else tell you otherwise.

As I discussed in the last chapter, we've had three centuries of society pushing dads to become workers and not parents. Because of this, the conventional wisdom emerged that mums are naturally better at raising kids, that dads aren't really needed by newborns, and that while dads have a role to play in providing for their families, mums are best placed to be *responsible* for their kids' development and any problems that arise.[17] Even public and private parental leave policies reflect these myths by dividing parents into 'primary' and 'secondary' caregivers. That's such bullshit.

Dads are meant to be co-pilots in raising kids. Equally involved, equally important and equally responsible. They have just as much flair and talent for raising kids as mums. They can handle *everything*, from nurturing a newborn all the way to guiding a young man into a volatile world. Dad and mum are like Goose and Maverick: the pair of you are badasses in aviators taking to the skies chasing glory. Dads are not in the control tower on the ground in some support role, just hoping the plane lands safely.

As I said at the start of this chapter, Julia and I had zero knowledge about raising kids before Aila was born. Four years later, we split our family responsibilities down the middle. Neither of us knows more, or excels more, than the other. Neither of us is the gatekeeper for the children's wellbeing. We can do all the same tasks, and can pick up the slack if something happens to the other one. When one of us gets sick with the latest daycare superbug, normal service at home is not thrown into chaos. We back each other, and believe in each other as parents.

In blue-collar families where the mum and dad have conflicting work schedules, especially shiftwork, dad may already be doing all the different kid-related tasks. Overseas studies of families in the United States, Germany and Norway, for instance, show that men who work the night shift can do more childcare as a necessity while mum is working the day shift, even if they may hold 'traditional' beliefs about gender roles.[18]

The importance of being co-pilots only grows with time, when your kids' development becomes more complex than just feeding, cleaning, dressing and playing with them. As we'll see, our young boys need a lot of support and nurturing to grow into young men, especially considering the types of challenges they'll confront in the 21st century. My dad was a loving, caring father, but he was not equipped to deal with the emotional side of raising a boy. His father hadn't done that for him, and emotional support wasn't considered part of the job requirement for a dad in the 1980s—that's why there were mums. Needless to say, I didn't have much idea what it took to be a man when I was a teenager on the verge of leaving high school. I could have used a little guidance on that front.

When you get to the tricky challenges of parenting, it'll pay to be a co-pilot who, alongside your partner, can counsel and advise your kids together, from a place of mutual knowledge, trust and understanding. That's what getting stuck in is all about—it means doing all the parenting things, including the hard, emotional, angsty stuff, the awkward conversations and the heart-to-hearts. Our boys could use a few more heart-to-hearts with their dads in life.

By diving into the all-consuming world of daddying, I also discovered that parenting is a skill you can develop, not a job you're naturally good at (or not). Like any other major life skill, it involves a ton of on-the-job training and applying yourself to the role. By doing different things, and with a shitload of trial and error, you gain experience. From that experience, over time you build expertise. Along this journey you may doubt your capabilities and question your instincts or judgement. No doubt there'll be times you look skywards and ask, 'Honestly, what the fuck am I doing here?'

That's certainly how it is for me. There are days I feel like a general, anticipating my kids' moves and moods, marshalling things with precision while keeping everything running to plan. Other days I feel like some chump who's completely wrapped around his kids' little fingers and has little idea what he's doing. But then some emergency or crisis inevitably crops up—most likely a sick kid—and you're all over it. Experience points gained once again.

Perhaps before you even realise it, you're Liam Neeson in *Taken*, with a particular set of skills, waiting to be deployed whenever it's time. You're ten steps ahead of any unfolding scenario and virtually working on muscle memory as you cook dinner while simultaneously cleaning the kitchen and watching your toddler climb the couch out of the corner of your eye. Whatever is required you can do blindfolded, backwards, underwater, even without coffee.

What I've said so far in this chapter is not exactly the parental equivalent of the Higgs boson particle breakthrough. It's something that lots of research has already shown us. I'm certainly not the first dad to have this parental epiphany in the wee hours of the morning. Yet time and time again, the cultural image of fatherhood presented to us in the media and in our communities reinforces the idea that it's completely acceptable for dad to be a well-intentioned, incompetent fool. Daddy Pig, from the British kids' TV show *Peppa Pig*, is the classic example of the bumbling and oblivious father who loves his kids dearly but can't do much for them practically, leaving it all to Mummy Pig (who relies heavily on the overworked Miss Rabbit). One episode even has Peppa having to rescue her father from getting trapped in a soft play centre (eye roll). Outside of soporific toddler television, there's Phil Dunphy on *Modern Family*, who I think is absolutely hilarious thanks to the comedic brilliance of Ty Burrell. He's always trying to be the likeable, fun dad who is woke to his kids' interests, while their mum frantically runs from chore to chore to keep the household together. Of course there's Homer on *The Simpsons*, who for the first few seasons was presented as the apathetic, ignorant but loveable dad, but more recently has become a zany whackjob. I watched a lot of *Home Improvement* in the 1990s, where Tim Allen's character loved nothing more than goofing with the kids and drooling over power tools. (I also watched a lot of *Family Ties*—Steven Keaton is probably still one of the best portrayals of a caring, involved father we've seen to this day, but he remains an exception to the rule.)

The worst thing about these portrayals is that they make dad's incompetency loveable and almost charming. He might not know how to take care of his kids, but he sure does love them. Thank god for Bandit in the smash ABC kids' show *Bluey*. Overnight he's become a model of fatherhood towards which a lot of dads are working, myself included.

In addition to pop culture depictions, celebs themselves reinforce notions that dad hasn't got what it takes at home. For example, take this interview with Russell Brand back in January 2019. He spoke to a journo from the *Sunday Times* in London about his role in caring for his two very young daughters. He waxed lyrical about being a dad and the supreme joy he found in family . . . aw, how lovely and sweet. Then the interviewer got down to the nitty-gritty of parenting. This section of the interview is pretty hilarious—it's a back and forth between the journo, Decca Aitkenhead, and Russell:[19]

So when I ask what length of time he's ever looked after his two children by himself, the answer is rather a shock. 'That's a good question, isn't it? Well, OK. The two of them? Well, not long, not long.' How long? 'Um, I've done like, a night. But they're asleep then.' Has he spent even 24 hours in sole charge of his children? He looks at me as if I must be mad.

'No. She wouldn't go away for 24 hours, Laura. She respects and cares for their safety too much. Yes, I'm very, very focused on the mystical connotations of Mabel's beauty and grace. Not so good on the nappies and making sure they eat food . . .'

Why doesn't he do more of the practical parenting? 'I'm still of a romantic and reflective and, possibly, to give it its proper name, a religious disposition. That's my world view. That's not necessarily what you want organising pragmatic, bureaucratic, managerial stuff.' Like remembering to pack the nappy bags and carrot sticks? 'Oh totally, Laura does all of it. It turns out that she is extremely well versed in the nuances and complexities of child-rearing. Me, I am dedicated to it, devoted to it, but I am still surprised when it's like, "Oh my God, this is f****** really hard and it's so exhausting." The younger one, I just feel inept so quickly like with the crying.'

I have a mental image of Russell Brand in his lounge room surrounded by burning incense, levitating off the ground while he meditates on the cosmic natures of his daughters, possibly with a golden glow resonating off him, while his wife Laura runs around after the kids. I like the guy—he was really funny in *Forgetting Sarah Marshall*. And I completely believe him when he says he's devoted to his kids. And in his defence, he mentioned later in the interview that he does the drop-offs for daycare and the like. But his answers above are a classic example of the problem with the contemporary fatherhood narrative. He's not confident doing the hands-on dirty work, doesn't spend lots of time caring for his kids on his own, is amazed at how hard it is when he does, wants credit for being a devoted parent, and feels his wife is just better at it than he'll ever be. Unsurprisingly, Russell's answers caused a stir on social media and among other parents.

Eddie Murphy has spoken before about how much he loves his kids. In *Comedians in Cars Getting Coffee*, he confessed to Jerry Seinfeld about going into his bedroom and crying all day after one of his kids moved out of home. However, he also said in an interview in 2016 that he doesn't change diapers because he would be horrible at it and that's not fair to his child.[20]

It's actually liberating when you work out that parenting is a skill and not something you either inherit from your parents or you don't. Seeing parenting as a skill helps you realise that you're not going to raise kids the same way you yourself were raised. It is not your destiny to be your father. Luke Skywalker didn't turn into Darth Vader. Being an amazing father comes from within you, and you alone are in control of what type of dad you become. There may be certain things your father did that were awesome that you seek to emulate, but you can ditch other elements you didn't think worked so well. You can be selective, and choose your own future.

I loved the fact that my father was always present at my school activities to support and encourage me. That's something I definitely want to emulate. Whenever I was nervous about how

I'd perform on the day, it was such a huge reassurance to have Dad there barracking for me. I also knew how hard it had been for him to attend a lot of those activities, given how demanding his job was and how much overseas travel was involved. Weeks at a time he'd travel to Tokyo, Detroit, London and Frankfurt. He seemed to spend most of the 1990s flying home on Saturday mornings from overseas business trips. He'd traipse off a plane into the morning sun after flying all night, bone-weary and bleary-eyed, and get home to slump on the bed for about two hours' sleep. He'd then take me to school sport all day. He was my number-one ticket holder at athletics, cricket, rugby and my brief stint doing cross-country running. By standing jetlagged at an oval for one entire day of his precious weekend, he was showing his love and pride.

My dad's determination to be present like that was a rejection of his own father's indifference and absence from similar activities. It's always staggered me that my grandfather never went to watch my dad's school sport. He took no real interest in anything my dad did. When Dad broke his arm playing rugby at school (let's assume making a heroic diving tackle to stop a winger scoring in the corner, thereby winning the game for his team), his dad wasn't on the sidelines to rush the field, comfort him and take him to hospital. Just a bunch of other families wondering where this boy's parents were. Another family drove him to have his bone reset, and then home at dusk. I can only imagine how crushing the whole sorry experience must have felt for my dad. No dad to hug him and tell him everything would be okay. To tell him that he was so brave and tough for dealing with the pain on the way to hospital. To distract him with dad jokes or funny stories. No promises of ice cream after the cast was put on. Just loneliness and sadness.

As I choose my own adventure, I'll take some of my father's example, and do some other things differently along the way. It'll all be part of the parental toolbox I'm building up. Now I can't wait to take Aila to her sports class during the week, and cheer her on every time she smashes the ball with her racquet or drives home a winning goal. I love my boy's swimming lessons on the weekends, when I hop in with him, blowing raspberries on his tummy as we bob around the pool together, singing songs with the instructor.

I hope they'll be excited when I flag the prospect of Auskick with them when they're older. I'd love for one of them to end up running onto the SCG to debut for the Sydney Swans.

The caring dividend

You don't have to take my word for it that getting stuck in when you're raising kids can be such a winner. People far wiser than me, steeped in scientific knowledge, have been researching the impact that fathers have on the development of their kids. They've found that a big dividend comes with being an involved, caring father who is hands-on at home.

It's worth mentioning at this point that the field of parenting and family science is a mixed bag, to say the least. For harried working parents, it can be impossible to work out what information has a reliable, robust evidence base supporting it, and what information is glorified opinion and should be treated with scepticism or even caution. On so many topics in childhood development, from feeding to screen time to sleep routines, there is lots of literature that makes sweeping generalisations about childhood development but that is in fact based on limited scientific evidence.

One thing I've learnt is that this field tends to split into hard science (like biology) and 'parenting science'. The hard science tends to focus on children's physiological and cognitive development, and is more rigorously verified—things like how a kid's body grows over time, or how their brain changes. This literature is more reliable. The 'parenting science', however, is all the other stuff out there about raising kids, written by psychologists, therapists and teachers. This is the stuff on sleep routines, screen time, eating habits, cranky toddler meltdowns, adolescent angst and sexuality, just to name a few topics.

Crucially, a lot of parenting science is based on one-off studies, small studies or studies with unrepresentative or homogeneous sample sizes, given the fact that over 300,000 babies are born in Australia, and about 130 million babies are born globally each year.[21] In these studies, researchers observe a particular trend or pattern, and then tend to extrapolate from it and say it could apply to *all* children on average, because 'it's science' (Ron Burgundy–style). The conclusions of competing works in the field are often contradictory or contested within professional circles.

It's not that these studies are worthless; they often find something that is incredibly interesting and should be explored further. It's that they shouldn't be promoted and disseminated as gospel truth to time-poor, information-hungry parents looking for answers.

A telling example is the science behind *The Wonder Weeks*. The sales pitch of *The Wonder Weeks* is that it itemises the 'developmental leaps' babies go through in their first twenty months, so parents can understand why their bubba might wake up one day super-fussy, irritable and behaving differently. *The Wonder Weeks* tells you that your baby's brain is rewiring with each developmental leap.[22] During one leap, he or she is beginning to understand shapes and sizes, the next time it's understanding depth and distance, and so on. It offers structure in those unpredictable and chaotic first months of a newborn's life. You can buy the book or have the app handy on your phone to refer to when things get hairy.

A friend recommended the *Wonder Weeks* app to us when Aila was born, and we thought it was awesome that we could know so much about our baby's growth. How comforting, right? I would steel myself for when our baby would go into a leap, expecting the worst sort of behavioural regression—but nothing much actually happened. I began thinking that our daughter must be abnormal, at one end of the bell curve. I didn't doubt the science, not for a moment.

It turns out that the *Wonder Weeks* idea was developed by a Dutch husband-and-wife team, Frans Plooij and Hetty van de Rijt, about 40 years ago.[23] They were studying the interactions between mother and baby, and the effects on infantile development. The only thing is, they were mostly studying chimpanzees.[24] According to the *Wonder Weeks* website, after observing how chimps got on with one another, they 'realised that these regression periods were likely to occur in humans as well'.[25] It was only in 1992, about twenty years after they started studying chimps, that they published findings based on human interactions.[26] Three years later, one of Plooij's doctorate students did her own research, looking to prove the existence of 'leaps' in infants, and could not.[27] She then tried to refute the concept of the leaps as an unproven theory. According to local news sources, Plooij tried to stop her work from being published but was ultimately dismissed from his teaching job, and left academic life.[28] *The Wonder Weeks* products are still going strong, with a website and a dedicated team for 'worldwide rights and product development' promoting the book and the app to eager parents.[29] The company also stands by its research, saying it has been verified by separate studies across Europe.[30]

Treating the parenting science literature with a healthy degree of caution is a sound way to go. In 2018, British journalist and author Oliver Burkeman did a critique of baby manuals and ultimately concluded that they're less about how to raise a baby than about giving parents false comfort that they can control a chaotic, unpredictable situation with the right information, and that the 'correct answer' exists out there somewhere.[31] Alison Gopnik, an author and professor of psychology, has observed that the sheer fact that the parenting literature industry is so enormous is a demonstration of its own failure: if we genuinely knew the answers, we wouldn't need an endless stream of books with 'silver bullet' solutions.[32]

But let's get back to the topic at hand—the caring dividend from being an involved father. For starters, nurturing your young boy has a huge impact on his psychological development. Neuroscience research shows that the brains of babies and young boys are extremely sensitive to the environment they grow up in and the relationships with carers during the early years.[33] Environmental factors heavily influence their ability to develop basic life skills. Our kids may have some of our precious DNA, but there's still a huge chunk of expanding brainpower for you as their dad to mould that goes well beyond genetics. The more you are there in their lives as they start to grow up, the more influence you will have. You are Obi-Wan, helping them take their first steps into a larger world, literally and metaphorically.

Secondly, you can start the nurturing process from day one (not six months later, as I was told). It's commonplace now for dads to have skin-on-skin interaction when their bubba is born, which, according to some research, can have a huge impact on the bonding between you and your son.[34] Skin-on-skin bonding can raise dad's hormone levels, such as oxytocin (associated with trust), cortisol (associated with sensitivity to bubs) and prolactin (associated with bonding).[35] In addition, studies suggest that the more a dad does the caregiving, the quicker and more noticeable the hormonal change.[36] I remember doing skin-on-skin with both my kids, feeling their squishy, soft, red, sticky bodies warming my chest, sending adrenaline racing through my body as I fell in love with them. It was magical, and perhaps helped us bond in the way the science suggests.

Thirdly, we now know that the early years of a kid's life are crucial to their long-term development. During their first five years, kids are like freshly laid cement. Around 85 to 90 per cent of a child's brain development occurs in this period, when most of the neurons develop and the brain is most receptive to new information.[37] A child's environment, experiences and relationships in their first 1000 days of life, from conception to age two, are especially significant for their development.[38] These early years are pivotal for kids because they develop life skills like problem-solving, thinking, communicating, controlling their emotions and forming relationships.[39] This in turn helps them get ready for school and the new environment that awaits them in a different learning environment.[40]

On top of this, there is a growing body of work that demonstrates the lasting, positive impact fathers can have on their boys if they're involved in their early childhood. A 2008 Swedish study concluded that a father having more direct interactions with his young kids helps improve their 'social, behavioural and psychological outcomes'—basically, they're more ready for the wider world and can fit in with greater ease.[41] A 2011 study published in the *Journal of Paediatrics and Child Health* found that greater fatherly involvement in the early years was linked to kids being more competent in social settings, having increased empathy, more positive self-esteem and self-control, better interaction with their siblings, and better progress at school.[42] The more you as a dad are around at this early stage, the more benefit your kids will derive, and the richer their development will be. Research also suggests that more involvement by fathers has positive long-term effects on the mental health and wellbeing of young boys and adolescents, in particular in relation to alcohol, tobacco and drug use.[43] Looks like getting stuck in early might save you some hassle and heartache further down the track.

There is also some emerging science showing that a dad's brain develops to be a better parent when he's involved with his kids early. A 2014 study at Bar-Ilan University in Israel showed that fathers who were the primary caregiver experienced an increase in activity in their emotional-processing systems, causing them to experience emotions similar to those typically experienced by mothers who are breastfeeding newborns.[44] The study suggested that there's a neural network in the brain dedicated to parenting, and that the network responds to changes in parental roles. This test showed the same result in homosexual male couples as well. If you're responsible for the baby, then the chances are that your brain is adjusting so you can perform that role even better. Researchers at Yale University in 2014 found similar results to their counterparts in Israel, but also concluded that involved fathers tended to be more emotionally responsive, better at multitasking and increasingly perceptive at detecting their baby's needs.[45] (I may just have found the scientific basis for my 'get stuck in' philosophy; I should probably get to work on my app to flog it all over the world.) The Yale study also showed that making complicated decisions became tougher—but hey, that's parenthood.

Getting stuck in as a father is also a sure-fire way to strengthen your relationship and your bond with your partner. Anyone with kids will know the strain they put on your relationship. You're exhausted and stressed, frequently at the point of bickering with each other, and have little time to hang out together as a couple, and even less time for intimacy and sex. Julia captured the challenge neatly one day when we were wrangling a provocative toddler and a screechy baby and things between us were getting a little heated: she turned to me and said, 'Sometimes I feel we're less like husband and wife and more like grumpy flatmates.'

It's clear that you do a great service to your relationship with your partner when you're active on the childcaring front. American research published in 2016 shows that when a father more evenly shares childcaring with his partner, they have a healthier, stronger relationship and a more satisfying sex life.[46] The research is not suggesting that men should only do this in the hope of getting lucky. In 2019, a so-called 'social media influencer' in California posted a photo of her passionately smooching her man while he grinned and held a sign saying 'Helping with housework so you can get lucky is called choreplay'. Plenty of people called this out as bullshit, but many others thought it was genius. Everyone has to march to their own beat, but I'd have thought nurturing your kids, tending to your home and helping your partner feel better about life should be its own reward. Why does everything need to end in a blowjob?

Being an involved father means you'll develop mad skills, you'll find *your* best version of fatherhood, you'll have a great bond with your kids, you'll help them learn better and become more socially adjusted and ready for the world, and you may even help rewire your own brain to be more attuned to their needs. Plus you'll strengthen your relationship with your partner as you each carry the 'mental load' of parenting, helping ensure that neither of you goes off the deep end due to exhaustion and stress. I'd say all of these benefits represent a fairly sizeable dividend for being an attentive carer. But it's missing one thing.

When our dads care for kids as co-pilots, they model to our boys and girls what equality actually looks like. They teach them that equality isn't just something you agree with in a survey, or the topic for a speech on International Women's Day. You demonstrate that equality matters every day. You'll show them that mum and dad are equals by cleaning the house, feeding the fam, nursing an infant, doing daycare pickup, volunteering for the school canteen or taking care of a sick kid during the week. You'll also take more of the emotional responsibility of parenting on yourself and off your partner's shoulders. That'll help create a happier household, and in that event everybody wins. You create equality at home, and you send your kids a powerful message during those crucial early years, when they're starting to form their worldviews, that will resonate with them forever.

If your kids grow up thinking that mum and dad sharing the caring and the housework is nothing special, then you've done your job as co-pilots and deserve to be on the Australia Day honours list. If all our kids start seeing this as totally normal, then we really will have taken a giant leap forward as a community.

The last thing about getting stuck in is that you can do it at any stage on the fatherhood journey. Similarly, any father, or father figure, can do it. Just because you may have been working hard to keep the family clothed and fed when your kids were really young doesn't mean you can't do more caring now they're older, or that you won't be as good at it as a dad who has been doing it all from day one. I'm not saying that there is only a small window in which you can influence everything, and that if you miss it, you're doomed. This chapter is about enlivening dads to the amazing world of caring, and the lasting, positive effects it can bring.

And if your children are all grown up, well, maybe you can get stuck in helping with the grandkids when they arrive. Fathers young and old around this country can do amazing things for our kids, and especially our boys, if only they believe in their caring and nurturing abilities just a little bit more.

BEING PRESENT WHILE ALSO BEING BUSY

SCOTT CONNOLLY, MELBOURNE

If you're a working father and you're looking for a role model, you could be looking for a fair while, given the low numbers of Aussie dads who work part-time, take parental leave or use flexible work arrangements. Scott Connolly was fortunate that he had a couple of leaders who helped him understand the importance of balancing family and work, no matter how challenging it could be.

Scott is Assistant Secretary at the Australian Council of Trade Unions (ACTU), and has three kids, including a six-year-old son. 'I was really fortunate because some of the senior leaders ahead of me were working fathers,' Scott says, 'and they role-modelled what it was like to be an attentive, active parent as well as a diligent worker. I could learn from their example – it was enormously helpful.'

Scott has an extremely demanding job, so if he wants to be involved in his kids' lives, he has to make up his work hours elsewhere. 'It comes down to a choice about what is important in life, and particularly what are the non-negotiable priorities,' he says. 'I wanted to make conscious, deliberate decisions about my family and my career in order to avoid getting trapped in situations I didn't want. I also strongly believe in equal responsibility in parenting, and supporting my wife in her career.'

Scott is driven to be such an involved parent in part because he and his wife experienced tragedy when their first child was stillborn. 'I feel every moment is incredibly precious and to be appreciated,' Scott says. 'I really want to experience all the joy of raising kids and provide the care myself. If this means doing work before the kids get up and after they go to bed, I don't mind.'

Scott's son is bursting with energy and enthusiasm, so Scott finds plenty of physical outlets for him, even if it is hard working a busy job and living in a townhouse. His son is now in primary school, and starting to be more exposed to more things in life. 'As a parent, it is a huge challenge to be across all the points of influence in your child's life, especially as my son is on the cusp of stepping into social media,' Scott says. 'Realistically, I cannot control all these different elements, and knowing that mental health problems are presenting earlier in the lives of children, I'm conscious of teaching my son how to handle it himself, to give him the tools and confidence to handle different experiences, especially online.' Scott sees the next six-year window, up to when his son becomes a teenager, as critical. 'I have this period of time to build mental fortitude and resilience in my son, and to teach him how to learn from his mistakes.'

Scott is determined to make sure his son sees the bigger picture of life. 'The responsibility to raise a man and to get the structures in his life right is actually quite scary,' he says. 'I want my son to understand that he is part of something bigger, that he is part of a community. I want him to find the best version of himself, and to also find a way to make a positive contribution to the community, in whatever form he chooses.'

Scott sees that things are starting to change for Aussie dads in blue-collar industries, but admits it's much more difficult to help them restructure their work. 'For guys working shifts in the construction or manufacturing sectors, for example, it is so much harder to help them find time to be at home caring for children,' he notes.

Now Scott wants to take the conversation about how to help dads beyond the office kitchen. 'In our society we've outsourced parenting to schools, daycares, extended family, nannies, and encouraged parents to work more,' he argues. 'We need to seriously think about how we organise work and utilise labour so that people don't feel exploited and disconnected from their families. We shouldn't just accept that the way things are now is the way they ought to be. That involves all of us.'

If Scott's leading the revolution, I'm there. I just need at least an hour or so to pack all the kids' things.

4

TIME TO BE
A DAD

The latest generation of fathers could be the one that transforms once and for all what it means to be a great dad. They can be the ones getting stuck in to parenting from the moment their kids arrive. They can be the ones who collect the caring dividend, and help create and maintain an equal home, where mum and dad split managing the household fairly. Instead of viewing it as a second job behind being the breadwinner, today's dads can see fatherhood as a lifelong calling, and look to wrap their work around their family rather than squeeze their family into the spaces work allows. They can teach their sons that to raise kids and care for them is one of the manliest things you can do. But it'll take work to embed such a monumental transformation in our community.

Road to the revolution

On first inspection, it looks like things are moving in the right direction. Most dads in Australia—about 80 per cent, in fact—do take time away from work when their kid is born.[1] Young dads in particular want to put family at the centre of their lives. In 2017, Nielsen conducted a survey of millennial Aussie dads. It estimated that of the 877,000 millennial dads, 83 per cent believed family was more important than career, and 58 per cent said they had a good work/life balance.[2]

This shift in attitudes seems to be supported by some behavioural changes. Research by the Diversity Council of Australia found that young fathers want more flexible work arrangements, with 79 per cent preferring to choose their start and finish times and the same percentage preferring to work a compressed week.[3] The Council also found that 37 per cent of young fathers had 'seriously considered' leaving an organisation because of its lack of flexibility.[4] The same thing is happening in other parts of the world. In the United Kingdom, a 2019 survey of 2000 dads aged between 24 and 40 found that one-third of dads had changed jobs since becoming a father, and another third were actively looking for jobs that would give them a better work/life balance, meaning that two-thirds of those dads were looking to improve their work/life balance so they could be at home more.[5] Studies also show that the men choosing to be stay-at-home parents have less traditional views of gender roles, seeing caring as every parent's responsibility.[6]

Fathers are starting to get more vocal advocates as well. Men in the media spotlight are starting to speak up about how much they love fatherhood and how they handle being a dad (not just Russell Brand waxing lyrical). To name a few examples, Thor

(Chris Hemsworth) and Wolverine (Hugh Jackman) have spoken publicly about how to maintain as normal a family life as possible while leading life as a megastar. Crooner and TV presenter David Campbell fills his Instagram pages with joyous images of him playing with LEGO or watching *Star Wars* with his three kids. And the Pied Piper of toddlers all over Australia, Jimmy Rees—better known as Jimmy Giggle from ABC Kids—uses his Insta account to show the beautiful chaos and long days of having a toddler alongside baby twins, and how he juggles his work and family responsibilities. There are plenty of others. These blokes help normalise the idea that men can actively care for their family while holding down a job too.

In 2019 we saw a bunch of global and Aussie companies upgrade their parental leave policies in an effort to encourage fathers to do more caring. Spotify and Diageo now each offer six months' paid parental leave to mums and dads, and have ditched outdated notions of 'primary' and 'secondary' carer. Telstra has done something similar, offering sixteen weeks' paid parental leave to both parents equally. Norton Rose Fulbright, a law firm, offers eighteen weeks' paid leave that can be taken up to two years after the birth of a kid—and workers are eligible to use this leave from day one. Financial services firm Deloitte is encouraging its men to take eighteen weeks' paid leave at the birth of their children. ING became the first bank in Australia to offer its employees fourteen weeks' of paid parental leave, removing the primary and secondary labels as well.[7]

Given the emerging change in personal and corporate attitudes, perhaps there won't be reprisals for young dads taking time to be a father and not a worker. Perhaps there will be a clean transition to a new way of doing things. In June 2019, Ipsos Mori did research in the United Kingdom showing that only 13 per cent of men thought taking paternity leave had a negative impact on a man's career.[8] This finding should give us hope that a change is happening now. Perhaps the fatherhood revolution, fueled by flat whites, rolling prams and sleep deprivation, is underway already, and domestic and workplace equality beckons. Maybe, within a few years, seeing a dad taking care of his kids during the week will be a wholly unremarkable thing.

Or maybe the revolution is a lot further away than we'd like—if it's coming at all.

The 'demographics is destiny' argument is often used to argue that change is inevitable because the views of the younger generation are simply different from those of the earlier ones. But unless you're Thanos, you can't just overturn 300 years of social and economic engineering with a click of your fingers. As I explored earlier in this book, the Industrial Revolution left a hell of an imprint on our society, and on the role of men. Men continue to occupy a rigid role in the family, and our workplaces still reinforce that role. Our dads remain tightly tethered to their jobs and the pressure to earn, as well as the identity a career so often gives them. They struggle to break free as a result. In fact, the way we work, and the way we structure our time, still has a lot in common with the way things were done in earlier times, despite the fact we're two decades into the 21st century.

Tethered to the workforce

It all starts with the fact that most fathers are working most of the time. About 90 per cent of Aussie dads with children under fifteen are employed, and about 92 per cent of these dads work full-time.[9] Compare this to mums, of whom 65 per cent are employed, and about 42 per cent of those work full-time.[10]

Dads still work long hours—on average, 46 hours of paid work a week—with some recent studies showing that more than half our dads are working up to 50 hours a week.[11] Mums, by comparison, do about 20 hours of paid work each week.

From the moment their kids are born, working dads find it hard to take time out from their jobs. When a brand spanking new bubba comes into the family, Aussie dads rarely or barely change their work behaviour, mostly continuing to work the same hours in the same manner.[12] This includes taking very little leave. Aussie dads are entitled to two weeks of pay at minimum wage (about $740 a week before tax, at time of writing) from the federal government, the 'Dad and Partner Pay'. But only about one-third of eligible dads use this scheme.[13]

The numbers of men taking parental leave to be the 'primary caregiver' are minuscule: just 5 per cent of dads become the parent most responsible for a newborn.[14] That's just one in twenty dads. Not only are Aussie dads not taking primary caregiving leave, they don't even know they can—only one in four dads are even aware they're eligible to take primary parental leave.[15] I certainly didn't realise I could take primary parental leave for either of my kids when I was talking about family arrangements with Julia.

Australia's parental leave schemes, both those funded by government and by companies and other organisations, are way below what comparable nations offer. When it comes to parental leave, we give days to dads, and months to mums. Dad and Partner Pay is well below the OECD average of 8.4 weeks of paid parental leave for fathers.[16] Our share of men taking parental leave is tiny compared to other OECD nations like France, Canada, Norway and Portugal.[17]

Northern Europe leads the way in the generous public parental leave schemes it offers, and in its encouragement for men to take several months off to care for their young kids. Since the mid-1970s, Sweden has been breaking the stigma on fathers as childcarers. It currently offers 480 days' paid leave to be shared between both parents. Ninety days are preserved for mum, the same amount is exclusively for dad, and the remainder can be divvied up as the couple prefers.[18] Swedish dads often take six months or more off work to care for their kids, so it's totally normal to sight dads out with their kids at the shops and playgrounds during the week. Norway and Iceland have similarly generous schemes for both parents too.

Now let's consider the leave offered by private companies. Generally, Australian employers aren't offering much to dads at all: in 2017 only 39.3 per cent of large private organisations provided 'secondary carers' leave, and the average length offered was 7.3 days.[19] Our leave packages are so small that they act as a disincentive to men, warning them off from taking time away from work to care for young kids. They reinforce to men that they should be back at work 'getting on with it', not caring for kids at home. Compare that with the fact that mums, on average, take 32 weeks of maternity leave before heading back to work.[20]

If the revolution is here, it's not evenly distributed. Even if dad is mad keen to take parental leave, depending in which industry he's in he may not have access to decent employer-based schemes. It's within pockets of white-collar industries like law, accounting and management consulting that the most generous employer-based leave packages are emerging and where the distinction between 'primary' and 'secondary' carer is beginning to disappear. A lot of traditional, male-dominated blue-collar industries still offer little paid 'primary carers' parental leave. Australia's Workplace Gender Equality Agency (WGEA) found that in 2018, only 33.4 per cent of all manufacturing companies, 28.6 per cent of agriculture, fisheries and forestry companies, 27.2 per cent of construction companies and just 11.9 per cent of road transport companies offered paid parental leave for 'primary carers'.[21] Those proportions shrink further when you look at 'secondary carers' leave. The two brighter spots are mining, where just over half of all companies offer paid parental leave, and utilities (energy, water, waste and gas) where 71.7 per cent of companies offered paid parental leave, but that proportion is down sharply from 86.3 per cent in 2014.

Many dads would like to take more leave but are reluctant to do so. In 2014, the Australian Human Rights Commission (AHRC) surveyed 1000 dads who had claimed the Dad and Partner Pay. A total of 85 per cent of the surveyed fathers had taken less than four weeks of leave.[22] Three in four fathers said they would have liked to have taken more leave. A total of 54 per cent of fathers surveyed extended their time at home by taking other leave in addition to Dad and Partner Pay.[23] Of those who wanted to take more leave but didn't, 57 per cent said it was because they couldn't afford more time off.[24] Who could blame them, given that a male breadwinner on average earns almost $35,000 a year more than a female breadwinner?[25] There are lots of families in which sharing the caring is not economically possible because of the poor parental leave entitlements offered to men.

Some dads feel burnt by the experience. One in four dads in that 2014 AHRC study experienced discrimination in the workplace when requesting or taking parental leave, or when returning to the workforce.[26] Of those, almost half said they received negative comments and attitudes from colleagues or bosses, or were discriminated against in relation to their pay, conditions or duties.[27]

Worryingly, the numbers of dads accessing parental leave does not seem to be improving with time. In 2018, four years after the AHRC surveyed men who had used the Dad and Partner Pay scheme, the company Circle In—a start-up enterprise assisting parents in the workplace—ran its own poll asking dads how much parental leave they had taken generally. They found that 75 per cent of dads had taken some form of parental leave, but half of those dads only took one to two weeks.[28] So it seems that dads still measure time off work with the kids as a short-term indulgence, not an entitlement they deserve as parents.

Our dads are even finding it really hard to work just a little bit more flexibly so they can be at home with the kids while they're awake. About 60 per cent of working fathers use no flexible working arrangements to help care for children (versus only one-quarter of mums not using flexible work).[29] Although more companies are starting to promote flexible work, they don't exactly do it wholeheartedly. By June 2018, seven in ten organisations surveyed by the Workplace Gender Equality Agency had flexible working policies, but only one in four provided manager training on flexible work, less than one in twenty set targets for employee engagement in flexible work, and less than two in 100 employers set targets for men's engagement in flexible work.[30]

Remember how I mentioned that the Diversity Council of Australia had found that 79 per cent of young fathers preferred to choose their start and finish times? Well, that research also showed that only 41 per cent actually did so.[31] And of the 79 per cent who preferred to work a compressed week, only 24 per cent did. Given how hard it is for dads to reshape their hours even a little bit, very few dads contemplate part-time work arrangements as it's seen as a bridge too far.[32]

It's not a huge surprise, then, that men are starting to feel that workplaces and policies treat them unfairly or exclude them. In its study, the 50/50 by 2030 Foundation found that over 40 per cent of all male respondents agreed with the statement: 'Gender equality strategies in the workplace do not take men into account.'[33] Young men especially feel excluded, with millennial and Gen Z males—the same crop of young dads who say they want to put family ahead of career—significantly more likely to agree with the statement: 'Men and boys are increasingly excluded from measures to improve gender equality.'[34] The Circle In poll also found that one in two dads believed their workplace wasn't supportive in encouraging fathers to take parental leave. Forty per cent felt that their workplace's parental leave policy was not equal for men and women.[35]

The upshot is that most dads are forced to adjust to life with kids by spending a lot of time away from them. And even when they are at home, many dads still feel the relentless pressure of work. Longitudinal studies of families have shown that one in two dads misses out on family events because of work, and one in four fathers often work weekends.[36] Even when they're at home, one in five dads say family time is pressured and less fun because of their job.[37] Sixteen per cent of dads say their work and family life is *never* in balance.

Even our kids agree that this is a dilemma for the family. In a 2017 study of the experiences of children aged between ten and thirteen, more than one-third thought their father worked too much, and one in eight wished dad didn't work at all.[38] Kids were most concerned about their dads working on weekends, the intensity of dad's work, him being unable to vary start and stop times, and his long hours. Two-thirds of kids did say they had enough time with dad, which is good, but if they're used to dad being the dominant breadwinner, then what they consider 'enough' might well be less than they expect of mum.

Even if dad does move to more flexible working arrangements, that might not always produce the assumed benefits. In a lot of white-collar industries where all you need to do your job is a laptop, a smartphone and reliable internet, 'flexible work' can often mean you don't spend all your time at the office, but you continue to carry an enormous full-time workload. Dads like this often end up taking work home, and work long hours after the kids are in bed. In that same 2017 study, children were more likely to say dad worked too much if he worked outside standard daytime hours, including in the evenings or on the weekend.[39] In fact, if dad worked 'non-standard hours' like this, children were more likely to say they wished he didn't need to work at all, and less likely to say they had enough time with him. So you might be able to physically be more present with your kids by bringing work home, but they will notice the extra burden you're carrying.

So many Aussie dads are dealing with significant amounts of stress as they juggle their work and family responsibilities. A 2019 study revealed that the dads with the 'highest psychological distress and poor mental health' are the ones dealing with challenges like working more than 50 hours a week, and having no access to flexible work, no job security, no control over workload, or no access to family-related leave.[40] According to this research, about one in three dads experiences work–family conflict.[41] There's a growing body of evidence that when a father is grappling with a conflict between his professional life and his family life, his mental health deteriorates, along with his relationship with his partner and his parenting capabilities overall.[42] Understandably, this can have a negative impact on his children's mental health as well. And the longer the work–family conflict goes on, the worse everything else gets in the family. So even when dad is celebrating his kid's birthday, cheering from the sidelines at a sports field or goofing around on a lazy Sunday, his smartphone is a ticking time bomb. Being stressed and distracted by work while you're trying to enjoy some family time at home is such a common fatherhood experience that it barely registers as a problem.

Five years of *House Husbands* on Channel Nine has failed to add glitz and glamour to the stay-at-home dad's life. In the 2016 census, just 80,000 families had stay-at-home dads.[43] That's less than 5 per cent of two-parent families. What's more, the proportion increased by less than half of 1 per cent (0.4 per cent) since the previous census in 2011.[44] Less than 2 per cent of families with a child under one year old have a stay-at-home dad; by comparison, there are half a million stay-at-home mums.[45] The Australian Institute of Family Studies, one of the leading national research agencies examining the lives of Aussie families, admitted that there is 'only weak evidence' that many more dads are stepping out of the workforce to stay home.[46] The numbers of dads working part-time so they can spend more time caring for their kids is no better. About 4 to 5 per cent of fathers work part-time, compared to more than 40 per cent of working mums.[47]

But change has got to start somewhere, right? You might argue that I should be celebrating the 80,000 stay-at-home dads who are demonstrating a bold new way of being a man. But that would be disingenuous. A lot of stay-at-home fathers are there not because they've deliberately stepped out from work to care for kids. It's because they're struggling with hardship. Over half of stay-at-home dads are classified as 'not in the labour force' largely due to health or disability issues, or because they've quit the labour force altogether, and another 30 per cent are at home because they are unemployed.[48] In fact, often the whole family is doing it tough.

In two-parent families with stay-at-home dads, half the mothers only work part-time hours.[49] These families are highly likely to be battling low incomes or joblessness, or struggling to find stable suitable work, so the real conversation needing to be had is about economic disadvantage, not parenting preferences. In the meantime, these families demonstrate unending perseverance and resourcefulness to push through this hardship in raising and loving their kids.

Why is the pace of change so slow? If young dads want more time with their kids, what's taking so long? The AIFS argues that 'very strong gendered patterns' remain the default option in heterosexual, two-parent families, and so stay-at-home dads are way outside the norm.[50] According to the AIFS, it's also possible that while people are supportive of dads doing more care in theory, in practice they don't want that arrangement for their own families, and prefer to stick to what they think the genders are good at.[51]

Our deeply embedded social and economic structures are matched by equally strong cultural messages that men shouldn't be carers, that they suck at it, or that wanting to raise kids instead of work full-time is unmanly or a dereliction of their duty as a breadwinner.

The reality is that change won't come easily to dads. Maybe a revolution is possible, but it's not just around the corner. Aussie dads are going to have to fight for more time with their families. This is a fight I have been in for four years now. It's a gruelling battle, but it's worth it.

Breaking the system

All of the above statistics resonate with me because of my journey so far as a working father. I've taken parental leave a couple of times. I've used flexible work. I've reshaped my work arrangements to better suit my family, and I've experienced the dilemmas of work–life conflict. I've even changed jobs because of my desire to maintain a work/life balance. I'm one of the 4 or 5 per cent of fathers who work part-time.

To be in such a small minority, especially as a white, middle-class, thirty-something man in Sydney's Northern Beaches area, is certainly an interesting change of pace for me. I don't know one other dad who works part-time in order to do caring during the week. Over the past four years, everywhere I've looked—my bosses, colleagues, close friends, neighbours, even my accountant—I see hardworking fathers doing long hours and handling lots of professional responsibility. I wrote earlier about my father's and grandfather's professional lives; uncles on either side of my family have been ambitious doctors, business owners and real-estate agents. My cousins are busy opening restaurants and wine bars or climbing the corporate ladder.

Then there's me. I work four days a week at a national charity, I'm home by 6 p.m. every work day, and I goof around with the kids every Wednesday. I'm always running low on holidays or sick leave because I use it for family emergencies. I don't really socialise during or outside of work because I need to leave on time to get to daycare or home. And I don't travel for work unless I absolutely have to—and even then I try to do it all in one day. Every day, I'm stress-testing the system we've built for our fathers, and waiting to see whether it will break.

Sometimes I like being a novelty in the workforce; other times I feel isolated. Sometimes I get a nagging thought in the back of my head that I'm failing in my duties to my family, and I've even heard that sort of thing said straight to my face.

Like most men, until the birth of my first child I had only ever held full-time positions, most of which demanded long hours. But when I found out Julia was pregnant for the first time, I wanted to rearrange my working life to suit my family. I wanted to heed the advice I was given by my friend and 'get stuck in' to fatherhood from day one. I also wanted to support my wife during her maternity leave, and then help her get back into the workforce when she was ready. I wanted to ensure she didn't have to sacrifice her career just because she was the one who gave birth and could breastfeed.

After a long series of discussions, Julia and I agreed that I would seek to take three weeks off at the birth of Aila, and that at the end of her nine months of maternity leave, I would take three months' extended leave to be our daughter's full-time carer. After my three months was up, I would ask to return to work four days a week. It took a fair while to arrive at this decision, but it was one we were really happy with. When I nervously pitched this scheme to my boss, he didn't bat an eyelid, and worked closely with me to make it happen. He even drafted a new parental leave policy for the company because of my request.

Now, I wasn't working at a large company with a big HR department and resources and personnel to spare. I was at a small, lean, not-for-profit organisation that ran on very little. The whole place ran on the labour of about five paid staff. Me being gone for several months would have a huge impact on everyone else. So I was also lucky to have an employer like this. At the time, I had friends who were getting laughed at by their bosses for wanting to be at home after the birth of their first kid, and other friends who were forced to say they had doctor or dentist appointments in order to go to their kids' school events because it was not an acceptable choice for the blokes in these high-flying commercial industries. I felt supremely lucky, to say the least.

The three weeks I took off when Aila was born in April 2016 remain some of the best weeks of my life. I didn't really sleep much, I drank way too much coffee and ate a lot of comfort food, I showered occasionally, I was rarely out of trackies, and I barely managed a single conversation with Julia where our baby wasn't the topic. But I'd never felt more like a man. Considering how hard her labour had been, and the ailments that had followed, Julia was glad I was there too. And I got my first on-the-job father training.

My workplace was incredibly supportive during that time, and genuinely happy for me. My phone wasn't buzzing with texts or emails, and there were no snarks about when I'd be returning to work, just a beautiful package of baby things—including a baby Swans guernsey and scarf—and lots of warm wishes. My new life as a working dad doing the juggle could not have started better.

So for the first year of my daughter's life, she always had one of her parents at home with her. My extended leave with Aila was glorious, exhausting, mentally consuming and about as hard as I had feared it would be. And I'd happily do it all over again. We did lots of excursions, including the time we went to the Sydney Aquarium on a stormy, wet day and seemed to be pushing against the entire crowd the whole way—only for me to realise that I'd taken us in through the exit and we were going the wrong way. Aila learnt to stand while I was taking care of her, and I learnt what it was like to change a nappy full of shit at a place with no changing table for dads. I didn't see many dads wherever I went during the week, and I often felt like a loner—but hey, I had my gorgeous little girl with me, making me look competent or powerless depending on what mischief she was up to.

It was April 2017 when I returned to my job four days a week and took care of Aila one day a week. My colleagues were excited for my return and I was fired up to be back doing work that I loved with a bunch of amazing people. I figured that opting for part-time might slow my career trajectory a bit, but I was more than happy with the choices I had made. I hadn't anticipated any other negative effects. With Julia also working part-time at this point, it was the first time we were both plunged neck-deep into the fight for work/life balance. It was also the time that things for me slowly turned into a train wreck.

Our family's weekly routine became a head-spinning combination of staying on top of home commitments, splitting daycare duties and scrambling to get things done at work before rushing home. I felt an urgency like never before, and the weight of multiple, important responsibilities. At the end of every day I felt a gravitational pull towards home that was irresistible, and I was increasingly stressed if I didn't make it back in time to do baths, dinners and settles. It felt like trying to spin plates on high poles, hoping to keep them all wobbling without any one plate crashing down.

One of my first 'uh-oh moments' at work was when it hit me that working part-time didn't mean a reduction in workload. Before kids, I was dealing with a big volume of challenging work that often required long hours, and because I loved the work I was more than happy to do it. But after kids, I was doing the same load in one day less each week. The work didn't stop coming simply because my hours had changed. If I'd thought I was busy before, that was nothing compared to the hyperspeed of being part-time.

The next 'uh-oh moment' was when Aila started getting sick at daycare, and as a consequence so did I. My wife and I valued each other's careers equally, so we took care of our daughter equally when she was unwell. So now not only was I contending with a high workload in less time, but my working week was regularly obliterated by hand, foot and mouth disease and other horrid toddler viruses. And there was nothing we could do about it—we were just in a new reality. The grandparents would help occasionally, but they'd invariably get a nasty secondary infection and so became (quite fairly) reluctant to take care of a sick girl. I took more sick leave over the next year than I had in the previous two. And my employer was noticing.

As the months passed, I got a good sense of what those fathers in all those studies were talking about. I was reluctant to stay late at work, to participate in meetings before 9 a.m. or after 5 p.m., or to travel unless it was absolutely critical. I would haul arse as hard as I could during the day, not taking breaks or procrastinating, in order to squeeze the most out of my time, but when my family needed me at the end of the day, that was it—at least until later that night when everyone was in bed. It gradually dawned on me that my employer, which had been so amazingly supportive to begin with, was growing frustrated by my attempt to do the juggle.

I started to get texts or emails with thinly veiled frustration about my not being there for 4.30 or 5 p.m. teleconferences. There was explicit frustration at my unwillingness to travel overseas for an international conference. I was questioned about how much leave I'd been taking. Even if I called in to a staff meeting while sick on the couch at home, there were exasperated sighs about me not being in the office. Life was already tricky enough, and as I realised my employer was starting to give me low marks for my performance, I unravelled. A job which I had long considered my dream started keeping me awake at night with stress and anxiety.

During my descent into what researchers would call 'high psychological distress', where I was in my therapist's office every one or two weeks to deal with how awful and fragile I was feeling, I had another uh-oh moment—I realised that there's pressure on parents to feel grateful for how their employers allow them to reshape their working life. As a part-time worker, you are daily combatting the perception that you're not doing as much work as the full-timers. (Of course, you're not getting paid as much either.) But I increasingly sensed an assumption that I should be eternally grateful for being allowed to go part-time—for being allowed to care for my family. And a pressure to repay that gratitude. It's like a whisper in your ear. *You're already not in the office as much as the others—why do you need more time off? Can't you get someone to help you? Can't you get your shit together better?* As one of the only working dads doing part-time hours, I was all the more conspicuous to everyone around me.

Between April and December 2017, my confidence in how I was handling the juggle nose-dived, and with it my self-esteem. I despaired going to work, dreaded every new email I received, felt more and more like a failure who couldn't keep up with everyone else. I spent most nights curled in a ball in bed dreading the new day. That's how fucking hard being a working parent and a part-time working dad can be. Before long I believed performing the juggle was well and truly beyond me.

My big, bold experiment to be a different kind of working father seemed to have become a total fizzer, and in such a short period of time. Was I breaking the system, or had it swiftly broken me?

Requesting backup

I became part of the statistics when I jumped ship heavily influenced by my work–family conflict. My experience in 2017 led me to start looking around for new work. I applied for a role at another organisation (still in the not-for-profit sector) that was designated part-time. It was the sort of role that women exclusively went for, not men. But the interviewers didn't blink when I put in my CV, and my bosses have been super-supportive ever since I started. The organisation I left behind still does fantastic work, is still staffed by incredible people, and now boasts a few more working dads who have taken extended time off to be with their young families. They continue to punch above their weight in helping their employees balance work and family, informed by their experience with me. As hard as it was, we all went on the learning curve together.

That's the role of pioneers—to go beyond the comfort zone in order to test old systems and create new ones. By trying things differently, pioneers see what works well and what falls flat. It's a bumpy road and one filled with risk, but ultimately it prepares the way for those who come behind them.

I don't mean to warn other dads off making similar choices to the ones I did. I never regret making the decisions to take extended time off work, to switch to part-time work or to put childcaring at the core of my being. But I do regret doing it so naively. My experiences are bittersweet for me, but my hope is that by sharing them, I'll help more dads take the leap with their eyes open. Because I don't want to be a novelty anymore. I want backup. I want to see more pioneer dads breaking the system and creating a more family-friendly one.

I'd love to see many more dads on the front line of change. To be the first in their organisation to apply for parental leave even if they're told 'it's only meant for women'. To be the first man to apply for a part-time role so they can spend more time looking after their kids. To be the first man in their team to tell their colleagues they'll be leaving earlier than usual so they can pick up their kids from daycare, or they'll be in later because they're going to the Father's Day breakfast. We need men sticking their necks out, demanding time to be a dad.

To help recruit this backup, I can share some personal reflections from my four years of spinning plates. My starting point is that doing the work/life juggle is hard on everyone, including employers. I remain extremely grateful that my previous employer was so supportive, but I lament that we didn't fully understand and respond to the reality of how my changed life affected my work. We thought that providing leave and officially adjusting my hours was all we needed to do, but that was just the tip of the iceberg. For all dads considering how to reshape their work life, try to think about *all* the things that will change when you have kids, and how that might affect your behaviour and decision-making.

One of the best things about pregnancy is that you've got the best part of nine months to plan your life and get ready for the baby hurricane. Expectant fathers have a decent window to think about how they want to run their life once they become dads, and to have conversations with their colleagues and bosses about restructuring their role and taking time off work. My advice is to use that opportunity productively—and try as much as possible to make sure it's all written down and agreed, to save the heartache of misunderstandings and wrong assumptions later. There are organisations dedicated to just this challenge, like Parents At Work, based in Sydney, and Circle In, based in Melbourne. Their whole job is to help you manage work and family. If you're finding it hard coming to an acceptable arrangement, you don't need to fight the battle alone.

Secondly, take the leave you are entitled to, be it public or private. Every Aussie dad has access to Dad and Partner Pay in the first year of their child's life. To be honest, it's not enough, it completely undervalues the role of dads, and the whole notion of having a particular, smaller leave load for dads is crap to begin with—but hey, it's (slightly) better than nothing. Take back some of those taxes you've paid via a minimum wage payment from your corpulent bureaucratic buddies at Centrelink. Check your access to paid parental leave policies from your employer, and if the policy doesn't exist, ask why not. Some of my mates have access to very generous paid parental leave packages, but they don't take them. Even if there's an implicit suggestion that such policies are only for working mums, be the pioneer who uses them. Be the leader and set an example. Organisational paid parental leave is awesome. The company will pay you to be with your family. Think of all those long hours and weekends you've worked where you missed out on fun things . . . now you can get it back by using your parental leave. (And that's to say nothing of the benefits to you and your family more broadly.)

One of the biggest things I've learnt from my journey so far is that I can't have it all. I just can't. I do not think I can have the massively successful, corner-office professional career, with all that entails, and simultaneously be a highly involved and engaged dad who is always there for his kids. In the previous chapter, I argued that dads can do (almost) anything a mum can do. But that doesn't mean they can do *everything*. Something has to give. My experience of the past four years has reaffirmed to me that time cannot expand. If I'm at work, I am not at home, and vice versa. Sure, I can video-chat with my kids if I'm travelling or working late, but that only makes me visible. It does not make me *present*. I can order the groceries online from work and get them home-delivered, but I can't cook for my kids and talk to them about their day. And no amount of daycare, nannies or family members babysitting will change this reality.

If I thought otherwise, I would have missed any number of amazing milestone moments with my kids: the first time Luke clapped, the first time Aila said a word, the first time Luke said 'dada', referring to me, the first time Aila brought home a painting she made at daycare. Those memories are etched into my soul and I wouldn't trade them for anything. Any dad thinking he can run on zero sleep for twenty years, kicking arse at work and at home at the same time, is heading for a breakdown. In the end, all I can advise is that all parents need to make a choice about the balance of work and family in their lives, so it's important to make it honestly and deliberately.

I'm hardly the first working parent to reach the conclusion that I can't have it all. Millions of Aussie mums have done the hard slog of working part-time and juggling family, but men today are not openly discussing this topic with one another. From the comfort of our workplaces, men have witnessed the decades-long debate about whether women can have it all, but we've never fully participated in the discussion. It applies just as much to working dads as to working mums.

The stats tell us that working mums have been sacrificing their careers for a long time, and dealing with a larger degree of stress and pressure caused by home life. When I started writing this book, my daughter was just becoming conscious of my work life. Whenever I tried to sneak off and hammer out some words, she would amble up to me and ask forlornly, 'Daddy still working?' Maybe I'm overly emotional, but it stung every time she said it to me. I don't want her to become one of the kids telling researchers about how she wished I worked less, or not at all, because she's so desperate to spend more time with me.

I'm only one voice. There are 5.4 million other Aussie dads we desperately need to hear from on whether men can 'have it all'. Every voice matters.

Another reflection is that I don't think a 'work/life balance' actually exists, at least not when you have children and teenagers dependent on you for almost everything. The term suggests that some harmonious division between work and personal life can be achieved with the right amount of organisation and individual efficiency. That's a furphy. I'm yet to have a perfectly designed and executed week where all the various challenges synchronised like cogs in a Swiss watch. In my experience, being a working father has mostly involved managing a series of never-ending imbalances as best as I can. Some weeks are dominated by major deadlines and projects at work, which can involve later nights or busting out the laptop in the evening, when I'm shattered after a few hours of toddler and baby time. Other weeks are dominated by family, because one of my kids might get sick and can't go to daycare, or Julia or I catch that same miserable bug.

As I started to realise the truth about balancing work and life, I also discovered that the juggle is fragile, even when you feel like you're in control and doing things pretty darn well. When I look back, it's remarkable how quickly it crashed for me and how immediately I came to cast myself as a failure. Prioritising caring alongside work as a dad remains contingent to a great extent on the goodwill and understanding of others in the workplace, and that support can vacillate or disappear. Working dads must be clear-eyed about the realities of what it's like. It's bloody hard, but you must back yourself that you're making the right choice for yourself and your family. We desperately need more dads to step back from the workforce and do more caring, because that's the only way we're going to permanently change the male breadwinner culture.

If you're on the cusp of taking the leap, check exactly what 'flexible work arrangements' your organisation really can offer, because that's another loaded term. 'Flexible' work can fail entirely to deal with the work–family conflict and the long hours that so many dads, and their children, have flagged as a major problem. It might be that 'flexible work', in your company, just means you're not required to sit in the office until late at night, phoning home to say goodnight to your kids. Unless 'flexible work' policies are accompanied by some boundaries that protect a worker's family time, then it's not a real solution.

Some parental bloggers, human resource specialists and working parents have started discussing 'work/life integration' as the solution to this dilemma. As a concept, this sounds very dubious to me. A lot of the people I've seen advocating it appear to come from white-collar industries in which devotion to clients is one of the core job requirements. I know people trying to do the work/life integration, and in my opinion it's a road to heartache. Work/life integration is about squeezing your work and family activities into the same available time. It means doing that conference call while putting the washing on, or sending an email from the rumpus room while your kids play on the mat in front of you. Of course, it also requires you to log on when they're asleep, or before they wake up, time you could be spending with your partner or doing some exercise. The idea of 'integration' destroys any remaining distinction between your personal and professional lives—they are as one.

The risk with a lot of 'flexible work' arrangements is that they lead to more work and less life. You think we'd be able to come up with a more durable solution that ensures the work gets done but safeguards time for families as well.

Our current model of the working week—the Monday to Friday, 9 a.m. to 5 p.m. routine—was devised by Henry Ford when he was building his Model T Ford in the early 1900s. No joke, he created the working week we're all still so devoted to over a century later. He determined that this was the most effective working schedule for his factory employees, and resulted in the highest number of cars being made with the smallest number of mistakes.[52]

The Kiwis have actually picked up on the fact that Henry Ford is dead and we don't make Model Ts anymore, and in 2018 trialled a four-day working week. The company Perpetual Guardian has 250 employees and piloted a work routine where employees worked four eight-hour days, with no reduction in pay. During the trial, staff reported lower stress levels, higher levels of job satisfaction and an improved sense of work/life balance.[53] It was so successful that the company implemented the system permanently. Shouldn't this sort of arrangement be our new normal? Isn't this really what 'flexible work' should look like for all of us?

Finally, dads need to support each other better. We need to open up to each other about what it's like to be a father raising kids, at the same time as dealing with pressure to be the breadwinner and to conform to the rigid role society has created for us. Fatherhood is a fraternity, but men aren't good at talking openly and honestly about what it's like to be a dad. It's as if we're members of Skull and Bones, knowingly nodding to each other without trading any real experiences or stories from our lives. Men can change the culture around working fathers if we can change the conversations we're having. Dads need a network so we can share our war stories and to relieve the pressure and chaos of daily life—and relive the moments of unbridled joy.

However, dads aren't gifted a community like new mums are. There's a fantastic system set up to help wannabe, soon-to-be and new mums. There's even a specialist organisation, the Gidget Foundation, that focuses on perinatal anxiety and depression in women during pregnancy and after birth. That same supportive, safe, informed space does not really exist for dads. We have to build it ourselves.

You've got your friends and your colleagues as a starting point, as well as that dad at the park who also seems sheepish about having a chat, but is probably as interested as you in shooting the breeze. There are some structures emerging but we've got a long way to go. Dad's Group is one of the largest social networks built for fathers, where dads can meet up with other local dads and their kids for a coffee. It has 3500 members in 100 locations.[54] There's a subreddit called Daddit which has over 140,000 members. Despite my initial suspicion, this feed has volumes of practical advice, from before birth all the way through a kid's development. If you've got a question, chances are it's been canvassed at length on Daddit.

No man deserves to feel trapped into working for his whole adult life and missing out on being a dad. Life is bigger than that. Lots of dads are already stepping up at fatherhood by stepping out of the workforce, and there are many big companies acknowledging the need for their male workers to take the time to be a dad. However, as I pointed out earlier, it's mostly white-collar workers who are enjoying improved work/life conditions. They are the ones closer to any big change in fatherhood. It's much harder for dads in blue-collar industries to find the time to be a dad, whether that's parental leave or more flexible work arrangements.

Plus, our national discussion and research on Aussie fatherhood favours the experience of white-collar dads over blue collar ones. We don't actively include in this conversation those fathers who arrive at the crack of dawn to work on construction sites, or in factories or warehouses. Or who haul cargo up and down national highways. Or who transport us around in planes, trains and automobiles. Or who work the night shift, or do FIFO (fly in, fly out) work. Or the fathers at home struck by illness or economic hardship, who diligently love and care for their kids without any of society's well wishes or praise. Where do they sit in our grand plans for the future of fatherhood? Are they included in our conversations about helping men have more time as fathers? Reforming fatherhood must be inclusive of all fathers, not just those who can work from home more easily. At the moment, we applaud the big multinational introducing better leave and conditions, or put the celebrity dad on a pedestal, but push to the side the stories showing how hard it is for many men in more rigid industries to provide for their family plus be an involved dad.

Are we really on the brink of a revolution in fatherhood? Even if, over the next ten years, the number of dads who stay at home and care for their kids doubles, they might make up, at most, 10 per cent of all two-parent families in Australia. Homes all over the country still overwhelmingly rely on fathers to be the primary breadwinner and mothers to provide both caring and a top-up of the family income. Plus, our public parental leave schemes are some of the least generous in the developed world, which means there's hardly any incentive for families who need two incomes to pay the bills. It's a massive challenge to break our current system and replace it with something genuinely different.

I worry, too, that we'll accept a little bit of change as a major triumph for gender equality—a few more companies offering a bit more paternity leave or more flexible work. A few more dads choosing to stay at home. A few more celebrity dads talking about fatherhood, or a reboot of *House Husbands* (blurgh). Is that what the revolution looks like? Is that the endpoint? Perhaps offering more flexible work reinforces to dads that they should indeed spend most of their time working. Perhaps providing dads with a little parental leave stops them asking for a lot more. Perhaps we're all supportive of dads stepping out of the workforce as some aspirational goal, but really we want them to stay in their traditional role because that's what makes us comfortable.

Children deserve to spend more time with their dads, and fathers deserve the chance to explore how great they can be as carers. There is no final victory until that is a genuine choice for all men. I was lucky enough to be able to make that choice, even if I encountered some rough patches as I embraced my dual role as a worker and a carer. I'll do whatever I can to help other men see that they've got a choice too. Maybe this uprising will unfold one father at a time. Even if it's a slow burn, it's worth fighting for.

FORK IN
THE ROAD

TIM HAMMOND, PERTH

How do you decide between your family and that terrific job you've wanted since you were young? What if, beyond that job, lay the prospect that you might one day become prime minister? In 2016, Tim Hammond was grappling with just such a dilemma: whether to leave his work as a barrister and run for federal parliament.

Tim was married with two young children, the eldest of whom was four years old. He took the plunge and won preselection for the seat of Perth, and was elected to the parliament in the September election. Smart, dedicated, passionate and hardworking, Tim was quickly identified as a rising star with a big political future. Within months of arriving in Canberra, Tim was already in the shadow cabinet. In 2017, betting agency Sportsbet had him at $4.50 to become the next prime minister from Western Australia, second only to Julie Bishop.[1]

However, by May 2018 Tim had given up on national politics and resigned from parliament. There was no scandal or controversy behind his decision. He hadn't collapsed under the immense pressure of the job. He was on the way up, and already highly respected on all sides. He headed back to Perth voluntarily. Why?

Each step on Tim's journey, from resolving to enter politics to deciding to leave it, was deliberate and thoughtful. When Tim was considering running, he sat down with his family to discuss it and make a conscious decision. 'We made the decision as a family,' he says. 'All the family members, including both our young kids at the time, put forward their views. We were prepared to jump together.' And jump they did.

The next challenge was one that a lot of fathers have faced: how to make a regular work commute manageable for a young family. Tim would be flying back and forth between Perth and Canberra – the equivalent of flying from London to Moscow. 'I knew it would be a different dynamic at home because of my inevitable absence,' Tim recalls. 'We put together a family plan to minimise my absence, using whatever practical strategies we could. Instead of taking the direct flight to Canberra, which left Perth on a Sunday arvo, I would take the flight to Sydney, which left at midnight. That allowed me to have a full day and evening with my family.' Once in Sydney, Tim would then get up at sparrow's to catch the morning flight to Canberra.

Tim found the transcontinental commute doable. But, he says, 'The real killer was my absence from home. Despite our best planning as a family, there were things I just could not anticipate about becoming an MP. Our eldest child really struggled with the transition and was just perennially sad. My work on parliamentary committees meant I was travelling interstate and occasionally overseas more than I expected, and spending more time away from home. On top of that, my local community rightfully expected that I was available to them when I was back home as well. I had no dramas with the travel and I knew that was part of the job. We just didn't predict the impact of my absence from home.'

Tim did structured Facetime and Skype chats with his kids. But he realised that however much he loved his job, it was having a negative impact on his kids' wellbeing. 'No matter what I did, it became unmanageable,' Tim remembers. 'I was becoming further disconnected from the dad I desperately wanted to be.' Then in early 2017, Tim was confronted with another curveball: the unexpected but joyous news they would be expecting a third child, a son.

Tim had a sliding-doors moment as he tried to look into the future and see what life might be like if he continued down this road. 'I would deliberately think: *What do I want my life to look like when I'm 80 years of age?*' he says. He didn't overly like what he saw. 'As dads, we can all think a bit harder about how we can best add value to our families. Is it really just working and earning? The best guidance I reckon kids can get is from their folks, and dads are such a big part of ensuring the next generation of boys get the life skills they need.'

His decision to step out of politics was as deliberate as his decision to enter it had been. Everyone in the family had their say again. He then pulled the trigger and decided to quit. 'Not for a nanosecond has it felt like the wrong call,' he says. 'I will forever cherish the reaction of my then six-year-old when she realised Dad was coming home for good.'

Tim was surprised by how supportive of his decision his electorate was. 'I was just hoping for an even split in the community between those who agreed and disagreed with me,' he says, 'but there was a very high level of understanding, which was a huge relief.'

What a refreshing scenario – a male pollie leaving to actually be with his family. A man putting his love of his children and his family first, at the time in their lives it mattered the most, and when he didn't have to. Now he has a new challenge: raising a little boy along with his two girls.

'It's unprecedented how kids are made to deal these days with so many fast-paced developments,' Tim says. 'I think dads can add huge value by being present and helping their sons be curious, giving them safe environments to explore and learn in.'

Tim Hammond may never be PM, but he's back doing what he loves: being an involved dad, and building beautiful memories with his family that he will cherish for his whole life. As the knight in *Indiana Jones and the Last Crusade* might say, he chose wisely.

5

BOY BIOLOGY

———

I'd never previously placed a huge importance on science. I know that sounds ridiculous, but it's true. I sucked at science as a kid, and it was the lesson I dreaded the most throughout high school. The closest I've come to science in the past decade is watching *Interstellar*. However, when Julia was pregnant the first time around, I, like a lot of partners, was suddenly immersed in obstetrics.

Each time we found out we were expecting, I immediately downloaded a couple of apps that gave me weekly updates on the development of the foetus, measuring its size against a random selection of fruit and veg. I would talk daily to Julia about how she was feeling and what was changing in her body. We did all the genetic testing on both foetuses. We did the antenatal classes to learn about labour and birth. And once our kids were born, we used the book *Baby on Board* to track their progress.[1]

About the time Aila turned one, though, I stopped paying attention to the science. It wasn't a deliberate decision. I guess I just thought that we'd made it through the first year, our daughter was alive and well, and from now on she'd just start growing up into being a kid. I didn't think I needed so much biological info in my daily parenting routine.

For the next couple of years, until late into Julia's second pregnancy, I didn't pay any attention to child science. Instead I operated on a couple of *very* basic assumptions. Firstly, that there was little actual difference between girls and boys, and that I would raise them in the much same way. I felt that the little kid in *Kindergarten Cop* had nailed the only distinction that mattered (much to the uproarious laughter of his classmates): 'Boys have a penis, girls have a vagina.' I believed that, as Luke and Aila started to grow up, the best thing to do was assume that they'd learn, behave and understand the world in the same way. Secondly, I figured there were only three stages to child development— they're babies, then they're kids, then they're teenagers—and that my job as a dad was to help my kids navigate these periods, adjusting my parenting style as they got older. Simples.

If I was giving these answers today on a game show, the big angry buzzer would be going off, telling me I'm wrong and that I didn't win the showcase.

In my well-intentioned desire to treat my son and daughter equally from the get-go, I didn't pause to ask whether there are significant differences between boys and girls that I should be aware of, physically, emotionally or intellectually. This started to change when I spent a precious Saturday in 2018 locked away in a conference room in Sydney's CBD, ahead of our son's birth, hearing some bona fide parenting experts—Steve Biddulph, Maggie Dent and Clark Wight—discuss what it's like to raise boys. Sitting alongside Julia, I'd decided to give science a full day to prove itself.

In a large amphitheatre usually reserved for evangelical sermons, the presentation blew me away. I was hit with some life-altering knowledge, and found that my basic assumptions were powerfully wrong. I learnt that boys have a unique developmental path that sets them apart from girls, and vice versa, and that there are a bunch of developmental phases that a lot of parents don't really appreciate. It inspired me to learn more before my baby boy popped out.

I think my experience is fairly typical. We reckon we're well informed as parents, but our knowledge tends to be pretty limited after our babies are no longer babies. Sure, there are hundreds of books you can buy, lots of podcasts you can listen to, and endless parental blogs, but how are busy dads meant to find the stuff really worth paying attention to? When it comes to parents understanding the science of children, it's all foetuses and babies. Our community places a huge emphasis on pregnancy and the first twelve months. But from that age the information starts to drop away. It's only as behavioural or physical challenges emerge later that we try to understand what is happening with our kids.

How about we actually help dads understand their boys *the whole way*, rather than just at the beginning or when there's trouble brewing? I feel lucky that I caught a bit of boy biology really early on, because now I understand that there are a bunch of biological markers for boys between their birth and their early twenties that are easy to miss without some guidance. But how many dads have been told about these? How can we expect dads to guide our boys on their journey to manhood if we're not giving them decent insight into the scientific secrets of boys?

In this chapter, I put aside my dislike for science to share some boy biology, and to explore what makes boys tick. This is absolutely not an exhaustive summary of the scientific literature out there, and—as I hope I've made obvious by now—I'm no expert. But I hope what you read here is compelling and triggers further thinking.

The science on boyhood is evolving constantly, and while it may not make raising boys any less challenging, it might make it more relatable, bearable and, dare I say it, manageable. I'll explore how dads can be there for their sons at these critical phases, and how they can help guide and teach boys on their journey to manhood. Getting this right is crucial for the next generation of men, and for the one after that. We've got to do better to light the way for dads, to help them understand what their boys are going through. How else can we get mature, resilient and emotionally healthy young men?

Let's start with a fun fact: all foetuses begin life as females. The Y chromosome is an add-on which helps give baby boys their boy bits.[2] So if you have a boy, congratulations—you've basically got your very own X-man!

Identity on a spectrum

How well does any of us understand the science of identity? I'm not sure if it's because I suck at science, if I was too busy staring at my phone during an antenatal class, or if I forgot to pick up the right pamphlet at the obstetrician's office, but I always thought that gender and sex were the same thing. You're born with a penis—hey, you're a boy! If you've got a vagina—ta-da, you're a girl! I envisaged a neat binary of boys and girls, the human equivalent of computer coding: 1 and 0. What I found out, pretty recently, is that it's nowhere near that simple, and I have a lot to learn.

When I actually bothered to look at the science, I discovered that instead of thinking gender was all about penises and vaginas, I should think of it as a combination of core components: biological sex, gender identity and gender expression. Biological sex is determined at birth by looking at your kid's bits. This is the element we all tend to understand: XX chromosomes means ovaries and vagina, XY chromosomes means testes and penis. If there's a mix of male and female chromosomes, you get someone who is intersex. (When I was a kid, someone who was intersex was called a hermaphrodite, as I tell Julia every single time we discuss this topic.) The biological aspect of the puzzle isn't exactly new information, but it's closely related to the other, less well discussed elements.

The next component is gender identity. Fundamentally, this is a person's deeply rooted sense of being a man, a women or something that exists in between these two positions. It comes from within the person—it's something they just intrinsically know about themselves. Science suggests that gender identity is pretty firmly established by about age three, but of course everyone's a little different.[3] So a person who is born with a certain biological sex but feels more deeply aligned with the other sex is *transgender*. A person who identifies with the biological sex they had at birth is *cisgender*. A person who identifies with both genders, or neither, is *non-binary*.

The third element is gender expression. Everyone expresses their identity through a variety of ways: how they walk, talk or dress, who they relate to, and how they identify with others. We refer to some expressions as more *masculine*, some as more *feminine*, and a combination of either set of typical traits we put under the banner of *androgynous*. In this last element, biology starts to rub up against culture and community, and individuals rely on their experiences of the world in an effort to build their identity.

That's a neat breakdown of basic gender science as I've learnt it. Perhaps too neat; in fact, science tells us that gender exists on a spectrum.[4] Lots of people might exist in two big lumps at either end, male and female. But between these sits a whole lot of splendid variation and rich individual experience. Gender is a complex amalgam of chromosomes, anatomy, hormones and psychology.[5] Intersex people or transgender people, for example, may be less common, but they are no less natural. The whole spectrum represents what it means to be human—and all boys sit somewhere on this spectrum.

For me as a newish dad, with young kids and poor scientific abilities, this was a huge new piece of knowledge. If fathers are to offer their boys a wider, deeper, richer version of masculinity, then we need to understand this spectrum, and help our sons find their place on it. As my tiny little fel starts to grow up and reach out to the world around him, I can listen to him, observe him and do my best to understand his version of being human. And in time I will help him to understand that all boys are on their own journey to understand their own identity. I can help him learn to respect his own identity and those of others around him.

Society is gradually catching up to the science and offering people more choice on gender identification. In 2013 it became unlawful in Australia to discriminate against someone based on their sexual orientation, gender identity or intersex status.[6] In 2014, Facebook introduced about 50 gender options to Aussie users.[7] In 2016, researchers from the Queensland University of

Technology teamed up with (believe it or not) the Australian Sex Party, AdultMatchmaker.com.au and adult industry lobby group the Eros Association to deliver the Australian Sex Survey.[8] When it came to nominating gender, its almost 7500 respondents could choose between 33 options. About 60 per cent of respondents identified as a man and 32 per cent as a woman; the remaining 8 per cent were scattered across all the other categories.[9] Coincidentally, the Australian census was held the same year, but the ABS was a tad more cautious than our Facebook overlords or the sex fiends, offering only 'other' as the additional category to 'male' and 'female'.[10] In early 2019, New York City introduced a law making it easier for transgender and non-binary Knickerbockers to match their birth certificate with their gender identity, as well as creating a new non-binary 'X' label.[11] Canada has done something similar with the identity labels on its passports.[12]

There's interesting stuff going on around the world that reveals an understanding of gender that is getting more sophisticated. No, I don't mean Caitlin Jenner having a new TV show. Close to home, Samoan society recognises a third gender, *fa'afafine*, whereby biologically male children can be raised as females who identify with being female, have female mannerisms and tend to have relationships with heterosexual men.[13] This is also a practice across Polynesia.[14] Researchers observed that in a region of the Dominican Republic, too, there are intersex children who at birth had no developed penis because they lack the requisite hormone. They are raised as girls until about the age of twelve, but then go through normal male puberty and develop a penis.[15] The trait is due to an enzyme deficiency that can be common in this area of the Dominican Republic but extremely rare everywhere else.[16]

Swedish society uses a third, non-gender pronoun, *hen*. It had floated around as a seldom-used word for decades, but in recent years was picked up and used by transgender people or people who did not wish to identify as male or female. In 2015, *hen* was officially listed in the Swedish dictionary.[17] Teachers at Swedish public preschools work hard to be gender-neutral in how they interact with their kids, and in how the kids play every day. They try to encourage children to explore their full range of behaviours rather than feeling they must conform to traditional boy/girl behaviours.[18]

It seems to me that all these examples point to different groups of people trying, however imperfectly, to reflect the complex reality of gender. No one has got it right, and lots of young men everywhere struggle with their gender identity. We in Australia have such a narrow vision of masculinity that life can be suffocating for young guys. It can be discombobulating or even confronting to get your head around it, but it's all part of the journey of being human.

This is where dads are so crucial. Even if we ourselves feel boxed into a limited understanding of what it means to be a man, or we're not familiar with the latest science, we can still show our boys a better, richer, deeper version of masculinity, one that allows them to be open about their identity. We can help them feel confident and safe in their sense of self, and to genuinely understand that they are accepted for who they are. Surveys tend to show that the present generation of young parents are more comfortable seeing gender as fluid than those from other generations.[19] A 2015 'Millennial Poll' asked 1000 people aged eighteen to 34 about gender: 50 per cent agreed that gender falls on a spectrum, while 46 per cent agreed gender is either male or female.[20]

One of the best gifts this generation of dads can give to the next generation of boys is the freedom to be who they want to be. I'd feel dreadful if my son, as an angsty teenager or even as a toddler, felt he had to hide who he really was from me because he thought I had particular expectations of him. I never want to trap him into a specific version of boyhood or manhood; on the contrary, I want to set him free, and help him feel completely comfortable in his own skin.

Being a boy

Before I had kids, the only stages of childhood I'd heard anyone talk about were the 'terrible twos' and the teenage years. I figured the period in between was just one long developmental phase. That's how I remembered my own childhood. Each year kids grow up a little more, get a little smarter, are more able to do things on their own and start to develop a really distinct personality—and then they enter puberty, when it all becomes chaos.

When Julia and I went to see Steve Biddulph and Maggie Dent give their workshop on raising boys, I didn't know much about their work. But it was on that Saturday that my understanding of boyhood started to shift. It went from being a foggy blur of personal memories and half-baked assumptions to a clear picture of a journey on a long and winding road. Parenting often feels like stumbling around in the dark trying to find the light switch, and that was the day I started getting closer to locating it.

Afterwards, with the arrival of my son getting closer and closer, I decided to get a better understanding of boy biology. Yeesh, parenting literature did not make that task easy. A simple Google search can quickly overwhelm you with the sheer volume of what's available.

The parenting expert industry is a mix of academic researchers, child psychologists, behavioural psychologists, medical doctors, schoolteachers, journalists, celebrity parents and ordinary parents, so it's important to keep your bullshit detector on high alert. It can be hard to sift through the books, blogs, reports, op-eds and scientific studies as you try to filter the authoritative from the personal and the random. Unsurprisingly, there is a lot of overlap between these categories. Something you think is based on slam-dunk, totally proven science turns out to be based on a study of a handful of kids 30 years ago, and is actually hotly disputed between competing groups of experts. Yet you can also find incredibly valuable pieces of information that can make a huge difference to you as a dad. I suppose the trick is to take what you find as advice, and not as hard and fast rules.

Similarly, while there are observable patterns across the population, every kid is different, and develops differently. They each have their personal challenges and idiosyncrasies that can challenge what the experts say. Critical thinking is vital for parents as they delve into this literature; taking everything at face value risks causing a lot of heartache and stress about why your boy doesn't conform precisely to the experts' behavioural models.

Nevertheless, delve in I did. What I discovered is that boyhood can be broken down into several stages that relate to a boy's changing biology. As they develop, their brain will rewire, and they will behave differently. And it starts early, really early, before you even realise you're going to have a kid.

According to the Centre for Community Child Health at the Royal Children's Hospital in Melbourne, the foetus and then infant is most adaptable (and also most vulnerable) from conception until about the age of two.[21] The foetus actively responds to changes in its environment, and can start reading the cues from mum's mental and physical state to determine the kind of world it will be born into; incredibly, it can even alter its bodily structures accordingly.[22] That means our biology changes in response to negative experiences, such as stress, trauma or poverty, and these changes can be passed on to children by their parents and grandparents.[23]

Studies have also found that baby boys can be more vulnerable emotionally than baby girls to bad things happening in their little world. This is due to their hormones. When boys are first born, their testosterone is already wreaking havoc and leaving long-term effects for parents to grapple with. Right after birth, a baby boy's testosterone levels are the same as those of a twelve-year-old boy.[24] So your precious, angelic newborn has something in common with spotty, grimy pre-teen Clyde, who lives down the street and seems to always be tripping over and picking his nose. The testosterone at birth is left over from his body's penis construction process, which takes place during pregnancy. (It can also mean baby boys can get boners—this happened to the son of a close friend of mine, who thought it was hilarious every time it happened.)

Testosterone influences a little boy's development, most notably by slowing his brain development relative to similar-aged girls. This is an important point. Because of this, boys take longer to develop the brain circuitry that regulates stress, meaning they don't respond as well as girls to negative things happening to them.[25] This can include trauma at birth, caregiving that leaves them in distress, or even prenatal maternal stress and depression.[26] This early developmental delay can leave them more vulnerable to mental health and behavioural problems later on. The science suggests that boys may be more vulnerable to autism, early-onset schizophrenia, attention deficit hyperactivity disorder (ADHD) and conduct disorders.[27]

Given that they start life a couple of steps behind girls, creating a safe, calm, loving and relatively stress-free environment for boys is crucial.[28] If you were looking for any additional reasons to take a decent chunk of parental leave and be an involved, caring dad from the get-go, here they are. The male breadwinner who is absent from home has done no favours in helping little boys deal with their developmental vulnerabilities. Nor has the way we narrowly define masculinity as a process of 'toughening up' young boys and teaching them to hide their vulnerabilities and problems. We're fighting against nature when we should be leaning into it. We need to work harder to nurture our little boys so they are emotionally healthy and resilient, with the knowledge that they start life a bit more vulnerable than their sisters.

This notion of baby boy vulnerability strikes a chord with me. According to this science, my little boy might very well be one of those kids with a predisposition to problems with emotional wellbeing and mental health. As I described in the Prologue, Luke had a tough entry into the world. His initial experiences of the world included Julia struggling with perinatal depression, being exhausted in the womb by a complicated labour, contracting a deadly serious virus at four days old, dealing with painful digestive problems when feeding as well as being woefully unable to sleep as a newborn. For the first few months of his life, Luke seemed so miserable that Julia and I wondered whether he was carrying post-traumatic stress from the birth. We certainly were.

At the time of writing, Luke is a year old, healthy, eating well, crawling constantly and flashing an adorable smile to make people's hearts melt. He seems great, but I wonder whether his shocking start to life etched into him a greater vulnerability that might get exacerbated over the years. I'll never know for sure. But at least I'm aware of the possible lasting effects and can keep an eye out for behavioural patterns that might suggest something is up.

Steve Biddulph talks about the first major developmental stage for boys lasting from when they're babies until they're about six years old.[29] They're sweet, cuddly little things whose eyes light up when they explore their world. They want to play, laugh and cause mischief. Apparently, during this time little boys usually bond most closely with their mums.[30] Everything is new to them, and their innocence and sense of wonder is infectious (and refreshing, when the dumpster fire that is life in the 21st century is eating away at you as a parent). Their brain is developing at the fastest rate it ever will, and every interaction with the world, and new sensation, creates millions of connections.[31] They learn best when they're playing, an awesome approach to life that, sadly, we mostly forget when we're adults.[32]

Within this zero-to-six age bracket, there are individual developmental phases worth mentioning. An important one is the 1000 days between conception and when the kid turns two. This developmental period of a child's life assumes a greater significance than almost any other, a finding backed by rigorous scientific research.[33] During this time, a child's brain is doing an incredible amount of risk assessment and environmental scanning.

Turns out that the foetus is a very cluey thing. As mentioned above, it uses cues provided by the mother's physical and mental state to 'predict' the kind of world it will be born into, and adapts accordingly. Individual family and community factors will significantly shape the development of a baby. For instance, the age, health and wellbeing of the mum and dad affect the embryo. After birth, when children do not feel safe, calm or protected, their brain develops neuronal pathways that are associated with survival before those that are crucial for future learning and growth. Experiences that shape this include essential items like access to decent housing and parks, a clean environment and a healthy diet. Not everything that happens in this first thousand days has a permanent effect on a child, but as they grow, their ability to compensate for these negative experiences and environments is reduced. The evidence is also 'overwhelming' that a child's exposure to family violence, even if they're not the direct recipient of abuse, can severely undermine their long-term wellbeing and potential.[34]

I hope my sharing this information is illuminating, and not scary. It shouldn't stir feelings of nihilism for dads who are way past the first thousand days with their sons. I certainly don't think my son's fate is sealed by the time he turns two, just like I don't think I will simply parent in the way I was parented. Fatherhood is a lifelong journey, and you have ample time along the way to be close to your son, to make up for past mistakes or sporadic absences from home. As we've seen, not every father can spend loads of time with his very young kids.

As I see it, the first thousand days, also acts as an early-warning system. It encourages parents to be attentive to the influences in their young boy's life from the get-go. It's helping me stay on my toes as a dad and remain mindful that each experience—each trip to the park, each piece of healthy food, each cuddle and play—adds another building block to my son's sense of himself in the world.

There are other individual phases in the zero-to-six bracket that get talked about by parents and experts all the time. There's the classic 'terrible twos', the more recent idea of the 'threenager', and even the 'full-on fours'. There are volumes of parenting literature dedicated to trying to categorise the patterns of behaviour you find in young kids, too much to get through in a lifetime. There are plenty of blog and opinion pages exploring parents' stories of raising threenagers, for instance.[35] Biddulph argues that the full-on fours could be due to a hormone release (luteinising hormone) in most boys around this age, when they become way more energetic and boisterous, and harder to keep quiet.[36] Getting them to behave or calm down can be an almighty battle. While some girls may show a similar pattern, it seems to be a phenomenon unique to boys.

Depending on which parents or experts you talk to, you'll get different responses about these so-called phases. Aila did not have the 'terrible twos' at all—it was an absolute joy watching her build her identity and sense of self, and I couldn't see what all the fuss was about. But I have friends who recount with certainty how their toddler became a threenager precisely as they blew out the three candles on the birthday cake. David Campbell explained his shock and frustrations when his twins became threenagers, calling it 'an attack on all you hold dear, orchestrated by two little people. There is no rhyme nor reason for the storm and it hits hard and fast.'[37] Another friend of mine with twins said that her son definitely experienced a major and dramatic change in behaviour when he turned four, and became very different from his twin sister.

I think parents apply these labels to kids because we're trying to find readymade explanations for behaviour that is new, challenging and confronting. We want a comfortable, reassuring answer to the question: 'What happened to my sweet little baby boy?' It may not help us in the short term, but having a reasonable-sounding rationale for dramatic behavioural change gives parents back a little control in an out-of-tilt home life. That in itself is helpful during tough times.

What these terms indicate is that during the time a boy is two to four years old, his parents may experience (suffer) some seriously infuriating and demoralising behaviour. During this time, little kids are carving out their place in their family and trying to stand on their own two feet—literally and metaphorically. They are gradually becoming more self-aware, getting more control over their actions, learning to communicate their needs and problems, and learning that they can have an impact on things around them. Their horizons are expanding with their ambitions to explore. Their desire for greater independence and control are restrained by their abilities, including how to deal with an explosion of emotions. That can lead them to be more angry, defiant, frustrated and overwhelmed.[38] On the bright side, they are more empathetic, compassionate and complex humans than we ever give them credit for.[39]

What about those four-year-old Rambos charging around the place? Biddulph argues that when boys are four, they need lots of physical activity because movement helps grow their brains. All kids need this, but the professional advice is that boys typically need it for longer than girls. Boys use physicality to express themselves as they are generally not as articulate as girls.[40] But instead of understanding what they're going through, we often start telling these boys they're bad or naughty—that they're making life difficult for everyone else. Worried parents might take the boy to a doctor or psychologist, and he might be incorrectly diagnosed with a behavioural disorder. Little boys can end up feeling pretty crappy for acting exactly how their bodies are urging them to.

Dads can be hugely important in teaching young boys how to play safely and respectfully of others, and help them learn to self-regulate, to talk openly about their emotions and to manage their feelings constructively.[41] This requires a fair degree of patience and consistency, and dads can also model that behaviour for their boys. It might be difficult, and require hazmat suits for Chernobyl-style meltdowns in the shopping centre or at the park, but dads can really help their boys get through this torrid time and emerge the stronger for it.

Once you're past the full-on fours, it's almost time for primary school. In the past decade or so, the age boys should start school has become hotly contested. We tend to start our kids at school at about five years old or a little younger, but there's lots of evidence that this is especially too early for boys. This is partly given how physical and energetic boys are when they're four or five and the importance placed on play-based learning over formal desk-based learning at this age. Within the OECD nations, primary school typically begins at six years old.[42] In Finland they recommend kids not to start primary school until they be closer to seven years old.[43] Research also suggests that four and five year old boys still tend to lag behind girls in brain development—by as much as twenty months.[44] That's a massive amount early in the life of the child, especially one about to start school. A lot of boys just aren't ready to be shoved on an assembly mat, or at a table, where they need to follow instructions, be quiet and pay attention.[45] Better for them to utilise that energy and business by playing and exploring. No teacher or parents wants a little boy to feel miserable or uncomfortable at school in his first year, and to dread going there.

There are experts encouraging parents to start their boys at primary school after they turn five years old, arguing that they're more likely to be ready when they're older. It's a topic where the research is not clear cut, and parents can find perfectly reasonable rationales for either delaying a boy starting school or keeping him in a cohort with slightly older peers. While studies regularly find that the older kids have better academic and behavioural outcomes in the first few years of school, it is not as clear cut whether there is a long-term impact. Certain studies have shown that younger kids catch-up to their older peers in the first few years of schooling, yet other studies find that while the gap may narrow, it is never completely closed over primary and secondary schooling.[46] Parents are starting to take note of the debate on this issue. A 2019 study showed about a quarter of children in New South Wales are starting school a year later than they are eligible.[47] Kids most likely to be held back from starting school by parents were 'boys, born closer to the cut-off date, who live in areas where others were being delayed, and come from relatively advantaged backgrounds'.[48] However, not everyone can afford to keep their boys out of school, considering how expensive daycare is for parents.

Even if you send your boy to school at around five, at least you should be mindful that he might have a very different experience of it from his sister, and help him do the best he can. Try to ensure he doesn't get labelled a problem child just because he can't sit still or pay super-close attention to what's going on.

The next major developmental phase for boys comes between six to fourteen.[49] This is when boys are going through primary school, and then transitioning to high school. They're getting bigger and formulating their distinctive personalities, and they're getting dangerously close to puberty and all its angstiness. As parents, you're relieved those toddler years are behind you, and you're adjusting to the school run combined with a little sport or drama on the side. You've also gone from getting personalised daily summaries from the early childhood carers on how your boy went at daycare, and instead you're picking them up from the bus stop or the school gate and trying to translate sighs and grunts into a narrative of how their day went.

In reality, this is a time of multiple transitions, not least the biological stuff. Actually this period is a whopper, especially for dads, although not many of us realise it.

Little boys, who tend to be devoted to their mums when they're younger, start getting increasingly attached to and fixated on dad. They'll crave his attention and acknowledgement, and do whatever it takes to get it. Biddulph argues that boys in this phase want to learn what it takes to be a man, and dad offers the nearest and best on-the-job training in masculinity. Sons are keen to discover the secrets of being a man as puberty comes knocking on the door.

There's a big danger during this phase that dad is being pulled in two different directions. His kids are getting older, going to school and costing more money, and dad himself is in the prime of his career, working hard, trying to get promoted and earn more moolah. For a boy born in 2019 in metropolitan Australia, it's estimated that it will cost his folks over $350,000 to put him through an independent private school, or almost $150,000 if he goes through the Catholic system.[50] Even if you choose the local public schools, it will cost you about $78,000! So right when his son desperately needs to learn from him, dad may well be working long hours to shore up his family's financial future.

If dad isn't around a lot during this period, the boy often locks on to the next available male in his life. It could be an uncle, an older brother, a grandfather. It could also be some douchebag down the street or an older kid at school. They will then take their masculinity cues from the dad-substitute, which may be really good—or not.

When I was a kid of this age, my dad tried his hardest not to work too late. He was mostly home by dinnertime, even if that meant he had to do more work later that night. However, he often travelled interstate or overseas, sometimes even for a couple of weeks. I remember him regularly ringing from a fancy hotel in some bustling international capital. I also remember how exciting it was when he came home—he was like Richard the Lionheart returning from the Crusades. He always had great presents or new pieces of technology he had been given, like pocketbook organisers or electronic language translators. He would ask me about school, come to my sport or other activities and be as engaged as he could. Then he would be away again.

When I look back now, it's fair to say that I had no clue what manhood or masculinity entailed. I was an only child who was very sensitive and took to heart everything people said about me. Without knowing what masculinity meant, I had a vague sense that I wasn't matching up. I don't think I ever tried to find a replacement for my dad—I just gleaned what I could from him. So I learnt that being a man was about working long hours at an office somewhere, and being married. I sought more answers from the mostly retrograde blokes who taught at my fancy private school, where masculinity was defined by sport and feats of strength. So I drifted during this period of life in which, according to Biddulph, it is so crucial for boys to get a rich experience of manhood. And I formed a shallow view of masculinity based on tired old tropes. I suspect a lot of boys at my school did much the same thing.

Importantly, it's not just that boys are looking around during this time for how to be a man—they're also feeling pretty vulnerable. At about eight or nine years old, almost the midpoint of this developmental phase, boys experience a precursor to puberty, a shot across the bow that warns of what is to come. It's called adrenarche, a cold-sounding name that could easily refer to a James Bond villain. It's also known as 'the emotional eights', which sounds more like a folk music troupe. This developmental trend is becoming better understood because in 2012 the Murdoch Children's Research Institute started following over 1200 Year 3 students, and has been closely tracking their development ever since. By 2018 the students were in Year 9, and the data was producing some pretty clear answers.

During adrenarche, which affects boys and girls, there is no physical developmental change, as happens during puberty, but a hormonal shift occurs that affects boys' emotional wellbeing and their interactions with close family and friends.[51] And it does seem to affect boys a lot more than girls.[52] Boys can be more easily upset, more emotional and more sensitive than previously. Young boys can feel more rattled and more vulnerable to the world around them.[53] They may be feeling a bit raw and vulnerable at this age anyway. They might have their first experience of bullying at school, they might start feeling pressure to conform with what their peers are doing, their individual differences might start being highlighted in their social groupings, and they will be trying to work out who their close friends are. Even understanding when someone is being sarcastic to them can be difficult.[54]

This can be a trickier age for boys than girls. Remember how I mentioned earlier that male babies tend to be more developmentally vulnerable when they're born? Well, by the time our little dudes approach adrenarche, the gap in their social skills compared to girls can become really apparent. Between the ages of seven and twelve, some boys can be a long way behind girls in social sensitivity, including understanding their own feelings, thinking through their actions and working out how to calm themselves down.[55]

Far from being a period of calm before the storm of puberty hits, these middle years can be rough on boys—and if it goes badly, it can really mess them up. What's more, it's about this age that boys start getting those nasty messages to 'stop crying like a little girl', and to 'toughen up and be a man'. They can get called out for being 'different' or 'weird', or even be subjected to physical attacks. Something as innocuous as wearing the wrong T-shirt or sneakers can see them treated as if they're an alien species. So at a hugely vulnerable point in boys' development, when they're wearing their hearts on their sleeve, our society has a tendency to take their hearts and stomp all over them. If we mistake their biological and emotional development for them being naughty or hot-headed screw-ups, we can do long-term damage to their wellbeing and their understanding of what it means to be a young man.

Testosterone tests

The final stage of boyhood is from about the age of fourteen onwards. During this time, puberty reigns supreme, and our boys are trying on the ill-fitting fabric of manhood for the first time. You may have thought the journey through the earlier parts of boyhood are fairly hazardous, but Biddulph believes that we fail our boys the most during this last developmental phase.[56]

While a boy's body has done some preparatory work in the lead-up to puberty, by the time he's fourteen it is all systems go. His testosterone levels will have increased by almost 800 per cent over his pre-puberty levels—the age of sweaty shirts and sticky bedsheets is upon you and your family.[57] And if your teenage boy feels his breasts are getting a bit swollen and tender, don't rag on him: in about 50 per cent of boys the testosterone levels get so high that some of it converts into oestrogen.[58] There is some evidence that environmental factors, including being in scary or violent school situations, may also have an impact on the level of testosterone in a boy's body—but that's still an area of emerging research.[59]

As his hormones are ramping up, his brainwaves are dying down. During this period, the brain prunes the synapses, removing connections between neurons, to make itself more efficient and ready for adulthood, but there is a lag effect for months when your boy may no longer be the rigorous intellectual he once was.[60] Our boys at fourteen are a real work in progress as they near adulthood.

Most of us have a clear picture of adolescent boys that's based on our own experiences and the reams of pop culture and media references that we're exposed to: they're horny, vacuous, vain, rebellious, disrespectful, impatient, argumentative, lazy, blah blah blah. Parents talk of 'enduring' adolescence and surviving its worst excesses, hoping that a decent young man will emerge out the other side. But how well do we, as parents, guide our adolescent boys in this final stretch to manhood? In this chapter, I've explored a bunch of biological markers to help us understand boys, but are we laying down markers for them to understand how to grow up and find their way to manhood?

Not really.

Manhood in Australia is pretty hazily defined. We don't really give any clear signals as to when it starts, and instead we celebrate a bunch of contradictory milestones. You can learn to drive when you're sixteen, vote and drink when you're eighteen, and most boys leave high school about the same age. We still celebrate 21st birthdays in a massive way, and over 40 per cent of people aged between twenty and 24 still live at home with their folks.[61]

By the time our boys are on the verge of being men, they have gone through a lot. They've gone from being cheeky, inquisitive toddlers to mopey, dopey teenagers looking for adventure. They've got on and off a lot of emotional roller-coasters. They're looking around for examples of how to be a man, trying to understand what it means and how to exemplify it in their own lives. But often they're not given clear signals about what to do. They leave high school, leave home, go travelling, get a job, start uni or TAFE, and we hope that as they muddle their way through these major transition points, they'll have somehow worked out manhood on their own. That's a bold parenting strategy for the next generation of young men. Is it really the best one?

6

GETTING REAL ABOUT MASCULINITY

I'm in a phase of fatherhood where as long as I keep my boy alive, I'm meeting the minimum job requirements. At the moment, he needs sleep, food, nappies and clothes. He needs to play and explore, and not become a zombie child hooked on screens. Boy biology tells me that at about the time my little fel blows out the candles on his sixth birthday cake, he's going to start wondering what it means to be a man.

Okay, so what do I show him?

When did I become a man?

I start by thinking back to what I was told when I was growing up. Problem is, I wasn't told much about manhood, what it takes to be a man, or how to know when I became a man. Ancient societies had initiations into manhood to let you know you'd arrived. Not so much anymore. My dad never really gave me the spiel about manhood. He tried to model it by what he did. He wore a suit, went to work, watched the news, loved sport. But even as I came to do those things in my twenties, I still felt more like a boy than a man. Doing them didn't make me feel manly, even if it was what my dad had done for all those years.

High school didn't make me feel like I was becoming a man. I straddled a couple of different social sets when I was a teenager. I was mostly in the nerdlinger camp, one of the studious kids trying to always get good grades and good reports, complying with the school's unending and often archaic list of rules. Instead of partying, I'd go to Sizzler (remember that?) with friends then see a movie like *Jurassic Park: The Lost World* up the road. Or I'd hang out at someone's house playing *Mortal Kombat* or *Mario Kart* and eat a bunch of chips, lollies and soft drink.

I was pretty good at cricket at school, so I was exposed to the sporty and cool kids who were partying and, I assumed, enjoying stellar dating lives with girls from the best and more self-important social cliques Sydney's North Shore could offer. I instinctively considered these guys, with their physical prowess and popular lives, closer to manhood than anyone else in my year. I remember sitting around with my nerd friends halfway into Year 12, getting drunk on Lemon Ruskis and lamenting how we didn't know any girls and the prospect of going on a date was utterly hopeless. I didn't feel very manly at that point—and even less so the next day, when I had my first hangover.

Even in my late twenties, when I was working in big corporate towers in my business suit and tie, I still didn't feel very manly. When people referred to me as 'sir' in a meeting, restaurant or a plane, I assumed it was out of politeness, or maybe irony. Most days of the week, when I looked in the mirror before heading to work, I saw an unsure little boy playing dress-ups in ill-fitting clothes, wondering when he'd get found out. It was like I was a boy operating an adult-sized automaton.

I still have no idea when I became a man. I'm not sure whether it was something I achieved, an age I turned, or a state of mind I reached. I felt great when I finished high school, when I lost my virginity, when I first voted, when I finished uni and got my first professional job, when I got married (these of course did not all happen on one action-packed day), but none of these occasions made me feel like I'd become a man. As hackneyed as it sounds, I'd say the first time I really felt like a man was when I became a dad, and I sensed the additional love and responsibility that entailed. I felt part of something far bigger than my dopey self.

That's not great, though. Here I am with no real clue as to when I became a man, and I'm now in charge of raising one. My confusion as a youngster about manhood happens to a lot of guys. Masculinity is a mystery for us, one that has only been partially solved by the time we're on the precipice of adulthood. Soon enough it'll be my turn to tell my beautiful boy what it means to be a man, and to help him become one. I don't want it to be a mystery to him, to leave him in the dark the way I felt I was. I don't want him to be uncertain whether he has 'what it takes' to be a man. I don't want him stumbling into manhood like I did. In fact, I want him charging full speed into adulthood with self-belief and confidence.

And I'd rather him not meet one particularly nefarious character: the 'real man'.

Getting away from the 'real man'

The existence of the 'real man' is one of the first things we as a community tell boys about masculinity. The 'real man' is the pinnacle of masculinity. He has a specific list of things he *does* and *does not do*. As a society, we are sending some pretty strong messages to boys about what it takes to be a 'real man': stoic, self-reliant, hardworking, physically and mentally tough, domineering and promiscuous.

If the 'real man' doesn't act in a certain way or do a certain thing, then no boy should ever do it. He is also a 'with us or against us' kind of guy. Real men don't cry, don't complain, don't feel sad, scared or insecure, don't show their feelings, don't feel lonely. So what do they do? They work, they hang out with mates at the pub, they bloody love sport, all the sport, and they don't muck around in the bedroom with intimacy or stuff like that. The 'real man' has a keen radar for fake men. If you breach his standards, no manhood for you! What's worse, because of your failure to act in the right way, the 'real man' might label you a wimp, a pussy or a freak.

Because the 'real man' believes in a prescriptive and narrow set of behaviours, he also has a major attitude problem himself. This is perhaps his most damaging influence on young boys growing up. In recent years, different organisations and researchers have been delving into the attitudes and values that young men hold in this country, to try to understand what the typical guy thinks. It's not all bad news—but it's not all that great either.

In 2018, Jesuit Social Services teamed up with researchers to investigate what young men actually thought of the 'real man' they'd heard so much about while growing up. They called it the Man Box Study. They asked 1000 men aged between eighteen and 30 various questions about social pressures to conform to a particular standard of manhood (neatly labelled 'the man box'), and about their own personal beliefs. One thing it showed is that young men feel a strong pressure to meet some objective 'real man' standard that is communicated to them. Two-thirds of them said that since they were a boy, they were told a 'real man' behaves in a certain way.[1] They were also asked to rank, using a scale of 1 (not at all) to 10 (extremely), whether the pressure from society to be a certain kind of man had shaped who they were today. More than half (51.5 per cent) chose a rating of 7 out of 10 or higher.[2]

If young men are feeling the pinch from the community to behave in a certain way, what kind of messages are they hearing? Those in the Man Box Study were asked about the pressure to conform on a range of issues—self-sufficiency, acting tough, physical attractiveness, gender roles, heterosexuality and homophobia, hypersexuality, and aggression and control—by saying whether they agreed or not with a series of statements. Here are some results that stood out to me:[3]

- 69 per cent agreed that society tells men to act strong even if they feel scared or nervous inside.
- 57 per cent agreed that society tells men it is very hard for a man to be successful if he doesn't look good.
- 56 per cent agreed that society tells men, not women, to be the ones to bring home money to provide for families.

- 56 per cent agreed that society tells men that a real man would never say no to sex.
- 54 per cent agreed that society tells men to figure out their personal problems on their own without asking for help.
- 49 per cent agreed that society tells men that someone who talks about his worries, fears and problems shouldn't really get respect.
- 47 per cent agreed that society tells men that a gay guy is not a 'real man'.
- 44 per cent agreed that society tells men that if they have a partner, he deserves to know where she is at all times.

The Man Box Study also showed that 64 per cent of men agreed that society tells them that being friends with a gay guy is totally fine and normal, so that's more positive (even though it means over one-third of respondents felt society wasn't telling them that).

The study showed that perceived pressures on young men come not just from the community, but from their own parents. Fifty-two per cent of the men surveyed agreed that their parents taught them that a 'real man' should act strong even if he feels nervous or scared.[4]

Here's the better news. The Man Box Study revealed that while young men feel pressure to conform to 'real man' standards, a lot believe they are able to resist such pressure, and live their lives differently. Below are the results from the Man Box Study about social pressure, including whether each young man personally believed the statement:[5]

54 per cent agreed that society tells men to figure out their personal problems on their own without asking for help.	27 per cent of young men personally agreed with this statement.
49 per cent agreed that society tells men that someone who talks about his worries, fears, and problems shouldn't really get respect.	25 per cent of young men personally agreed with this statement.
57 per cent agreed that society tells men it is very hard for a man to be successful if he doesn't look good.	42 per cent of young men personally agreed with this statement.
69 per cent agreed that society tells men to act strong even if they feel scared or nervous inside.	47 per cent of young men personally agreed with this statement.
56 per cent agreed that society tells men, not women, to be the ones to bring home money to provide for families.	35 per cent of young men personally agreed with this statement.
47 per cent agreed that society tells men that a gay guy is not a 'real man'.	28 per cent of young men personally agreed with this statement.
56 per cent agreed that society tells men that a real man would never say no to sex.	24 per cent of young men personally agreed with this statement.
44 per cent agreed that society tells men that if they have a partner, he deserves to know where she is at all times.	37 per cent of young men personally agreed with this statement.

So a lot of the guys in the Man Box Study thought that what society tells them about masculinity doesn't match the type of man they want to be. That's pretty good. But what was also clear is that a significant percentage of blokes *did* personally agree with these statements. Almost one in two young men think they need to act tough and strong even if they're falling apart on the inside and desperately want help. More than one in three think they still need to be the male breadwinner. And one in four thinks that if he's vulnerable to others and talks about his worries and fears, he'll get no respect.

The Man Box Study showed something else troubling: that those young men whose views most closely aligned to the 'real man' statements were often struggling within their own lives. In the two weeks prior to the study, 83 per cent of those who most closely aligned with these traditional statements registered 'little interest or pleasure in doing things' and 44 per cent had suicidal thoughts. In the month prior to the survey, 56 per cent perpetrated verbal bullying, 47 per cent perpetrated physical bullying, 57 per cent went along with someone making sexist comments or jokes, 66 per cent experienced verbal bullying them-selves and 52 per cent experienced physical bullying themselves.[6] These were self-assessments. Blokes holding more reductive, negative views about masculinity, and who were trying to be a 'real man', were not in a good way—and others were often in the firing line as a result. These numbers were all far higher than for the guys whose personal views differed from the 'real man' statements.

A 'real man' may not have the best attitudes to others and their feelings, especially women. The 50/50 by 2030 Foundation did a survey of over 2100 Aussies in 2018 to dig into attitudes on gender inequality and see whether anecdotal evidence from the community on discrimination and sexism held up.[7] Women were significantly more likely than males to see gender inequality as a problem, and to have been personally impacted by it in their careers. Men were more comfortable with people being offended or hurt, especially if it was unintentional (according to the person being offensive, that is). Men were more likely than women to agree that 'freedom of speech is important, even if it means offending someone', and that 'people are too sensitive about what is written online'. More men than women also agreed that people have different talents and skills based on gender, and that women are better primary carers than men.[8]

Also, many men didn't think these negative attitudes were their problem to fix—better someone else do it, even if it was their own sons. They thought schools, teachers, workplace relations officers and politicians had more responsibility to fix sexism than fathers and male primary carers.[9] If there is a problem with sexism (and many men aren't convinced there is), then just outsource it to some trained person to deal with it.

The risk that other people bear the brunt of men's bad attitudes through physical aggression or violence is deadly serious. The National Community Attitudes towards Violence Against Women Survey (NCAS) has been conducted periodically in Australia since 1987, and is the world's longest-running survey of community attitudes towards violence against women.[10] The latest survey, published in 2017, included responses from over 1700 people aged between sixteen and 24 years old, including 964 men. The results show that young people who don't really support gender equality, or understand what behaviours constitute violence against women, are more likely to support violence against women in certain situations. Of the men surveyed, 43 per cent thought it was natural for a man to want to appear in control of his partner in front of his male friends, and 57 per cent thought women mistakenly interpret innocent remarks or acts as being sexist. Although 78 per cent of men rejected rigid gender roles and stereotyping, 52 per cent thought women exaggerate how unequally they are treated in Australia.[11] Most alarmingly of all, one in seven of all those surveyed agreed that a man is justified in raping a woman if she changes her mind midway through hooking up.[12] Let that sink in: one in every seven men thinks rape is justified in some circumstances.

It seems to me that the 'real man' is a bit of a dick, to say the least. To cut him some slack, those traits may have helped him survive the turbulence of the twentieth century with its wars and Depressions and inflicted trauma. But almost two decades into the 21st century, he just sounds like the quintessential bully. We all know this guy, someone who inflicts pain and misery on those around him, whether in the schoolyard, the office, the pub or at home. He brushes off criticism of his behaviour as people being thin-skinned and needing to lighten up. At the same time, he is breaking on the inside, tremendously insecure in himself and taking it out on others whenever he can. If you get on his bad side, look out: it will get ugly.

Why does our society continue promoting this guy as the model for young boys? No one wants their son growing up to be a dick who always tries to act tough, wants to dominate any situation, makes others feel bad about themselves, but is secretly dying on the inside. Yet we still pivot to the 'real man', whether we mean to or not.

In February 2019, White Ribbon Canada released an ad called 'Boys Don't Cry'.[13] I can't watch it without feeling my stomach and chest tighten because it's so powerful. It starts with a father holding his crying newborn son. It then shows glimpses of the boy as he grows up. He is playing with his parents, being told to use his big strong muscles. He starts school as a sweet, shy boy and is told to be brave. He gets lonely, slumps against the classroom wall, then retreats in tears to his parents, who say, 'Why are you crying? . . . Boys don't cry, honey . . . Be a big boy, please.' He gets bullied and harassed by other boys at school. He witnesses his father using rage against his mother. He then decides to toughen up like he's been told. He does pushups in his room. He beats up another kid who was bullying him. His dad shrugs off his action as 'boys will be boys'. He enters adolescence and a glazed, hollow look falls over his eyes as he continues to work out and go to school. He starts heading to parties. The ad ends with him leading a drunk girl into an empty bedroom at a party, closing the door to the camera. The imagery, combined with a tense strings accompaniment, is chilling. We see a sweet baby boy grow into a 'real man' in less than three minutes.

Apart from being a sobering public service announcement, the ad also demonstrates one of the most insidious impacts of the 'real man': he fills the void we leave when we don't properly explain masculinity to our boys. When our boys are confused about what it means to be a man, the 'real man' sidles up, offering a masculinity filled with anger, insecurity, sadness and an ambition to best others at all times. If we leave our boys to muddle their way to manhood, like so many have done before, we risk them embracing the 'real man' stereotype. The ad is powerful because it shows how a boy's sweetness and decency can gradually slip away. It also shows how the 'real man' is dangerous *to everyone*, including the boy himself.

Dads have such a major role in helping our boys ward off the 'real man'. They're the first line of defence. With guidance, love and nurturing, dads can ensure our boys turn out healthier and happier. They can prepare boys to reject whatever stealthy messages on the 'real man' are being disseminated in the community. The Man Box Study shows that many young men already do this, but also that we have a lot of work still to do.

I sure as hell don't want my gorgeous little boy to think manhood is the 'real man' persona, and I want to make sure that if he does start whispering into Luke's ear, he'll know to show him the door.

So what positive image should I construct as an alternative to the 'real man'?

The same Saturday I heard Steve Biddulph talk, I also heard from a school principal from Western Australia, a guy called Clark Wight. As well as being a teacher, Clark has boys of his own. He's originally from Baltimore, Maryland—the home of *The Wire*. When he strode to centre stage, he asked all the dads in the room to put up their hands. That was about one-third of attendees. Then he hit us with a question: 'When you were young, how many of you were told by your dad that you had what it takes to be a good man?' Not many hands were left in the air. Mine wasn't.

With this simple straw poll, Clark had stumped most of the blokes in the room, including me. He demonstrated something so seemingly obvious, but so elusive: not enough fathers talk to their young boys about what it takes to be a good man. Clark said he only ever sees a few hands left in the air every time he gives this talk, no matter what part of the country he's in.

Mind blown. By the time I put my hand down in that seminar, I felt that I had found a powerful alternative to the 'real man': *the good man.*

The thing I really love about the good man is that he's welcoming. He's a 'the more, the merrier' kind of guy. He has a fundamental set of values that mean he respects and tolerates all different types of men. He's not defined by feats of strength or stoicism, or by how quickly he can make others feel an inch tall. He's just the type of fella you want to have a beer with because he includes you happily. He broadens what we consider masculinity to be, instead of defining it narrowly so as to leave out others.

As we've seen, dads are a walking demonstration for their boys of what masculinity is. They can set their sons on a path to being a good man or a 'real man'. From our simplest daily behaviours to our reaction to a crisis. From being at home with family chillaxing to how we work (and how we bring work home), to how we interact with people, play sport, drive, eat, cuddle our partner, drink, fart, you name it. Each time we do something, say something, express a feeling or vent a frustration, we add another splash of colour to the picture we're painting of masculinity. Whether we think we're just an average shmo or King Shit, we're modelling manhood for our boys. Sure, dads are competing with the latest pop culture prophet on YouTube or Instagram, but dads inevitably leave a more lasting impression than those fadistas. And our boys absorb it all, consciously or not.

My little fel is still only tiny, but whenever I enter the room his eyes light up and he follows my every movement closely. I've never seen someone look so exhilarated when I take off my shoes, stuff my face with food, open a bottle of wine, change into my trackies or put my keys away. Often I don't notice until I turn around and see him smiling and staring gleefully at me. Right from the start, he's sussing me out and reading my actions. Those actions will take on deeper meaning the older he gets.

There's a reason Clark Wight's simple question is so compelling. Even though our boys are watching dad, and dad is the nearest demonstration of manhood, they still tend to arrive at adolescence a bit confused about masculinity. Our dads might show us a *few* things, like how to shave, how to drive or how to pour a beer. But do they give us the full rundown? Are they showing their boys the path to being a good man, or reinforcing notions of what it takes to be a 'real man', either deliberately or by omission? The Man Box Study showed that young men feel pressure about being a 'real man' from those they are closest to. When masculinity is explained to teenage boys, it normally boils down to sex, not getting an STD and not getting a girl pregnant. If this is how boys view manhood, then it's being reduced to a set of actions, rather than being about traits and character.

So how can we do things differently? For starters, we can use boy biology to our advantage.

Basking as superman

As we've seen, it's when boys are between six and fourteen that they start to learn about being a man.[14] During this time, little boys often see their dads as heroic, near-perfect figures, capable of anything. These are the 'superman years', a time of love and admiration for dad. And dads can use their superhero status to do a lot of real good for their boys, instilling important values and traits in them that will serve them well in adolescence and then adulthood. It's when we can lay the foundation stones for their character.

Take something as seemingly straightforward as physical play. Kids love running around chasing one another, climbing on things, collecting sticks and other treasures, playing pretend and jumping all over equipment at playgrounds. Play and exploration is the biggest and most fun way they get to know their friends and experience the world. Good old-fashioned rough-housing and horsing around is also one of the most common ways that fathers interact with their sons. Play is not just an activity for kids, it's a way to understand the world. They get to experiment with cause and effect. That includes the physical and emotional reactions other kids have when they do something.

When young kids play together, they're like particles in the Large Hadron Collider, whirring past each other at increasing speed, each on their own path, until they inevitably bang into one another. It's no surprise that boys can be a bit more rambunctious than the girls they play with, or the younger kids around them. But excitedly pushing someone over in a game or punching them in the arm may not be much fun for the kid on the receiving end. It might hurt or come as a shock, making them feel sad. When dads play with their sons at a young age, they can teach them not only what is fun, but the importance of restraint and consideration of the physical space of others. Fun means fun for everyone, and that also means everyone needs to feel safe from unintentional harm. Dads can help young boys understand that their actions while playing have repercussions. That accidents happen, and they need to stop or slow down, take a moment and check on the person who may be hurt or not feeling so flash. While encouraging their sons to dream up imaginative, awesome games as they charge around the place, dads can show why boundaries matter, and why it's necessary to read other peoples' reactions and be considerate of them.

Aila is no shrinking violet. She's strong and tall and can mostly hold her own, but she's had the wind knocked out of her by overzealous boys who are just excited and happy. She's been pushed over, crash-tackled and had things thrown at her as part of a game she didn't realise she was playing. I once took her to our local park when she was just starting to use the big-kid swings for the first time. A little boy of about six or seven was eagerly waiting for a turn, standing right up against the swing she was on. She accidentally let go of one side of the swing to brush her hair and fell hard onto her stomach. The little boy waiting for his turn hopped right over her and onto the swing as she was still on the ground. He didn't hesitate even though she was lying winded, crying *underneath him* as he started swinging. I'm biased, of course, but I felt that wasn't very considerate of him.

It seems basic, but it's so crucial. Teaching young boys how to handle and control their bodies, even when they're bursting with crazy amounts of energy, and how to play with and around others, is a major life lesson.[15] It helps them see that they're one person in a wider setting, and to be conscious of others—that they can't just do whatever they want in the name of fun and adventure and ignore the consequences. If anything we pass on as dads has an effect later in life, *this* lesson has got to be a big one. Boys who understand physical restraint are less likely to be seduced by cheap talk from the 'real man' about the need to be domineering and in control at all times, especially in relation to women.

It's not just pulling up kids when things might go a little wrong. Dads need to be role models who show that same restraint everyday, especially when they play with their kids. If dad is overly physical or rough with his boys, hurts them a little and then tells them to toughen up, his boys will learn to push the boundaries of what other people find enjoyable. In the many awesome episodes of *Bluey*, there's one where the dad, Bandit, is pulled up by Bingo because he is hurting her as they play, and they work out together what Bingo's comfort level is for physical games. (The *Raiders of the Lost Ark* nod in that episode, where the kids run away from a giant inflatable gym ball, was especially great to me!) Small lesson, big ramification—and great show.

Dads model physicality when they do anything around the house—cuddle their partner, pat the family dog, do the household chores. If our boys see dad as Godzilla trampling everything in his path, they'll learn that's acceptable. If they see dad using strength where necessary but being gentle and soft at other times, they'll learn to moderate their own behaviour too.

Dads can also show their young sons how to express their feelings and emotions without resorting to physical outbursts or hurting others. Little kids like to hit, kick and throw stuff to show their displeasure. In those tender years when they've emerged from toddlerdom and are starting school, they can be full of emotions that they don't quite understand. Remember the research on boys going through the full-on fours and the emotional eights, for instance? A happy, calm little guy can be turned into a raging maniac because of even a minor setback, a small accident or being told 'no' by a parent. It may take hours for them to get their anger or frustration out of their system. They want to make sure everyone knows how upset they are.

Expressing their frustration through words and not physicality is a lesson many blokes still need to work on, because we've not been taught well. We still tend to tell boys and young men not to carry on, whinge or complain, and we too often tell them not to cry. We're not great at helping them handle disappointment or frustration, be it major or minor. The result is that many men still react like young boys when things go wrong. I've played cricket for most of my life, and for most of that time I've watched a very good friend (who's a handy cricketer, too) chuck major tantrums when he gets out. He throws every piece of batting equipment across the change room, and swears and stomps around as if he's just lost the Ashes. It was understandable when he was fifteen; not so much when he was 30 and still doing it.

It's not just that we haven't been taught well, we also see the wrong messages on the big screen. I love pop culture as much as the next person, but it's disturbing how often we see fighting and physical strength used to resolve problems. The Marvel Cinematic Universe now comprises over twenty movies that together have made over US$8 billion at the box office, but the solution to almost every problem in these films is to fight someone.[16] Even in *Captain America: Civil War*, when the superheroes disagree with each other on whether there should be limitations placed on how they use their powers to help people, they settle their disagreement by punching each other in a German airport.

Other films aren't much different. *Batman v Superman: Dawn of Justice* wasn't the greatest movie in my view, but the millions of kids who saw it heard a woman tell Superman that there was no way to reason with Batman, and that the only thing he'd understand was a fist to the face. One of my favourite movies ever is *Return of the Jedi*. Obi-Wan tells Luke that the only way he can become a Jedi Knight and reconcile with his haunted family past is to fight and kill his own father. When Luke says he simply can't do that, Obi-Wan is disappointed in him.

These examples may seem superficial, but they contain messages our kids take on board in addition to what they hear at home. So when they go to the park or the playground, it's important they understand that resorting to physical strength is not the way to show their hurt or anger, or to show someone you don't like them.

Our boys need to be taught that it's okay to have emotions, and that it's not okay to lash out and hurt others. It's one thing to say that to an upset boy; it's another if that same boy sees dad demonstrating that behaviour. If dad throws stuff at the TV when his team loses, punches the couch, bubbles with rage when something goes wrong or even takes it out on his partner or children, that's the lesson the boy will learn. Boys need to be shown how to use their words to describe what is going on inside them. They need to learn how to handle anger and frustration in a way that doesn't suppress those feelings, but articulates and expunges them in a healthy way.

We all get upset and angry from time to time, about minor and major things; it's how we handle it that shows our character. That may involve doing something physical, like taking a walk and shaking out their limbs, and it definitely means sometimes having a nice, big cry on the couch or in bed to really get it out. It may involve a boy talking about what's going on inside him.

These moments offer great opportunities for dads to help their little fels through whatever it is they're feeling, rather than leaving it to mum to be the default family counsellor. Part of dads getting stuck in at home is sharing the emotional and mental load of parenting. Helping young boys in times of distress and anger is a great way not only to show boys how to handle their emotions as a man-to-be, but to share in the tougher parts of parenting.

Perhaps one of the best things we can do for our boys is model the full array of healthy emotions that any man experiences. A boy needs to see how his father experiences joy and happiness, as well as how he handles sadness and disappointment. Understanding your feelings and knowing how to handle them is at the core being a good man, even if it makes the 'real man' recoil. Biddulph thinks helping boys to understand it is okay to cry is one of the biggest breakthroughs for manhood in recent years, and helps young men everywhere realise that revealing their feelings is not a display of weakness.[17]

Especially during the superman years, dads can show their boys that riding the ups and downs of your emotional state is part of being a man, and that understanding what you're experiencing and why can be a source of strength and resilience, not weakness. This may come in handy for the whole family particularly when the little boy hits the emotional eights, and will definitely hold him in good stead for adolescence. If our little boys have a decent grip on how to regulate their emotions as puberty comes knocking, the whole transition might be a little less scary (even if not less sticky).

I was a really sensitive boy all the way through school. I remember crying very obviously in the change room in Year 3 because the teacher had recently moved me in the classroom so I couldn't sit next to my best friend. There were only a couple of desks now separating us, but it felt like we were continents apart. I couldn't keep it together or act tough—I was just sad. My classmates were bemused.

I had many moments of sadness as a kid, like anyone does, where my vulnerable, open heart got the better of me. My mum would be the chief consoler, helping piece me back together. My dad had no idea how to help with my emotional states. He didn't get angry or frustrated with me, he just didn't know how to help me feel better. I remember thinking that this outpouring of feeling never happened to Dad, and that I must be weaker than him, unable to cope the way he did. How I would have loved a loving nudge from him to let me know I wasn't alone.

Today, as I approach 40, Julia would say I am still oversensitive. If she didn't give me a full-throated compliment when I pitched her any idea for this book, I would have sullenly slumped on the couch feeling scorned. At least I'll be ready and able to show my little boy that the spectrum of emotions lies at the core of manhood.

The superman years offer fathers a terrific chance to show their boys that strength comes from the heart. Dads can demonstrate how to have a generous nature. For mine, kindness is king. My dad has always been a kind man who was considerate and generous to others. He never told me explicitly that being a man meant being kind, but he modelled it in his life every day. He was a high-powered CEO but never stopped being kind to others around him. As the eldest son in his family, he took responsibility for the care of his ageing parents. Watching and absorbing his kindness definitely had an effect on me.

Kindness like this may in fact be more important than ever, because it seems to be in short supply in the adult world a lot of the time. Being kind is equated with being weak, or acting against your own self-interest, rather than as a virtue that helps keep society civil. Kindness is missing from the way we typically talk about manhood. The 'real man' is definitely not interested in kindness. It goes against the grain of being tough, stoic and having a winner-takes-all approach to life.

Little boys can start to understand kindness in many different ways, like learning to share things with other children, and by watching dad share his things as well. As adults, we're most comfortable sharing a plate of food or a jug of beer at the bowlo, but sharing our possessions or resources, or those of our community, isn't something we reflexively do, even as we ask our kids to share their stuff.

Parents everywhere can attest to how hard it can be to get little people to share things. And it's not just about boys: Julia and I are still trying to teach Aila that sharing does not simply mean other children giving their things to her. Many times I've seen her grab a piece of playground equipment, almost holding it to ransom while she instructs the other kid to share it. But sharing doesn't come naturally to anyone, let alone young kids, who don't really understand the idea that different people own different things.

I think sharing is a great way to understand kindness. At its best, the act of sharing is beautiful and powerful because it means acknowledging someone else, understanding their needs and giving them something that makes them feel happier or more content. For kids, it can be offering a friend a toy or inviting them into a cubby house. It's an act of inclusion that shows people that you see them, and that they matter to you. Given the dearth of kindness in the adult world, a dad openly sharing his things in front of his children—his food, his time, his knowledge—is a wonderful role model. Such small acts of generosity will leave an imprint on his son, making the selfish task of the 'real man' that much harder.

Being kind is closely related to being considerate and respectful of others. Our little boys look up to us to understand how to interact with the world around us. If we are polite and friendly as we go about our day, if we smile and are warm, if we actually listen to what others are saying to us, we demonstrate kindness. Saying good morning to the educators at daycare or the teachers at school, saying thank you to the shop assistant as we leave, waving at our neighbours, saying excuse me as we hop off the bus—it all adds colour to masculinity, like tiny brushstrokes on a large canvas.

The superman years are also where dad can show his little boy for the first time what loving others looks like, and how wonderful it is. Again, perhaps this is obvious, but with the prominence of 'real man' attitudes in our society, it is something dads have to model for their boys. Fathers showing their love is one of the most important things they can do.

The Beatles thought love is all you need, but not so the parenting industry. In their zealousness to give mums and dads all the answers to raising children, they seem to have forgotten about love along the way. Ezra Klein is a US journalist who founded the news site *Vox*, and became a father for the first time in February 2019. Not wasting any time, he's been a voracious reader of parenting books, and as he read he realised that so little of the literature explored love, showing love, or the act of loving family.[18] A fairly big oversight, I'd say. Klein dedicated a whole show of his podcast to exploring love and its impact on human development.

Dads can show their sons that men love, and they love deeply and openly. We can *demonstrate* how love is manifested in our character and our actions. Our boys shouldn't have to guess at love, they should be wrapped in it and see it up close. Everyone loves in their own way, and not necessarily with hearts on sleeves. We love our kids so much, so why hide it?

Boys can get so much out of seeing displays of love from dad. It may start with saying 'I love you' a lot, but it doesn't end there. It's the fondness when you play with your son. It's the warmth in your smile as he dances or jumps around in front of you. It's the way you cuddle him and kiss him. The way you hold his hand even when you're not crossing a street, because you want to. The attentiveness you show him when he is telling you a story. The way you read his moods and feelings and respond with patience. In fact, in the whole way we care for our sons, we can demonstrate our love. Leaving work a little early to be home for dinner demonstrates love. Making the school concert or the weekend game demonstrates love. The 'real man' scoffs at displays of intimacy; the 'good man' makes lifelong memories from them.

Of course, it matters how dad loves the rest of the family and his friends as much as his son. Loving his partner, his siblings and his parents with equal measures of kindness and sweet-heartedness teaches further valuable lessons to boys. Focusing all your love on your children to the exclusion of all others is counter-productive. Loving openly shouldn't mean the kid gets whatever he wants. No one wants to raise a precious little princeling who basks in his father's love and gets away with blue murder as a result. We're trying to show true love here, not how to indulge or coddle children to think that only they matter. We've all known those kids growing up where their parents, no doubt with good intentions, put them on a pedestal, and they carry that attitude into the rest of their lives. That's not what we want here.

The idea that a father's love can set young boys up for life might seem like a truism, but it is profound. Kids know they are loved, but something incredible can happen when that love is buried deep into their soul. It becomes unshakeable, and a limitless reservoir of strength and confidence. I'll come back to that in the next chapter.

This is not an exhaustive list of traits and virtues that fathers can show their sons while they're young enough to idolise them. It shines a light on what's possible, and how dads can start to define manhood in a more meaningful, inclusive way. A boy can learn that men are respectful, considerate, kind and loving. They share and are attentive to others. Men have physical strength but exercise restraint in using it the wrong way at the wrong time. They enjoy the company of their family and friends, but that doesn't mean making their loved ones the punchline. They're mindful of the world in which they reside. For me, these qualities beat anything that the 'real man' can offer.

If our boys enter their teenage years understanding that these traits are the hallmarks of manhood, we as dads will have truly done something heroic, worthy of the superman years we've experienced together.

The next stage, unfortunately, is where it can all go to shit. It's when our boys grow up a little more, stretch out more defiantly as they look for independence. Dad can become a pain, an embarrassment, a guy stopping you from having a good time. These years can put distance between father and son. Gradually, dad becomes fallible. Bye-bye, superman; hello, regular man.

Emerging as the good man

We all remember the time we worked out that our parents were in fact vulnerable humans with failings like everyone else. This moment rocks your world—especially if you find out your father is Darth Vader and he just chopped off your hand. But it's okay for sons to understand that dad has vulnerabilities and insecurities, that he screws up and doesn't have all the answers. In fact, it's great, because it shows that being fallible is part and parcel of being a man. That's a vital message during the teenage years, when boys can feel insecure and start experiencing pressure to look tough and in control.

Dads can show their sons that a good man understands his insecurities and worries, and has come to terms with them. He doesn't pretend they don't exist, nor does he bury them deep down in the hope they won't re-emerge. The 'real man' may do that, but the good man works through them as best he can.

Being an adult is hard, and as I approach 40 I still don't feel like I've got a good grip on it. When I was moving from being a teenager to a young man, I had even less of a clue. I muddled along from high school to uni, and hoped I would stumble on the secrets of manhood through some form of osmosis. And I had worries about life—loads of them, actually. When it came to working out how to be a man to fit the times, my dad trusted my school to tell me, as a lot of parents do. Dad also trusted Mum to handle the tricky emotional stuff, especially during my angsty teenage years. I didn't know what it meant to be a man in a community beyond school or home.

In Dad's defence, no one had prepared him for that kind of parenting. He was the breadwinner! He hadn't been taught how to nurture or respond to feelings, and he sure wasn't nurtured himself. So my relationship with my dad didn't yield many answers on what I was meant to do as a man.

I knew my dad best through the prism of sport. Sport was genuinely our shared interest and created the bonds of intimacy. Celebrations of victory and commiserations of defeat were acts of love. As a toddler in 1983, I jumped up and down on the couch saying, 'We won! We won!' to mimic Dad's excitement at beating the Yanks in the America's Cup. I buzzed with unbridled excitement when walking into the Sydney Cricket Ground with Dad for the first time in 1992 to watch Australia play India in the Benson & Hedges World Series (still the best one-day comp ever), and we then had an intense discussion about why my hero, Dean Jones, had been made twelfth man. I turned to him and cried in the stands at the Sydney Football Stadium when the North Sydney Bears lost the 1994 Preliminary Final to the Canberra Raiders after leading at half-time. Two years later I berated him in the second quarter of the 1996 AFL Grand Final for jinxing the Sydney Swans, paying less attention to the fact it was not Dad's guarantees of victory that brought them down but their on-field performance. This was how, over many years, we forged a bond.

As Dad was away a lot for work, our relationship became distant geographically and emotionally. Partly this was the normal teenage frustration kids have for their parents, but it went deeper than that. As my insecurities about myself grew,

I felt I couldn't talk about them with Dad or get a real response from him. We were stuck in a place where we were only able to talk about sport, and nothing deeper. Sport ended up crowding out a deeper intimacy. I could get decent insight from him about improving my outswinger, but not about how to handle my creeping anxiety and the loneliness that filled my soul. Invariably his advice was: 'You'll be alright . . . you'll work it out.' He may genuinely have believed I was more resilient than I felt, but it didn't exactly light the way ahead.

It's not good when teenage boys feel they need to handle their insecurities on their own, just like it's no good for a grown man. Steve Biddulph argues that teenage boys feel a need to put on a mask in order to fit in and survive.[19] That Man Box Study showed that one of the messages boys hear is the need to appear in control at all times, and that showing weakness or vulnerability is a sure-fire way to lose the respect of others. Teenagers on the verge of manhood, feeling insecure about themselves and their lives, should not be encouraged to act tough and bury their worries. And they definitely shouldn't believe that dad is impervious to feeling insecure and frail.

It's all too clear that suffering in silence can have deadly consequences: Aussie men make up an average of six out of every eight suicides each day in this country.[20] Beyond Blue says that, on average, one in eight men will experience depression, which is a major red flag for suicide risk. One in five will experience anxiety at some stage in life.[21] And boys aren't great at reaching out for help, and are becoming less willing to do so. Since 2007, the number of males contacting the Kids Helpline has slumped. One in three callers used to be boys (which itself was not a good ratio); now it's one in five.[22] Over three-quarters of callers are girls.[23] Eighty-seven per cent of calls received at the Kids Helpline are from people aged between thirteen and 25 years, those crucial years when kids are becoming teenagers and then adults.[24]

The importance of helping young men deal with their sense of vulnerability isn't theoretical for me. I am the one in five men who suffers from anxiety. For a very long time, I thought I was weak because I didn't seem as strong, brave or tough as the young men around me. I chastised myself for not being able to 'just get on with it' like my dad or my friends. I assumed that I was just a wimp struggling to grow up and be a 'real man'. After enduring my anxiety as a teenager, it became overwhelming in my twenties, leading to bouts of depression. At the urging of my mum, I finally went to the Black Dog Institute to get my mental health checked. I was diagnosed with clinical anxiety. Unsurprisingly, I'd been suffering from it for years.

Having anxiety is mentally exhausting. On bad days, it drains the life out of you. As a young man, I regularly felt a strong fear of failure. I started having irrational fears and worries, about my own health or my own life. Some of my fears were utterly bizarre even to me. I had a fear for a long time that I wouldn't be able to eat in restaurants without throwing up. Weird, right? Others struck more deeply at my sense of self. I had a fear about failing my High School Certificate—to the point that I was dry-heaving in the bathroom prior to my final exams. I feared that I would never find a decent job and would end up homeless and impoverished. And my life has always been secure, stable and privileged.

I went to a very religious school, and in my impressionable teenage years became frightened that I would burn in hell. That made me depressed for a period of time, to the point that I went to see a family friend who was a priest to discuss my fears. These were deep-seated thoughts, the dominant theme being a fear that I couldn't cope in my own life and was destined for failure and rejection. There have been many times, too many to count, where I have thought that some minor incident at school, uni or work would be the end of me. When I fall into this mode of thinking, I catastrophise irrational risks in my head. My anxiety is also very physical: I experience shallow breathing, feel a knot in my stomach, get sweaty hands and chest, am light-headed, feel nauseous. It's a trip.

My anxiety and fears have antagonised me throughout my working life, and I've seen therapists regularly to find techniques to deal with them. I'm well aware of my own vulnerabilities and how fallible I am. I understand the importance of seeking help and being open with my loved ones about it. One of the best things I've ever done is seek therapy when I feel particularly bad—it showed me that taking care of your brain and your emotions is just like getting a check-up for any other part of your body. I know my dad felt heartache and was deeply worried about what I was grappling with, but I don't think he knew how to talk to me about it, or what he could do to help. It was just something foreign to men of his generation.

I'm determined that my experiences of mental anguish as a teenager and as a man become an asset for my son. I will be open and honest with him, in the hope that he learns from my vulnerabilities and my past and emerges better for it. I can talk to him about what it's like to feel insecure, scared or worried about your future, and how you can draw strength and courage from facing such feelings head-on. I really hope he doesn't have to worry about clinical anxiety like I do, but if he's inherited that from me, or if he has other mental health challenges, then I'll be ready and able to hold his hand and help light the road ahead for him. I'll tell him very clearly that seeking help makes him no less of a man.

It's because of my experience that I believe so strongly that fallibility is a great thing for teaching boys about manhood. Understanding how to deal with your own insecurities builds emotional intelligence. Dads can model for our boys what it's like to feel scared or stressed, to worry about failing or what the future may hold, and to experience heartbreak or loss. Dads can show their boys positive ways to deal with these feelings, just like they showed them how to play with others when they were little, and how to show love and affection and be kind. It's about helping them understand that no one has all of life's answers, and everyone from time to time feels lost. Working out how to solve problems and overcome challenges, even if they appear impossible or overwhelming, is all part of being a man. It's how you handle them and bounce back that shows your character. That's a lesson I really wish I'd learnt earlier in life, as it would have saved me from a lot of stress.

So while the blinkers may come off our sons' eyes when they're teenagers and we become regular men rather than supermen, they can still know that dad is a great role model (even if he's also a cringeworthy embarrassment with his taste in music and frequent references to 1980s movies).

I may be a long way off this period of development, but I can see the silver lining among the grey clouds of fathering an adolescent son. I really want to help my boy find his place in the community, and to cast his eyes towards bigger horizons and grander adventures. It will be my last big chance to instil in him virtues that will last through his lifetime, and to get him as close to good man status as I can.

When I heard Steve Biddulph talk, he made the point that as time passes, most dads and sons grow further and further apart. He reckoned that in a room of 100 dads, only about ten would consider that they have a really close and warm relationship with their own fathers. That's a pretty heartbreaking outcome. If boys continue to see their dads as great role models (even if they don't want to admit it), then hopefully the bond between them remains close as they age. The relationship can mature into an adult friendship, characterised by mutual respect and admiration. And as our boys get closer to fatherhood themselves, they'll have an appreciation for what their dads taught them across all those years, both when he was the real-life superhero and when he was the ordinary bloke. Our sons will be ready to pass on what it takes to be a good man themselves.

Which brings me back to the effect dads can have on the wider world. If, day by day, bit by bit, household by household, we start talking with our sons about what it takes to be a good man, and modelling that behaviour for them, we'll have such a profoundly positive impact on the whole community. We'll send out into the world a bunch of emotionally intelligent, resilient, decent, kind, loving men who will live the example their fathers showed them as they grew up. They won't be as confused about what being a man means, feeling awkward while looking tough and trying to muddle through. They'll leave the 'real man' and his negative version of masculinity in the dustbin of history, a relic of the harsher experiences of men in the twentieth century. As dads, we'll have transformed what masculinity means for boys everywhere. If we achieve that, everyone's a winner.

BACKING ALL BOYS TO BE GOOD MEN

BERNIE SHAKESHAFT, ARMIDALE

It's hard enough understanding what it takes to be a man when you come from a stable home with engaged parents. What about when you've had a hard upbringing, or even when people have given up on raising you at all?

Bernie Shakeshaft is the founder and CEO of BackTrack Youth Works, an organisation dedicated to supporting disadvantaged young boys and turning them into good men with promising futures, no matter how long it takes. Bernie is an involved father himself, whose children are now all grown up. He recalls that his year at home with his kids was 'the best year I've ever had', and that he was active in his son's life when he was younger, coaching his soccer team. Since 2006, Bernie's helped over a thousand young people in regional New South Wales through BackTrack's programs. Many of the boys Bernie helps have experienced family violence or abandonment from a young age, as well as poverty and hardship. They've often been cast aside by family members, and are at high risk of ending up in the juvenile justice system, potentially derailing their whole lives.

The organisation Bernie created offers each boy long-term support, patiently assisting them with education, training and shelter as necessary. A huge part of this work is mentoring and modelling what it takes to be a good man. Bernie explains that for the young boys they help, BackTrack 'wraps good, sensible males around these kids and puts the right behaviours on display for them'.

'The boys we're dealing with don't know what the fuck it means to be a man,' Bernie says. 'They've experienced violence or abuse in the past, or seen parents with drinking or substance abuse problems. We try to role-model good behaviour for them, including helping them feel comfortable expressing their emotions and insecurities. This process is a slow burn and we have to be patient and understanding with them at all times. Where I'm from, none of us were shown this ourselves, so it's not easy. We were all taught not to display our feelings and to act tough.'

Bernie strongly believes that young boys need meaningful conversations with other men in order to become good men. 'It's up to us as men to change this generation,' he argues. 'There is a core, golden chunk about manhood that must be taught by other men. Problem is we still think of a good man as a hardworking knockabout bloke who has a few beers, loves sports and has a couple of kids. But are these really the attributes we want for our young boys growing up?'

He also thinks the transition from boyhood to manhood lacks structured guidance. 'We don't do initiation into manhood well. Our boys learn to drive, or enrol to vote, or go into a pub for the first time, and that's their experience of becoming a young man. We should be doing much more to initiate them. Every year as they grow up, we should be explaining to them how they're developing into a young man.' BackTrack talks the talk and walks the walk, having created a network of men for the young boys in the program to guide their transition into adulthood.

Bernie argues that raising a boy requires support from the whole family network. 'If you look at some of the mobs in the red centre, at a certain age the men take over the raising of the boys, and conduct men's business and initiations with them. The dads stay close to the sons in everything they do together. And when they get a bit older, the uncle system within the family unit means it's also not just up to dads to raise them.'

Bernie's experiences at work and at home have led him to ask a bigger question of our community: 'Can we sit down as a group of men and discuss what it takes to be a man?'

I sure hope so – my son is counting on it.

7

THE LOVE QUOTIENT AND FREE WILL

We talk so much about how to raise children, and how to get through the day-to-day, but do we consciously discuss *how* to best love and nurture? In the last chapter I said that it's good for our boys to see their dad love them openly, as it helps our boys understand the importance of love to masculinity. But our love as fathers can also be misguided, counter-productive, even overbearing and judgemental. Instead of loving our sons in a way that nourishes their souls, we may end up giving them a love that demands they conform with what *we* want for them in life, or what we consider appropriate for a boy and a young man.

I'm on a learning curve on how best to love because, regrettably, I am a relapsing helicopter parent. I've been denying it for a couple of years, but it's the truth. I am the hoverer at the playground. I'm the parent getting off the park bench the moment I can't see my kids amid the equipment. I'm the dad constantly saying, 'Be careful,' even when the risk of harm is pretty low. I'm the one who calls out to Aila from the top of the stairs, 'Are you okay?' when I can't hear her making any noise, because she's in front of the TV like a zombie. I'm the one telling her to slow down whenever she rides her bike to the park down the hill from our house. Even at our home, which has secure boundaries on all sides, I fret that my kids will somehow end up on the street getting splattered. I try to pull myself up from this overbearing fretting, and Julia is always telling me to relax. I battle my helicopter tendencies daily.

As my kids start facing more complex physical and social challenges in their lives, I know I'll have the instinctive tendency to intervene. What I might think is well-intentioned and appropriate could be considered heavy-handed, clumsy or over the top by my kids. And my intervention could do more harm than good, especially if I'm telling Luke how to act, behave or what life decisions to make.

Alison Gopnik is an author who has written a fair amount about how to love our children. She released a book in 2016 called *The Gardener and the Carpenter*. For Gopnik, the carpenter approach to parenting is when parents try to precisely carve a child into a specific person. They have a product design in mind, they work with the materials in front of them as best they can, and they determine how well they've done by checking the specifications on the final product. Gopnik says it's a very prescriptive way of raising your kids, with a high chance of disappointment and frustration because, unsurprisingly, the kids are going to be who they are going to be. Gopnik, however, argues that the carpentry approach is the one most commonly endorsed in the oodles of parenting literature out there.

She prefers to think of raising children as growing a garden. You tend to the patch of earth, ensuring that it's protected and nurtured. You put lots of labour into keeping it alive and healthy, trying to sustain a whole ecosystem of different plants. You adapt to unintended consequences, as plants can grow differently to how you expected, and you must respond to changing weather patterns. You don't have a specific finished product in mind, just the prospect of a beautiful patch of life.

According to Gopnik, the job of parents is not to try to make a particular type of child, as a carpenter makes a chair or table. Rather, it is to provide a 'protected space of love, safety and stability in which children of many unpredictable kinds can flourish'.[1]

Keeping the gardening analogy going, Australian psychologist and researcher Judith Locke wrote in her book *The Bonsai Child* how parents are increasingly raising children as if they were caring for a bonsai tree.[2] According to Locke, parents are generally over-nurturing. She says that over the past fifteen or so years, mum and dads have increasingly shown their love by removing all the challenges and obstacles in front of their kids, while at the same time instilling in them great ambitions for their future. They're making sure the road ahead is as easy and smooth as possible. As well-intentioned as these parents might be, their kids are not growing up with much resilience as they've never had to deal with much adversity. They may be well loved and nurtured, but they're a bit delicate, like a perfect little bonsai tree. As they turn into adults, they end up not just with a badly wounded ego but with an inability to weather life's storms.

What Gopnik and Locke are both exploring is how parents can love their children in a way that protects and nurtures them, but also gives them space to explore and deal with life. To make mistakes and fix their own problems, and in doing so prepare for the shit life is going to throw at them 24/7/365. They're helping parents find ways to nourish the souls of their kids, while letting their egos get a bit bruised and battered along the way.

Unlikely place to learn about love

I like what these two authors have to say. However, there's another idea about how to love your children that has resonated just as strongly with me. And it came from an unlikely source. Cue flashback.

A few years ago, Julia and I heard former prime minister Paul Keating speak at the Sydney Opera House.[3] (This was before we had kids, when we could actually do things at night without months of advance preparation.) I wasn't expecting him to talk much about his upbringing, just his time in office. Yet he started the night by recounting his childhood, and expounded on the topic of love. One thing he said in particular struck me hard and has stayed with me ever since.

Keating explained how his mum and his grandma gave him a limitless, bottomless reserve of powerful, unconditional love and support. He knew, deep in his bones, how well loved he was by these two strong women in his life. He could feel their love radiating. He described it as a protective suit that allowed him to charge into the fire. He said he felt complete, and that no matter what happened in his life, the adversities, the triumphs, the rolling barrage of opposition and criticism, he knew that there were at least two people who wholeheartedly believed in him and believed he was special. He said it gave him a deep-rooted confidence to set his sights high and try to conquer the world. He called it 'the love quotient'.

From this night I took one of the best ideas about fatherhood that I've ever received. What Keating described was something immense, powerful and uplifting. The idea of giving my children their love quotient has been stuck in my head ever since. It's the notion I go to when I feel the helicopter tendencies coming on. To me, it's a turbocharged version of what both Gopnik and Locke are talking about. It appeals so strongly to me because I feel a hollowness at my core where confidence should be.

I am someone who suffers from self-doubt and imposter syndrome. I'm always wondering whether I'm good enough, whatever the circumstance. I've already mentioned my fear of failure, and it certainly hasn't gone away the older I get. The fear changes shape, from fear of failing the HSC to fear of losing my family or my job. Many times in my life I have turned away from an opportunity or a risk because I thought I couldn't do it. Now, not everyone can be a prime minister, but I want Luke to feel the love quotient at his core so that he's emboldened and resilient.

As dads can be amazing carers of children, they can also provide the love quotient just as superbly as mums. Just because PJK got his love quotient from his mum and grandma doesn't mean Aussie dads can do it any less brilliantly. We have evidence that more emotionally involved fathers make a noticeable difference to the development of their kids. Studies out of the United States over the past ten years have demonstrated that fathers who are more sensitive and supportive end up with children who develop better social skills and language regardless of class, race or ethnicity.[4] If dads provide the love quotient to our boys, it will reinforce positive notions that being a man means being a loving carer, a nurturer and a provider of emotional strength and intelligence. And it may contribute to their cognitive development as well.

Dads can be that deep reservoir of love that emotionally nourishes a child, enriches them, fills their soul and gives them the confidence to take on the world, chart their own adventure and deal with the setbacks and difficulties that are sure to come.

The great thing at the centre of the love quotient is that it's a liberating, empowering love. Which brings me to my next big point. In the last chapter I discussed how amazing and important it is for dads to help boys to become good men. But it will be a life half-lived for our good men if they are not free to be who they really want to be in life. We're discounting our own handiwork if we're showing boys what it takes to be a good man while also limiting their choices in life. We might think we're acting out of love, but are we helping our boys be who they want to be, or are we narrowing life's possibilities for them?

If I hop into the DeLorean with the Doc and hurtle forward twenty years, I'd be overjoyed to discover that Luke is a good man, but I'd lament that fact if he also felt unable to pursue what he really wanted in life, and be who he really wanted to be. And I'd feel a thousand times worse if that was because of pressure I'd put on him as a helicopter parent, carpenter or bonsai trimmer.

What's in a face-paint?

Boys make decisions about who they're going to be every day of their lives. These start out as small choices: which toys to play with, which clothes to wear, which games to play. Those choices get bigger and more important as they grow up—which subjects to choose at school, which activities to participate in, which friends to hang out with, who to ask out—all the way up to the adult stuff like choosing a degree or pursuing a career. If we're going to give our boys the love quotient, it involves allowing them to make these choices without imposing on them an expectation of what boys and young men 'should do'. What we can do as dads is help them lay the groundwork for a fulfilling and satisfying life of their choosing, not ours.

A small example of how this can go pear-shaped comes by way of an American clown. No, not the president—an actual clown who paints kids' faces at birthday parties. In 2017, a Twitter thread went viral from a lady who is a clown for hire in the United States.[5] She had finished entertaining a bunch of kids at a party, which included face-painting. She wrote about her interaction with a four-year-old boy who wanted to get his face painted. He asked for a butterfly. His mum interjected: 'No, he doesn't want that.' The clown asked whether she should paint the butterfly anyway, given that was what the boy had asked for, and of course butterflies are beautiful. The mother's response was swift: 'No, give him something for boys.' The mum looked to the father for backup, asking him whether he wanted his son to have a butterfly on his face. No prize for guessing his answer. The little boy ended up getting a skull and crossbones painted on his cheek.

Once the face-painter had complied, she tried one last time, asking the boy whether he'd also like one little blue butterfly on his face. He nodded meekly. But even a small, blue butterfly wasn't acceptable to the mum, who sternly told the face-painter that she had the final say, not her son. So back to the party went this little boy with his skull and crossbones, wishing he had a butterfly, feeling bad that he'd asked for it at all, thinking he'd done something wrong, and knowing his parents were disappointed with him. The face-painter said she saw this all the time; she wanted to draw people's attention to the fact that these experiences, however small they seem at the time, end up having a multiplier effect on boys as they grow up.

This example shows how easy it is to typecast boys when they want something even slightly outside what we, as adults, consider normal. I feel really sorry for that boy, who liked butterflies and wanted one on his cheek as it would make him happy. Do his parents love him? Of course they do. But they were also projecting onto him some invisible standard about 'what boys should like'. It was bad enough that they made their son feel crappy; it was worse that they made him feel like he wasn't a normal boy.

The standards imposed on boys can be so arbitrary that we're not even sure why they exist or where they come from. Take clothing choices for boys. Whenever I go to a major chain like Target or Big W, all the astronauts and dinosaurs are in the boys' section, and all the bunnies and ballet dancers are in the girls' section. When I take Luke out in any pastel-coloured clothing— really, anything that isn't blue or green—I get at least one friendly person telling me, 'Oh, she looks so gorgeous—what's her name?'

Putting a boy in blue and a girl in pink is not some deep-seated biological preference, by the way. At the end of the nineteenth century, all little kids were put in what were essentially white dresses. A nice, easy, practical outfit—what more did you need for a small human that would frequently vomit, poo and stain their clothing? There's an adorable photo from 1884 of little Franklin Delano Roosevelt as a two-and-a-half-year-old. This guy went on to be the longest-serving American president in history, winning four consecutive terms, leading the nation through the Great Depression and World War II. A man's man, am I right? In the photo, he sits with his curly blond locks in a nicely tailored dress, with leather shoes and a hat with a marabou feather. Totes cute, but by today's standards dangerously girly, to the point that you half-expect someone to ring child protection services accusing the parents of abuse. But Roosevelt's parents weren't forcing him to act effeminately—it was just the style at the time.

Then, around the time of World War I, pink and blue became heavily promoted as appropriate for boys and girls respectively.[6] Here's the thing—they were talking about pink as the manly colour for boys, and blue as suitably dainty for girls. A trade publication produced for department stores in 1918 said: 'The generally accepted rule is pink for the boys, and blue for the girls. The reason is that pink, being a more decided and stronger color, is more suitable for the boy, while blue, which is more delicate and dainty, is prettier for the girl.'[7] It was around the 1940s that manufacturers started promoting pink for girls and blue for boys. And here we are now, still doing it—and thinking it's based on some irrefutable science about what our kids like to wear. But the honest truth is that we're making this shit up as we go.

Boys and young men still cop abuse for having anything to do with the colour pink. In 2007, a teenage boy in Canada was badly bullied for wearing a pink shirt to school. To counter this bullying, two other boys and some of their friends headed to a discount store and bought 50 pink shirts, handing them out to their peers to wear in sympathy. One said that when the boy being bullied arrived that next morning, 'it was like a huge weight was lifted off his shoulders'.[8] Pink Shirt Day in Canada is now a major day to highlight how bad bullying can get for kids in school, and it's even taken off in New Zealand. It's got a foothold in Australia, with the Upper Hunter Shire Council in New South Wales joining the campaign in 2019.[9]

We encourage men to wear pink for one day during the annual cricket Test match played at the Sydney Cricket Ground.

For just one day, the national men's team dons a 'baggy pink' instead of their normal baggy green, while media figures wear striking pink blazers. Almost everyone in the crowd rocks up in pink. Of course, the event is about raising money for the McGrath Foundation, which funds nursing services for breast cancer sufferers, a thoroughly worthy cause. Yet maybe we're inadvertently sending a message to boys that it's okay to wear pink on that one day, because you're supporting women, but that isn't what men *really* wear.

What will my reaction be if Luke chooses to wear a pink bunny rabbit jumper when he's six years old? Or wants the cool Wonder Woman shirt? Or pyjamas with Jessie the Cowgirl from *Toy Story*? Should I freak out and tell him to choose 'something for boys', or should I tell him he looks terrific and made a great choice?

And while we're talking about arbitrary standards, what happens if my boy doesn't just ask for a butterfly on his cheek but instead dabs a bit of make-up on his face from mum's supplies in the bathroom? Or starts wearing it regularly as a teenager? The male grooming industry is worth over $26 billion globally.[10] About one in five Aussie men uses make-up.[11] Yet a lot of people still see this as something to freak out about. Before Luke was even born, a very close family member told me they would feel 'disturbed' if he was playing with make-up the way his big sister does. If he did, that would mean there was something wrong with him.

Seriously? Why project on to my boy a hand-wringing anxiety about something he does for the sake of adventure, fun and exploration? And if he does like to wear make-up, what's the big deal? Every day before I leave for work I put on moisturiser. I've also used fudge in my hair (with varying degrees of success), oil in my beard and concealer on my acne. Should people be disturbed about my behaviour?

What if we rebrand make-up for boys so it sounds more in line with traditional masculinity. Recently I saw an ad on Twitter for 'war paint'.[12] Produced by an English company, this is make-up for men who are struggling with their looks and want a boost in their self-esteem. Problem solved! Wearing make-up as a man may be effeminate, but wearing war paint—well, that's plenty tough! The model on the Twitter ad was a super-toned and buff dude, with a decent beard and a cool fade in his hairline, powerfully applying his 'war paint' in front of the mirror—a not so subtle suggestion that the model could be me if only I had the balls to wear war paint too (plus work out three hours a day and get a sleeve tatt). If my boy starts wearing make-up, should I just tell everyone it's war paint to validate his decision?

Cars or dolls?

The same arbitrary distinctions occur when we talk about toys. There's been loads written about whether boys and girls naturally like to choose different toys, or whether they learn preferences as they grow up and respond to social cues. A 2014 study by the University of Western Sydney and the University of California explored the toy preferences for babies aged between three and a half and five months. Now, this feels awfully young to explore 'preferences' in humans whose main form of communication is drooling and screaming, and who can barely grip something in their tiny hands. Nevertheless, the researchers showed these bubbas images on a screen, and measured the time and frequency with which they looked at them. The study showed that boys were more attracted to dolls than toy cars and other mechanical objects.[13] Other studies, too, have suggested that boys start reacting negatively to dolls at the age when they start being taught dolls are intended for girls.[14]

These studies may only be suggestive, but they're interesting and useful to throw into the discussion. Given that kids understand the world through play, it should be no surprise that researchers have found that different toys teach kids different skills. Playing with dolls can teach nurturing, caring, empathy and language skills, while playing with blocks or LEGO teaches spatial awareness and design skills.[15] Without us realising it, we're laying the foundations for the choices our kids will make in school and beyond.

In 2012, Top Toy, the Swedish franchise holder for Toys R Us, put out a Christmas catalogue picturing boys caring for a baby doll while a girl takes aim with her Nerf gun (not at the baby), in an attempt to make the outrageous point that all toys are for everyone, and kids can decide what's best for them without parents telling them what boys and girls should and should not play with.[16] A year later, they had doubled down by moving to make their physical stores gender-neutral, with another round of advertisements showing a boy and a girl playing with their Nerf weaponry together.[17]

What does this say? Fun is fun is fun, and boys and girls both like fun equally (and I wish I'd had a badass Nerf gun as a kid). Since 2012, there's been a campaign running in the United Kingdom called Let Toys Be Toys.[18] It's all about encouraging retail chains to ditch the gender-differentiated toy departments and marketing, and to sell all toys to all kids. That includes dissuading retailers from selling pink and blue toy kits, to girls and boys respectively.[19] The campaign noted a 70 per cent drop in boy/girl toy categories in online stores by 2016, and the boy/girl signs in physical stores have almost disappeared completely.[20]

Global toymaking juggernauts like Mattel and Hasbro are now deciding to drop gender labelling and just market all their toys to all kids.[21] In Australia, chains like Target, Toys R Us and Kmart intend to replace the pink and blue toy aisles as well.[22] We've still got a way to go: when I take my kids to the big chains at the local mall, there's a noticeable array of pink and blue toys, just like there remain major differences in the clothes department.

How about the superheroes and action figures which boys love when they're young? As at the writing of this book, Aila's favourite characters are (in order) Spider-Man, Sheriff Woody, Queen Elsa and Buzz Lightyear. She may be a pre-schooler who is starting to be influenced by those around her, but she doesn't pause for one moment to think she couldn't be any of those four characters, not just Elsa. She has two different sets of Spidey pyjamas, a Spidey robe for cold mornings, a talking Woody doll, a Woody hat, *Toy Story* pyjamas, two Queen Elsa dresses plus her wand and crown. Aila dressed up as Spidey for Book Week in 2019, and because she loves all four *Toy Story* movies went as Jessie the Cowgirl for Halloween that October. She's also come in to our bedroom a few times with a mask pretending to be Batman, or donned a cape to be the Man of Steel. I love it every time she does this, and I never want her to feel self-conscious about it.

So what should I do if one day my little boy comes down the stairs to 'Let It Go', telling me he's Queen Elsa, creating sentient snowmen out of thin air, building magnificent ice castles, and ruling over his kingdom like a monarch with divine right? Am I meant to spring into action and tell him 'that's not what boys like' and encourage him to dress up as Spider-Man or Woody instead? Wouldn't it be better if I was right there dancing by his side, singing the song or complying with his royal decrees, just as I did with his big sister?

In early 2019, a Norwegian dad named Ørjan Burøe posted a video of himself and his son dancing around their house to 'Let It Go', both wearing Elsa dresses. They've got big smiles on their faces and are having a ball.[23] Within two days of it being posted the video had nearly a million shares.[24]

It created such a buzz that Ørjan was asked to appear on *Good Morning Britain* to explain why he'd done it.[25] One of the hosts, Piers Morgan, queried whether Ørjan thought he was a better father because he danced in dresses with his son while Piers himself liked playing footy with his boys. Ørjan was warm and gracious in his response, and even gave Piers his own Elsa dress to give it a go himself. He also had to explain to the panel why Elsa was in fact a superhero in her own right, and not a dainty Disney princess from yesteryear.

Full marks to this champ! I want my little boy to look up to and respect strong women, just like Ørjan's son does.

And there are so many to choose from at the moment. In late 2018, Roy Morgan polled 2500 Aussie kids between six and thirteen, asking them to name their favourite superhero. Wonder Woman won by a mile, with Batman a respectable second and Spider-Man a distant third.[26] And that survey didn't even include the brilliant women from the *Star Wars* movies: Leia, Rey and Jyn Erso. Is there any reason why Luke can't fill his young, giddy head with aspirations to be Queen Elsa, Wonder Woman, Leia, Black Widow or Supergirl?

Choosing their own adventure

What about when boys get a little older, and start activities outside of school? We want to encourage them to pursue whatever makes them happy and lights a spark inside them, even if they're things traditionally considered as girls' activities. Australia is on a bit of a roll watching so many women's sporting codes become professional and entering the mainstream. The popularity of the AFLW is amazing, and I cannot wait until the mighty Swans create their own women's team—I'll be at the first home game with Aila and Luke, all of us donned in red and white. The Matildas are one of the most popular sports teams in the country, period. And the Australian women's cricket team have covered themselves in a lot more glory than their male counterparts recently.

I remember very clearly the judgement made about boys at my high school who chose the 'wrong' sports or activities. If you played soccer, tennis or did cross-country instead of rugby during winter, you would be on the receiving end of sustained harassment that you were a wuss, or a string of homophobic slurs. The same went for the other extracurriculars the school made boys choose. When I was fifteen or sixteen, boys had to choose whether to join the cadets, the Air Training Corps or the school orchestra. Choosing cadets was what the 'strong, brave boys' did; those who were girly or scared chose Air Training Corps (no amount of references to *Top Gun* would convince your peers otherwise); don't even mention those who chose orchestra. (Spoiler alert: I was one of the unmentionables in the orchestra, screeching away on a viola with minimal talent and poise.) When I left school twenty years ago, I thought men who did music or drama were less manly and weaker than those who played rough sports. I had a very narrow and prejudiced definition of what 'normal' boys did. How could I not think that, having been exposed to these attitudes daily for a decade at school?

Let's look at dancing, for instance. When it comes to athleticism, physical strength, endurance, hard work and competition, dancing ticks all the boxes. So when boys choose to get into dancing over a sport like footy, why do they get hit with derision about being effeminate? What about a dance form that's considered *really* girly, like ballet? A professional male dancer can train for eight to ten hours a day, and then give a two-hour evening performance, six days a week.[27] Compare that to sports stars who prep all week for one game on the weekend.

Danseur is an American documentary following the lives of several young male ballet dancers.[28] They talk about their love for dancing, and the sacrifices and costs that their passion has demanded. One of the boys observes that every day he trains four times more than his peers who play football, and he is fitter and has better muscle tone than any of them, yet he's labelled a 'fag' and a 'sissy'. Another says it's only his love of ballet that helps him overcome the constant stream of abuse he gets off the stage. These guys may be physically strong, but they need an enormous amount of mental toughness just to make it through the day and deal with the perception bias and judgement of others.

I've loved cricket my whole life. It's also the only sport I've ever been any good at. I was a fast bowler at high school, liking nothing more than getting the new red rock to cause opening batsmen some discomfort. By Year 12 I was playing serious, tough, competitive cricket, and had (for a brief time) become the best fast bowler at my school. I was even selected in a combined schools' team because I had such a good final season. I'd sledge and intimidate the batsmen, and fire myself up before each match by listening to 'Sunday Bloody Sunday'. Then, after I'd worked all that aggro and teenage machismo out of my system during the game, I'd go home and put on my Mariah Carey CD and pine over girls who didn't know I existed. Honestly, when I was seventeen or eighteen, I couldn't hold a candle to the fortitude of the ballet dancers in that doco.

What about careers and jobs for my kids? Firstly, do they feel they can dream about any career at all when they're young? We know that by pre-school age, children are already thinking about what they want to be when they grow up.[29] They see mum and dad go to work, they interact with educators at daycare, and their shows are filled with characters doing all sorts of things like flying spaceships, putting out fires or even being professional archaeologists who somehow work from home (I seriously don't know how Bandit got himself on such a good wicket).[30] But even though they're still so young, kids are already ruling out jobs that they don't think conform with their gender, and they form stereotypical opinions on occupations and careers based on their experiences with their family, friends and others in their lives.[31]

Because we know that kids form views on occupations so young, there is a big push on around the world, including in Australia, to introduce career education and information in primary school, before students' opinions harden. That way, by the time they reach high school and pick electives, they can choose the right subjects for the future they really want for themselves. A key aim in this is to break gender stereotypes that hang over certain industries.

'Inspiring the Future' is a UK campaign that is trying to do this for young Brits. In 2016, it ran a social experiment where a classroom of young primary school kids were asked about their views of three professions—fighter jet pilot, firefighter and surgeon—and were then asked to draw an image of each of them.[32] Sixty-one pictures showed men in each of these roles, while only five showed women. Then into the classroom walked a real fighter jet pilot, firefighter and surgeon so the kids could see for themselves. They were all blown away to see three women take off their helmets or masks and introduce themselves.

Career ambitions for girls and young women are expanding. I know that Aila can choose any industry, even the male-dominated ones, and go in there and turn the place upside down. The numbers of women in management positions is increasing across most industries.[33] I feel I can put my hand on my heart and say to my girl, 'You *can* be whatever you want,' and not have a deep-seated reservation that I'm misleading her. Doctor? Pshh, too easy. Engineer? You betcha! Professional cricketer? Absolutely—and can you get me some free tickets?

Here's a question: at the same time we're telling our daughters they can be anything when they grow up, are we telling our sons the same thing? Are we encouraging boys to enter traditionally female-dominated industries—healthcare, social assistance and education, for example? In fact, the proportion of women in these three fields has increased over the past twenty years.[34] Yet these industries also have some of the highest jobs growth in the country.[35] A common theme across them is that serving and caring for others—young children, the elderly, people with a disability, the sick—is at the core of the work.[36] These industries are also much more immune to job losses from automation than typically male-dominated ones, such as construction, engineering and manufacturing. As people are starting to consider the prospect that their job will one day be given to a robot or an AI system, it makes economic sense to encourage our boys to think about working in these fields. Yet men struggle to see them as genuine career options.

The NPR podcast *Hidden Brain* looked at the employment choices American men were making after the global financial crisis. In the aftermath of the GFC, there was a deep recession and skyrocketing unemployment across the United States, with tens of millions of families losing their jobs, homes and retirement savings.[37] Even though men were desperate to work, the so-called 'girly' industries were still off-limits, despite the fact some of them had the highest growth rates in the country.

One young man, Robert Vaughn, saw through it.[38] By his early twenties, Vaughn had done four years in the US Navy (even the 'real man' would have approved of that), and now he wanted a career where he could put his physicality to good use. He was advised by someone to become a nurse. Nursing was one of the fastest-growing fields in America, but only 10 per cent of the workforce were men. Being a nurse risked your manliness. Vaughn's first thoughts were of tottering around the white halls of hospitals, cleaning things and holding people's hands while he took their temperature. What he found was a gruelling, fast-paced, physically demanding role that required urgent decision-making. He often had to use his strength to subdue patients going berserk and threatening violence to the staff. Vaughn loves his job as a nurse, even if plenty of men still call him a wimp or a weakling.

Why do we keep feeling the need to impose on boys, across their whole lives, a set of arbitrary standards about what they should do and how they should act? Why do we fear it when their choices run contrary to the stereotype? The answer is that there's a deep insecurity at the centre of traditional masculinity.

Jennifer Bosson is an American psychologist who has done a lot of work on the influence of stereotypes on people's personal decisions and behaviour, and her research led her to the conclusion that 'manhood is something that is hard to earn, and easy to lose'.[39] As men, we like to think of masculinity as being clearly defined and very durable. The reality is it's fragile. Men carry around their masculinity like it's a delicate Fabergé egg which can be easily chipped, scratched and damaged, and a major event can see it shatter into pieces.

We can see this in the daily choices, big and small, that boys and young men make every day. Whether it's getting a butterfly painted on your cheek, wearing the 'wrong' clothing colour, worshipping Queen Elsa for her powers, loving to dance or choosing to be a nurse, if boys step outside the narrow lanes our society has established for them, they risk having their whole identity brought into question, which can cause their self-worth to plummet. One act or decision as a man that bucks the trend can undermine your masculinity in the eyes of others.

As fathers, we love our sons endlessly, but at the same time we risk pushing them down a narrow path that is not necessarily one they would choose for themselves. We become carpenters, trying to build a model man according to our own design specs. We try to clip and shape the perfect bonsai tree that we can put on our mantelpiece.

But why would we want to make our boys' experience of masculinity as fragile as the one we ourselves grew up with? Why not let our boys tell us what they like and want without fear of intervention? From the time they're toddlers to when they become young men, boys should feel encouraged by their dads to make choices that reflect who they are.

That's what the love quotient is all about. It gives our sons a strong sense of self-belief to take action in their own lives and decide things for themselves. As I said at the start of this chapter, the love quotient is about instilling in boys a deep resilience and belief in the decisions they make, because, unfortunately, they're going to need it.

In mid-2019, author Clementine Ford shared an interaction she had at a speaking engagement. A mother told her that her boy, in first grade, suddenly stopped asking to take strawberry milk to school—it turned out he was getting teased by his classmates because it was pink. Ford asked men to share similar experiences on Twitter. Lots of blokes shared stories about being teased, bullied or harassed by classmates, family and colleagues for doing things considered girly, effeminate or abnormal. This included such wild and dangerous acts as playing netball at school with the girls, rolling your school socks at the ankles instead of folding them, liking the pink Power Ranger, and watching *The Powerpuff Girls*. For men, it also included doing things like drinking tea out of china cups, or buying a Mini car.[40] Too often, the scorn came from family members.

If our sons are going to make life choices that defy convention in this way, they'll inevitably draw derision and opposition from some others. That's why they need their dads beside them, radiating love and belief. Paul Keating said the love quotient wrapped him in a protective suit, and our boys can experience the same thing and meet scorn with conviction, not letting the opinions of others get them down. They will emerge the stronger and better for it.

The love quotient is all about confidence and belief, but it should also be about doubt. I don't mean teaching kids to doubt themselves, but doubting the invisible but powerful boundaries that surround them in everyday life. Bruce Pascoe is the author of *Dark Emu*, a ground-breaking book examining the economy and society of Indigenous Australia before colonialism.[41] Pascoe argues that children need to be instilled with doubt as the 'wisest of all our skills' because doubting inspires a 'generous thirst for investigation' that leads to the challenging of conventional wisdom.[42] Society imposes on kids a lot of arbitrary rules about who they're allowed to be. We need our sons to question and challenge these rules, and ultimately to break them down, because no one benefits from them. We don't want our boys shuffling off to the corner when they're teased for doing something that makes them happy but is considered 'not for boys'. We want them to be like those Canadian high school students who put on pink shirts in defiance of bullying, and forced others to reassess what they were thinking. We want our sons to ask: 'Why?'

In 2017, a mum in Tennessee, Kimberly Jones, posted a video of a discussion she had with her son after school one day. He'd been badly bullied about his looks, and taunted that he had no friends. With his heart aching, he sat in the car and asked his mum, 'Just out of curiosity, why do they bully? What's the point of it? Why do they find joy in taking innocent people and finding a way to be mean to them?'[43] Within a couple of days, he'd had a string of public figures reach out to him to offer empathy and support, including Captain America himself. (I love Chris Evans so much.)[44]

I'm not a dope; I know standing up to this sort of thing can be unimaginably hard and challenging, especially when school is all about fitting in and acting cool. That's where dads can make a difference. We can be the endless reservoir of love, positivity and confidence when things get hard or brutal for our boys. We can walk through the fire with them, and question the invisible rules. We can help our boys be free.

Together, let's give our boys an unshakeable, unconditional, immovable love, and in doing so empower them to seize the day. Just like with our daughters, let's instil in our sons a sense that they can truly do and be anything. And let's shatter the invisible, arbitrary and unnecessary rules surrounding boys' choices, and let our sons decide for themselves.

8

HAVING THE WOLF BY THE EAR: TECH AND THE INTERNET

My kids are at that wonderful stage of life where the world is one massive playground. Every place and every item offer the promise of adventure. They are young, happy children. They know they are loved and cared for, and their naivety about the world is like a snug, warm blanket wrapped around them. Simple things, like opening the garage door with a buzzer or hearing music come out of a bluetooth speaker, are still astonishing, bordering on magical.

But when I think about them as older kids, at the age where they become exposed to technology and the internet, it puts a large knot in my stomach. Watching the glow on my son's face as the full power of the internet emanates from some handheld device for the first time will, for me, be like watching him stare into the Ark of the Covenant. As I've said, I have many worries, and plenty of them are irrational. And I've got a tendency to helicopter over my kids. But honestly, nothing makes me more concerned for their health and wellbeing than tech and the internet. It's where I feel the most lost as a father. Because there are no easy answers, and a long list of problems.

Hold or release?

Our family routine already involves lots of tech. We've got two smart TVs, two smartphones, multiple laptops, and three streaming services. We let Aila and Luke watch ABC Kids in the morning while we make coffees and breakfast, do some tidying up, get their bags ready and have showers. Similarly, we use it in the evening so we can get dinner ready and clean up after. We constantly take pics of the kids on our phones to send to family, and Aila loves watching videos we took of her as a baby. We order our groceries online, we Skype with overseas relatives and we use Spotify for our four-person dance parties in the living room. I expect our reliance on tech will only grow as the kids get older.

When it comes to handling tech, I don't want to be a puritan. I want a balance between the online world and the real world, and for my kids to understand the importance of keeping their feet on the ground in both.

We've all heard the stories about what can happen to kids online—how what they experience on the internet can drive kids to depression and even suicide. The omnipresence of online bullying is an enormous challenge for all our kids, as is managing screen time and access to devices. But the parental discussions about tech tend to stop there. The reality is that bullying and addiction are only the beginning of the conversation. The impact of technology and the internet has more sharp angles to hurt you than a ninja star. Here are some of the other big worries rattling around in the back of my head: device separation anxiety, FOMO, addiction to gaming and gambling, exposure to porn, the risk of sexual harassment, the erosion of privacy, and the proliferation of misinformation. Wherever there is technology, these problems lie waiting. And technology is everywhere. I'm going to focus on how these specific challenges impact boys, but I'm well aware the dangers are just as real for all kids. In many ways, Aila will be the guinea pig in my family for our approach to tech, and Luke will be the beneficiary of our trial and error with her.

As a community we tend to discuss individual pieces of this jigsaw, like what to do about one specific game, or one particular app or device. As I write this book, we're all worried about the game *Fortnite*. By the time you read this, we might have moved on to the next concerning game. We've got to step back and look at the bigger picture. There will always be a new game or social media trend to worry about, but the impact being made by tech and the internet on our society is lasting, and every Australian family will have to deal with it.

To make matters more difficult, we have no real precedent for how to handle these problems, or what the long-term damage may be to our boys. We're riding the first crest of this wave, and we don't know what will happen when it breaks on the shore. It seems to me that warping the mind of a boy has never been easier than in the current era, and technology supplies seemingly unending ways to stop a boy from becoming a good man and to turn him into something else. And almost every day, there is a new app or piece of tech that poses a fresh challenge.

As a dad, I feel overwhelmed. Where should I start if I'm going to get a handle on this? When discussing the problem of slavery in the United States, Thomas Jefferson used the metaphor of having the wolf by the ear—'we can neither hold him, nor safely let him go'.[1] That's how I feel about technology and the internet. To take a hardline approach on access to devices and the web might mean driving my son's online activity to places I can't see—a mate's house after school, or his phone in the playground at lunch. Allowing him free and regular access to these things while I hover over head won't be any better. Either approach sees me staring down at a growling wolf, gnashing its fangs.

We need our boys to develop positive, healthy identities outside of the digital world, and they need to have the resilience to withstand the more sinister, seductive temptations of being online. Because as helpful and hilarious as the internet can be, when it gets dark, it can get dark really quickly. Being a boy these days means being discerning and judicious about tech. Our sons need to learn how to weigh up the various offerings of the internet, to work out what is dangerous and what is fake—and, crucially, how to ask for help when they think they need it. As dads, we've got to find a way to allow boys access to technology without being domineering or slack. If we put our heads together, surely we can find ways to enjoy the awesomeness of the World Wide Web and the devices that dish it up, while still making sure our boys are mentally and emotionally okay.

Bullying delivered to your home

Luke and I stand on either side of a digital ravine. Like a lot of youngish dads today, I knew life before the internet and before smart devices took everything over. I remember heading down to the dark and musty computer labs at school to use Netscape Navigator in the 1990s. Then I would go home and use Microsoft Encarta 95 on our home computer to do my homework, which I wrote in an exercise book. Only in Year 12 did I start using the internet alongside my textbooks for studying. I hadn't even heard of MSN Messenger, which was about the only chat service teenagers were using. When I turned eighteen, midway through Year 12, my parents gave me a Nokia 3310. I remember discovering the text function as I was walking home from the beach one day, and I loved to play Snake to procrastinate. I was amazed when someone showed me you could set hit songs as your ringtone. And I remember a friend sending me a link to Facebook, which I had never heard of before, in 2006.

I was probably part of the last generation of teenagers to know a life that wasn't reliant on tech for daily interactions. Luke is a member of one of the first generations to grow up online. He will grow up with the internet heavily shaping his understanding of the world, his attitudes and values, and his interactions with most other people. He'll know no other way, and my old-timey stories of what it was like 'back in my day' will no doubt elicit eye rolls and sighs rather than gasps of wonder. We may not yet know the long-term impact of this profound change, but we know a lot about what is happening in the shorter term.

For starters, kids now have a lot more ways to bully someone. Sadly, cyberbullying is a daily experience for a lot of Aussie kids. Devices have unleashed the potential of round-the-clock bullying, from the time they wake up and get ready for school, all the way until they finish their homework and hit the hay. It takes away the safety of the family home as well, with kids able to be bullied even when sitting next to dad watching a movie. They may always feel vulnerable, on high alert for that buzzing from their device notifying them that the latest taunt has arrived.

Boys are on both ends of cyberbullying, being victims and perpetrators. Boys cyberbully other boys, and they cyberbully girls too. The exact numbers are hard to pin down, but the consensus among researchers is that between 10 per cent and 20 per cent of children and young people under eighteen years of age experience cyberbullying each year, with the percentages varying between younger and older kids.[2] We don't know definitively whether more boys are cyberbullied than girls, or vice versa, or whether more boys are cyberbullies or vice versa.[3] Different studies in this area have reached different conclusions. However, it's an extremely good bet that the prevalence of cyberbullying is underestimated, given that some of the studies are now over ten years old, and cyberbullying tends to be underreported.[4] Just think of all the apps and new tech released in the last decade—and remember, the first iPhone was released in 2007. Cyberbullying means kids can wage war on two fronts: online as well as in person. It's estimated that 84 per cent of students who are bullied online are also bullied in person.[5] It gets more acute in the teenage years, with young people over the age of fifteen more likely to be involved in online bullying.[6]

When I first tried to imagine cyberbullying, I instinctively thought of boys sending nasty messages to other kids, calling them names and teasing them. Until I started looking around, I didn't realise how creative they could be. A 2016 report on cyberbullying to the New South Wales parliament listed a few of the main types of cyberbullying; they included 'happy slapping', where someone is filmed being physically assaulted, with the video then being distributed to other kids in order to humiliate the victim further; 'masquerading', where a perpetrator pretends to be the victim and posts a bunch of stuff online, even sending offensive messages under their name from accounts that look legitimate; and 'outing', where a perpetrator manipulates a victim into disclosing personal information, which is then publicised by the perpetrator to embarrass them.[7] So we're a long way past yelling something nasty at lunchtime—these actions are methodical, targeted and sustained over an extended period of time. It was enough to push the New South Wales parliament into action: its members passed laws in 2018 making cyberbullying an offence punishable by up to five years' jail time.[8]

The cyberbullying done by boys tends to be vicious. Boys are more likely to post offensive material to social media sites, send nasty or abusive emails directly to people, or coercively sext others.[9] One of the most common methods is to repeatedly send offensive or violent messages to the person. These can include memes telling victims to kill themselves or get raped. Honestly, I'm still getting my head around this weapons-grade level of abuse. And it's not just directed at kids their own age. Teenage boys are taking their anger out on anyone they can find online. I follow a few high-profile female journos and authors on Instagram and Twitter. They regularly highlight the volume of offensive or violent messages they receive from teenage boys in particular. Additionally, boys who are themselves victims of cyberbullying are often threatened with physical aggression and violence from the perpetrators.[10]

Cyberbullying is particularly cruel as the perpetrator often doesn't witness their victim's reaction and how miserable it makes them. They don't see the victim becoming withdrawn and detached from their family as they hole up in their room for days, sliding into a deep, dark place. Sadly, the family does not always see it as well, as the victim often puts on a brave face while inside they are falling apart, and with some boys trying to maintain a tough, unfazed image even if their world is crumbling. A 2014 study from the University of New South Wales' Social Policy Research Centre found that girls were reporting cyberbullying more than boys.[11] Similarly, a 2016 study from the University of South Australia found that a higher proportion of boys claimed to never have been bullied, with the researchers stating that, 'Arguably a denial that one has been bullied is consistent with a macho image that some boys wish to project'.[12] Well, the 'real man' doesn't get cyberbullied, does he?

In February 2009, Allem Halkic jumped off the Westgate Bridge in Melbourne to commit suicide. He was seventeen years old, and the only son of Ali Halkic. His devastated parents discovered that a perpetrator had been cyberbullying and stalking Allem online. The police uncovered a series of abusive messages on Allem's computer and phone. Ali said 'the sense of security of having your child at home . . . exposed us . . . everything was happening between 10.30 at night and 3 AM'.[13] Ali said it only took two months for his gorgeous boy to become destroyed by cyberbullying.[14] Ali became one of the founders of Bully Zero, an organisation dedicated to preventing bullying and saving more people from taking their own life, yet he fears a decade after his son's death that cyberbullying is worse than ever.[15] It may be because cyberbullying is insidious: it can creep into your children's lives and take hold before you're even aware there is a problem.

On top of bullying, there's sexual harassment, cyberflashing and cyberstalking. Sadly, this is where our boys run a huge risk of being the main perpetrators. The *Sydney Morning Herald* ran a piece in 2019 about how a sixteen-year-old girl was AirDropped a 'dick pic' while on a school excursion to an art gallery.[16] The stranger who did it also sent her a picture of two rotting rats, just to really mess with her. The fact that these offensive images were AirDropped meant he was physically very nearby. (Some classes use AirDrop to share lesson content, so a lot of kids have their settings open.)

In a 2016 survey of 600 Aussie teenage girls aged fifteen to nineteen, seven in ten agreed that girls are often abused and harassed online.[17] A total of 58 per cent also agreed that girls received uninvited or unwanted indecent or sexually explicit material.[18] This is the sort of stuff that the 'real man' would think is all fun and games, and a demonstration of how tough and masculine he really is. We have to help our boys resist the pressure to join in this sort of ugly behaviour.

Women are not the only victims too. Another survey conducted in 2016 by university researchers asked 4200 people aged sixteen to 49 about their experiences of 'image-abuse', the sharing of intimate or sexual photos without consent. While women tended to have far more troubling experiences than men, it also found that gay and bisexual males were more likely to have been the victims of image-abuse than straight men.[19]

New phobias

Every parent is familiar with the daily battles with their kids about screen time. And everyone has their own approach to it. There's loads of scientific literature examining the effect screen time has on kids and what to do about it, even if the advice is only realistic if you're inside a science lab. In an extreme case from Jiangsu, China, in 2019, a two-year-old's excessive use of screens gave her permanent eyesight damage.[20] But have you heard of nomophobia? It was the *Cambridge Dictionary*'s word of the year in 2018.[21] Nomophobia is the fear or worry of being without your phone or smart device, or unable to use it. The term comes from 'no-mobile phobia'.[22] It even covers the angst people can feel when they're in an area with bad mobile coverage.

Nomophobia is, to put it mildly, an emerging area of research, and not all scientists are convinced of how serious it is. Given that nine in ten Aussie teens have a mobile phone, it might be more real than we'd like to admit.[23] According to a study published by *Men's Health* in 2017, almost three-quarters of the Aussie guys surveyed admitted to having their phone at hand throughout an entire day.[24] Some international researchers are pushing for nomophobia to formally be listed as a diagnosable mental health condition.[25] Others still are examining how we use our devices for everything, including the capturing and recalling of personal experiences; they argue that we've begun projecting our own identity onto these objects and treating them as extensions of ourselves.[26]

In 2019, a research team studied the phone habits of over 700 Aussies, using a scale to work out who were 'problem users' and comparing this to data from 2005. People were asked whether they agreed or disagreed with 27 different statements, such as 'I lose sleep due to the time I spend on my mobile phone', 'I find it difficult to switch off my mobile phone' and 'I feel anxious if I have not checked for messages or switched on my mobile'. Those aged between eighteen and 25 were the most problematic users.[27] While more women than men were identified in this survey as problematic users, the researchers questioned whether this was because women were more aware of their phone habits than men and more willing to discuss it openly.[28] From what we've now seen regarding men's ability to be open about mental health and even bullying, it's a very fair question to ask. The results weren't all rosy for men in the survey either. For instance, the number of men agreeing that they lost sleep due to the amount of time they're on their phone had increased, as did the number of men agreeing that their productivity had decreased as a direct result of the time they spend on the phone.[29]

Once we're used to having an infinite amount of information and services at our disposal, we can find it extremely hard to turn away. I'm definitely guilty of being overly attached to my phone. I use it for everything and I take it everywhere. It's my best friend when I need to multitask, and it's rarely out of my reach. Even when I'm watching Netflix on the couch after the kids are asleep, I'm aimlessly browsing Twitter or Instagram. If I honestly answered the 'problem user' set of questions, I would definitely come out at the top of the curve. So I'm not exactly setting a great standard for my kids to emulate when they begin asking for their own smartphones.

I reckon we should cut our kids a little slack, as the things they love are being specifically designed to keep their attention. We know more about the chemical reaction from getting positive reinforcement online. When we get a bunch of likes, shares or comments, we get a dopamine hit in our brains.[30] Some platforms like to give users a steady stream of notifications to keep them stimulated; others withhold them and then send a larger bunch of notifications to give us a bigger buzz. Some Silicon Valley insiders have revealed how apps and social media platforms are actively designed to trigger these responses.[31]

Nomophobia is closely related to a couple of other doozies, 'FOBO' (fear of being offline) and 'FOMO' (fear of missing out).[32] Quality scientific research on these new challenges is still scarce and the analysis tends to focus on differences in age groups rather than gender. However, in 2015, the National Stress and

Wellbeing Survey looked at FOMO among Aussie teens and is one of the best studies available of the extent of the problem.[33] It found that about 56 per cent of kids aged thirteen to seventeen were heavy social media users.[34] Fifty-one per cent of teenage boys were heavy users, and one in five was on social media constantly throughout the day.[35] FOMO for teenage boys was consistent across the different age groups studied.[36] The survey also found that over half of Aussie teens connected to social media fifteen minutes before bedtime every night. Almost 40 per cent connected both in the presence of others, and within fifteen minutes of waking up. One in four teens was on social media when eating brekky and lunch, every day of the week.[37]

As you would expect, the survey also found that the higher the social media usage, the higher the chance of anxiety and stress courtesy of FOMO. A whopping 90 per cent of heavy social media users admitted they were afraid of missing something if they didn't stay connected to their online networks, and 78 per cent admitted they felt worried when they couldn't access their accounts.[38] Being on the inside of what's happening was really important for these teens too, with 78 per cent of heavy social media users saying it was important that they understood their mates' inside jokes, with 60 per cent worried that their friends were having fun without them.[39] As people move from being teenagers to young adults, their FOMO follows them, and can get even worse. And this survey was from five years ago, so I'd wager that the results would be at least the same, if not higher, in 2020.

Getting hooked to a device can provide an easy ramp to other compulsive or addictive behaviours as boys become young men. In the land of the punt, gambling is the obvious example. The days of needing to head to the TAB or pub to place a bet are gone.

In 2014 it was estimated that at least half of all sports betting was done online, and that number has surely grown in the years since. Studies show that men place bets wherever they are: at uni, at work, at home, even at the match itself.[40] Devices give us the opportunity to place live bets on sports matches, play online poker, even online pokies. According to HILDA (Household, Income and Labour Dynamics in Australia Survey) data, men gamble more than women, and their tendency to gamble increases with age.[41] Just over 20 per cent of men aged between eighteen and 24 gamble, but that increases to over 50 per cent for those aged 45 to 54. It's easy to think young men are placing a few small, cheeky bets on their phone, however they wager almost as much in one month as men twice their age. There are also 200,000 problem gamblers in Australia, and a link has been established between problem gambling and the incidence of family violence, something that is being investigated further by researchers.[42]

Gaming has a culture

Ever since the 1980s, one of the classic conflict areas between parents and kids has been video games, with concerns about young people getting hooked on gaming. I loved games growing up. I played a bunch with friends. I had a first-edition Game Boy, which I played until my thumbs hurt. As a teenager, I loved (loved loved loved!) *Age of Empires*, which appealed to all my nerdy desires. You got to build up and take control of one of the great civilisations from ancient history, from the Bronze Age to the Iron Age, and there were loads of missions and challenges to complete. I regularly loaded it up to play for one hour only, or to finish a particular challenge, and ended up with bleary red eyes in the wee hours of the night after playing for five or six hours. I would get so lost in the game that time just fell away. My mum frequently heckled me for 'still playing that bloody game'.

When I was fourteen, we went on a two-week family holiday to Hawaii—the only way Dad could get rest from his work was to be physically removed from the country. Even as I swam at the beach and dived around the amazing pools at the resort, my mind was racing with different *Age of Empires* scenarios, and I couldn't wait to get home and keep playing. When I was approaching my final two years of high school, I decided to get rid of my copy of the game as I was nervous about my ability to switch it off so I could focus on my schoolwork.

I know my experience was shared by millions of boys all over the world. But the Game Boy and *Age of Empires* are beta level compared to the sophistication and seduction of games now. They've got cinematic editing and production, extraordinary detail and design, endless character choices, a myriad of imaginative worlds to explore and conquer, and the real kicker: an online community of gamers with whom to share your triumphs and tragedies.

Mum and dad may not get how amazing your favourite game is to play all through the night, but your international cadre of fellow gamers sure do. Kids report that 'massively multiplayer online' games (MMOs) give them a stronger sense of community and attachment to their fellow gamers than the real world, so logging off is like being cut off from your friends (hello, FOMO and FOBO).[43] Even if your folks do try to shut you down, they might not realise that these games are available on many different devices, not just your Xbox or PS4. Gaming technology is evolving rapidly and will keep getting more sophisticated, more sensory and more alluring. According to Australia's eSafety Commissioner, six in ten kids aged eight to seventeen have played online multiplayer games, and one in two kids has played with people they haven't met in person.[44] Online gaming tends to be more popular with teenage boys. They are happier than teenage girls to play anonymously online as well as play with people they have actually met, and make in-game purchases to boost their gaming experience.[45] The Commissioner estimates that about 200,000 Aussie kids have experienced in-game bullying, which is doubly sad as many kids play games online to escape bullying in the physical world. About one in four boys who were bullied within a game retaliated, a higher proportion than the girls who did likewise. Aussie male gamers tend to play longer each day than female gamers too.[46]

How about watching other people gaming after you've finished for the night? It took me a while to get my head around this trend. Why on earth would kids want to watch other people gaming? But if that's your main interest and they're your people, why wouldn't you? When I finished playing cricket on the weekends, I'd go to the pub with my mates and watch the cricket, whatever match was on. If you love something, you want more of it. So even if I eventually win the daily struggle to get my boy to log off from the game, there's a great chance he'll kick his feet up and watch others game for hours. Talk about winning the battle but losing the war.

This type of spectating is massive in the gaming community. At the writing of this book, one of the most prominent platforms for doing this is Twitch, designed exclusively for people to watch other people play video games. And it isn't some numpty website—Amazon bought it for US$970 million in 2014.[47] You can watch individual players or you can browse people playing particular games. It has over 15 million daily users and between 2 million and 3 million daily broadcasters. The top ten individual gamers on Twitch have followings ranging from 3 million to over 14 million people. It is also a platform tilting heavily towards males. The top ten gamers are all male. Over 80 per cent of Twitch's audience is male, and 55 per cent are aged between eighteen and 34.[48]

Worrying about boys' gaming behaviour is causing constant headaches for parents across the country. We tend to think of the problem in terms of addiction and the flow-on effects, and sure, addiction is a big risk. Boys are more susceptible to becoming compulsive gamers than girls.[49] In May 2019, the World Health Organization officially recognised gaming disorder as a diagnosable addiction disorder.[50] Parents everywhere fear that their sons are more tired, more irritable, more distracted, more anxious and more withdrawn because of gaming.

The United States already has a therapeutic retreat dedicated to dealing with gaming addiction, reSTART, located among the lush, coastal wilderness of Washington state.[51] At the centre, teens are cut off from their devices and the virtual world. They're put through a program to reconnect them with the real world, while they try to tackle the underlying reasons they game so compulsively.[52] reSTART has fielded 20,000 calls from concerned parents since opening. Aussie families are also on the hunt for clinical help for their wayward, addicted children, and some of the most shocking examples of gaming addiction come from teenage boys threatening violent retaliation unless they're allowed to plug back in to the virtual world.[53]

But the problems associated with heavy gaming among boys and young men run much deeper than not being able to switch off the console more regularly. Because gaming is a community, it has a culture, and so creates and promotes a set of values and attitudes. They're not pretty. Let's start with the rather mild views emanating from heavy gamers. In 2018, the 50/50 by 2030 Foundation did a survey on community attitudes to gender. It found a link between gaming and traditional views of gender: among millennial males who played video games for an above-average length of time, 62 per cent held traditional views on gender.[54] This included 46 per cent of young male gamers agreeing that 'women should not be out in public places after dark', 43 per cent agreeing that 'women prefer to stay at home with young children', and 43 per cent agreeing that 'women are best suited to be the primary carer of children'.[55]

Why are young male gamers apparently so regressive in their social attitudes? For one thing, female characters in 1980s or '90s video games were often not portrayed in a positive way. They were damsels in distress who needed saving—prizes to be won at the end of an adventure. Typically, they had no agency and were just objects.[56] Alternatively, female protagonists were often simply the male character made a bit more girly—like whacking a bow on Pac-Man. The male character remained the default choice, with the female character being a deviation from the norm.[57] Many 'retro' games from this era are today getting a second lease on life, and as a result so is the 'damsel in distress' trope.

In more recent games, women are often portrayed in a far more sexualised way, so as to excite the straight male gamer on the other side of the screen.[58] It can get really graphic and violent as well, like in the *Grand Theft Auto* series; some games will even suggest, directly or indirectly, that female characters have been sexually abused or assaulted.[59]

One thing to have emerged over the past few years is that the gaming community has a problem about including women, despite the fact that almost half of all gamers are female.[60] There's a lingering bias among male gamers that women are not as good at gaming, even though studies (and common sense) have proven that's bullshit.[61] But there's also an insidious segment of gamers who argue that women are not just poorer gamers, they also cheat and hack to get an advantage, they're poorer coders,[62] even that they should not be part of the gaming community at all. This nastiness was revealed to the wider world during the 'Gamergate' saga in 2014.[63]

Gamergate started with a game in the United States, *Depression Quest*, made by Zoë Quinn. As soon as the game was released, Quinn started receiving hate mail from other gamers telling her the game wasn't entertaining (even though within about a year it had been played 1 million times).[64] This turned into outright personal attacks on Quinn when an ex-boyfriend blogged that she had previously had a relationship with a gaming journo who reviewed her game. Pretending concern for journalistic ethics, male gamers started incessantly attacking Quinn. Eighteen months later, someone on the website 4chan threatened to hurt Quinn, badly: 'Next time she shows up at a conference we . . . give her a crippling injury that's never going to fully heal . . . a good solid injury to the knees. I'd say a brain damage, but we don't want to make it so she ends up too retarded to fear us.'[65] This was one of many physical threats she received. Then people started posting her personal details on the internet, including her home address, phone numbers and bank details. For her own safety, Quinn was forced to leave her home and couch-surf for a period of time.[66]

As female gaming journos spoke out and advocated change in the gaming community, they too have been subjected to vicious threats. Some left the industry, but others soldier on, targets in an online firefight.[67] Sometimes the threat of a firefight is disturbingly real. In October 2014, American gaming critic

Anita Sarkeesian cancelled a talk she was going to give at Utah State University because of a terrorist threat that if she spoke, they would commit 'the deadliest school shooting in American history'.[68] Sarkeesian also had to leave her home amid Gamergate due to the seriousness of threats against her.[69]

This stuff terrifies me. When I was a teenager, gaming was a hobby I mostly did on my own. It wasn't a way of life or a refuge from the world, and it didn't teach me my personal values. Like I said at the start of this chapter, I'm on one side of the ravine, Luke is on the other. Talking about how to prevent our boys from getting hooked on gaming is the tip of the iceberg. As parents, we've got to get our heads around the murky culture of the gaming community, and appreciate how it can affect the attitudes and values that our boys hold—from the outdated but more banal 'women are better carers than men' all the way to 'women gamers should be expelled from our community by whatever means necessary'. Research into these issues is still emerging, and as yet we don't know the extent of the impact.

Shared hatreds

The internet is full of many different communities, and they're not homogeneous. Some groups cluster around shared passions and interests, or shared life experiences, but also shared dislikes or hatreds. The incel community is one such subgroup, whose members gravitate towards one another due to their shared hatred. It's for men who feel that they 'suffer' from the oppressive yoke of 'involuntary celibacy'.

Exemplifying the shape-shifting nature of the internet, the original incel community sprang up in the 1990s during the dial-up era, and was a civil, supportive, open place where awkward men and women could socialise and ask each other questions about dating.[70] But it's metastasised into a rage-fuelled mini-cult of men who think they're socially oppressed and cruelly spurned by evil, manipulative women. They talk about violent revolution against women and people generally, all because no one will have sex with them.[71] There's a whole lexicon and social theory developing among incels as to why certain men and women have sex and others don't, and it has a distinctly racial bias built into it as well.[72] It's estimated that about 80 per cent of identified incels are in Europe and North America—but this is the internet and so no one really knows for sure.

This community would be less concerning if not for the fact that self-declared incels have perpetrated violent physical attacks in North America over the past five or six years. One went on a shooting spree in California; another drove a van over ten people in Toronto. But that sort of violence doesn't really happen in Australia, though, right? Not so. Incels boast in their online forums about sexually assaulting women on a daily basis—groping them on public transport, harassing them in offices, you name it. They fight their revolution wherever and however they can.[73]

One former incel, a teenage boy from Denmark named Andreas, recounted his experiences in an interview with *Vox* in 2019. It started innocently: he was a lonely guy looking for comfort. He'd been a victim of bullying and had been dumped by the only girl he'd ever gone out with. He fell into a bad spot and stumbled across the incel forums. At first he thought it was a supportive community that helped him while he felt really bad about himself, but the more time he interacted on the forum, the angrier and more hate-filled he became. He eventually unplugged from the forums, he told *Vox*, but not before he'd developed a seething hatred of all women that he was still trying to expunge.[74]

Then we've got to get our head around the fact that computer algorithms are starting to lead, and manipulate, people's online behaviour. Search engines, social media sites and video platforms all use algorithms to determine users' preferences and recommended content or products. My Google, Instagram and YouTube accounts are filled with articles, videos and retail items based on my search history and previous activity. I get stuck in my own bubble as much as the next person, and I've disappeared down many YouTube rabbit holes, often with hilarious consequences. I've also let Aila watch YouTube clips of her favourite shows or songs.

But it's not always so amusing. There are videos designed for children that are clearly addictive and tailored to their sensory appetite, and there are also unofficial videos of popular toddler shows like *Peppa Pig*, *Thomas the Tank Engine* and others featuring disturbing or violent images that can scare the kid watching them, who has no idea it's fake.[75] We're talking about seriously messed-up stuff like Peppa having her head chopped off.[76] These can pop up as recommended viewing within only a few minutes. Videos like this are churned out by production teams because they get hits and are ripe for advertising, which is where the money lies.[77] YouTube's algorithm dominates what people watch: it's responsible for more than 70 per cent of the overall time spent on the site.[78]

Keeping an eye on your toddler while they watch YouTube clips is one thing; what about a teenage boy on chat sites and social media platforms? You don't know what algorithms are guiding the things your boy reads or watches, or how it can spiral out of control. In 2015, Calab Cain was 21 years old and had dropped out of university in the US state of Virginia, when he went onto YouTube looking for advice about what he should do next. Over the next few years he watched approximately 12,000 YouTube videos, which, as he admitted in an interview with the *New York Times*, led him down an 'alt-right rabbit hole'.[79] The YouTube algorithm kept recommending videos that were slightly more negative, and over time the content Calab was watching became more and more extreme, and his views became more radical and conspiratorial as a result. But he found a sense of belonging in this world, and stayed for a few years as a member of the alt-right. The journalist who covered the story, Kevin Roose, argued that Calab's story was common across the country.

In August 2019, the *New York Times* did a month-long investigation into how YouTube radicalises people; its journalists were shocked to discover how frequently the algorithm used by YouTube deliberately led people towards hate-fuelled, far-right vloggers and conspiracy theorists. It's not because YouTube is pushing a political line, it's because anger, fear and doubt suck people into watching videos online, and the videos of right-wing extremists trigger these emotions. Even when people were looking for information on their own health and wellbeing, YouTube was more likely to take them to anti-vaccination videos and the like.

This isn't small fry: in Brazil, which is YouTube's second-largest market, those who campaigned to get the current (and far-right) president elected credit the site with changing the national conversation ahead of the election.[80] There is now a big push to get YouTube to remove content that is extremist or that promotes violence against other people.

Zoë Quinn's and Calab Cain's experiences in America, or Andreas's journey in Denmark, may seem like they're a safe distance away from the bedrooms and studies of suburban Australia, but our boys are not isolated from this toxic torrent.

The internet is everywhere, and the amount of content it offers is growing on a mind-bending scale. In 1994, the year I began high school, there were 2738 websites worldwide.[81] When I left in 1999, there were over 17 million. Today, the figure is over 1.6 billion. That's a lot of information to enlighten someone—and a lot of dark alleys to get lost in.

All this makes our jobs as fathers that much harder, and the challenge will only heighten as the gaming world evolves, as online communities continue to splinter or go further underground, and as content providers refine their algorithms to maximise engagement, whatever the cost.

What's real?

The proliferation of fabricated information online is another huge challenge. Donald Trump may have weaponised the term, labelling everything he finds disagreeable as 'fake news', but it existed long before him. The internet has long been replete with bullshit, but today the fake stuff is getting way more realistic. Recent tech developments have made it so freaking easy to disseminate content that looks legitimate but that is in fact utterly false.

We may be more accustomed to doubting what we read and being advised to check sources, but what about what we see? In September 2018, a photo did the rounds that appeared to show Trump trying to save a guy trapped in the floodwaters caused by Hurricane Florence. Most people saw it for the nonsense it was (Trump was also handing the guy a MAGA cap in the doctored photo), but it still got shared over 275,000 times on Facebook with the caption: 'You won't see this on the news . . . make it go viral.'[82] The original photo was of first responders to flooding in Texas in 2015.

Now, that particular example might seem like it's only for real suckers, but what about 'deep fake' videos and portraits? This is when real footage is manipulated to change the nature of the video. It can put different words in a speaker's mouth, change the way they talk or move, even generate an entirely different scene.[83] This technology is being used on world leaders and public figures—for now. But it can be applied to any scenario and to any person. Deep fake portraits and videos will only get more realistic as our kids grow up.

Young people are now less likely to get their news from mainstream media channels and instead rely on social media and the opinions and experiences of their friends. A 2018 study demonstrated that young Australians aged eighteen to 34 have the highest trust in news found on social media and on search engines.[84] They're actually going to the places where misinformation is far more likely to exist.

Sometimes fake news is just people stirring the pot, but often it's people pushing a particular agenda and trying to influence opinion. Being able to discern fact from fiction is a critical cognitive skill for our kids if they're going to stay grounded in reality. They will need to learn to question what they read, see and hear. But at the moment, they don't feel confident about pulling this off. A 2017 survey of 1000 young Aussies aged eight to sixteen examined how they get news. Roughly one-third said they could distinguish fake news from real news. But one-third felt they could not make this distinction, and one-third were uncertain about their ability.[85] So our young people are dissing newspapers and other old-school news platforms, going to those places on the internet that offer volumes of unregulated content, and as a result feeling uncertain about what's real and what isn't.

While we're discussing real versus fake, there is of course the problem of 'catfishing'. Someone sets up a social media account, finds a few suitable photos for their profile, and bingo—we've got a new 'person'. Such an identity can then be used to lure, scam and harass victims. Catfishing was the subject of an indie doco in 2010, and there's even an American TV show where two guys help people who have fallen in love online to find out whether the person they're involved with is real or not.

Like all things on the internet, catfishing is getting more advanced and more despicable. All parents should take notice of the tragic circumstances around the legal case involving Lincoln Lewis, son of the rugby league star Wally Lewis. Lincoln was a *Home and Away* star who was impersonated by a catfish on Facebook.[86] This person had created an elaborate plot to ensnare women into thinking they were in a romantic relationship with the actor, with the intent of causing psychological and emotional harm to them. The full story is horrifying, with the catfish having used a range of fake characters to play out a sick drama. The catfish also used sophisticated video and photo manipulation to make the relationships seem as legit as possible. The catfish turned out to be a 29-year-old woman from Melbourne: she was eventually caught and tried in 2019, but not before one of her targets committed suicide. The other was left with severe anxiety.[87]

Data cashcows

While we are trying to help our boys work out what is real, we've also got to help them understand how tech and internet affect their private identities. There are a couple of major things boys need to understand: that all their online movements create individual pieces of data, that this data is collected by private companies, and that it is then sold to yet other companies for the purposes of advertising, marketing and god knows what else.

I'm not sure any of us, adults or kids, really understands this permanent undercurrent of our everyday life. We currently produce approximately 2.5 quintillion bytes of data globally each day.[88] The extent of how our every move is tracked to create a personalised consumer profile is not exactly known, mostly because the tech giants don't tell us exactly how they collect and sell our data.[89]

Our sons need to understand that any information they voluntarily put online about themselves, and about their friends and family, is a ripe target for data mining. As soon as we go online, we're cashcows for multinationals like Google, Amazon and Facebook. The global data market is more valuable than oil now.[90] In 2019, one estimate had the global data market worth about US$26 billion, and digital display advertising worth about US$121 billion.[91] Our most private data can be bought and sold time and again to companies we've never heard of. The main aim right now is to market products back to us, using the data to ensure that the marketing is targeted and attractive and pricks our interest.[92]

It's not exactly clear what data mining is being done. In 2017, Facebook was in hot water over whether it was offering advertisers the chance to target 6.4 million young Aussie and Kiwi users during moments of mental and emotional vulnerability. The *Australian* newspaper uncovered a document seemingly prepared by Facebook for advertisers, highlighting the platform's ability to micro-target ads when young people felt 'worthless', 'insecure', 'stressed', 'defeated', 'anxious' and like a 'failure'. The average age of the targeted users was sixteen. Facebook denied this, saying the research breached its protocols, and its research on minors is never used for ad targeting.[93]

In 2018, after an investigation by *Gizmodo*, a tech-focused media outlet, Facebook admitted that it was mining uploaded address books to identify contact information for other users that was not public.[94] It had previously denied the practice. Back in 2012, Facebook experimented on 700,000 of its users for one week, altering the algorithm showing users' status updates, to determine what effect pushing more positive or negative messages would have on the emotional state of users. It didn't take an investigative journo to uncover this: Facebook proudly published its results in a medical journal.[95]

Data mining is done on all the social media platforms young people use. And we're producing a ridiculous amount of data on social media. Currently across the globe, Snapchat users share over 527,000 photos, users watch more than 4.1 million videos, 456,000 tweets are sent, and Instagram users post over 46,000 photos—*every minute of the day*.[96] We may just be dicking around online or aimlessly browsing, but we leave a clear trail of identifiable footprints for others to follow.

The longevity of what we post online is also a concern. Our boys might be posting things they think are hilarious when they're young, but they may well come to regret them in future years. We all do stupid shit as teens, but now all that shit lives online for families, friends, partners or even employers to look at.[97] I am incredibly relieved that my every movement and thought as a teenager wasn't permanently stored on the internet. As a result, a debate is happening across the world, including in Australia, about whether people have 'the right to be forgotten' and the right to demand that companies expunge a user's personal data upon request.[98]

Courtesy of social media, teenagers are growing up with an instinctive understanding of the benefits of having a personal 'brand' which they can leverage online.[99] Some boys now want to be YouTube stars or Instagram influencers, monetising their identity and life experiences for everyone to see. We are living through the first wave of social media influencers, so we have no idea what effect such personal exposure will have on their lives and careers in the long term. Some young people may become the next wave of shrewd entrepreneurs; others may be haunted by their online posts for years. We just don't know.

The erosion of our privacy through data mining is penetrating our offline lives as well. These days we have devices sitting in our homes that listen to us 24/7, with our consent, and add our conversations to their data profiles on us. In early 2019, Julia and I started ordering our groceries online via Woolworths and getting them delivered to home, in a bid to save a bit more time. One week, without us ordering it, Woollies gave us a Google Home Mini, free of charge. We were surprised, and it also seemed a bit weird, if not outright dodgy—a naked attempt to obtain more data about us by listening to our conversations. We put the unwrapped box on the shelf and forgot about it. The next week, we were sent another one—again for free. Tempted by the suggestion a second time around, we set it up and started to use it.

The sleek little disc sat in our kitchen for a couple of weeks. I started asking it about the weather in the mornings. When we were short of hands, we asked it to start playing music for the kids. It only took Julia or me shouting out, 'Hey Google!' half a dozen times before our toddler cottoned on and starting asking Google for things herself. Not a good sign.

One day we asked the Mini very directly: 'Hey Google, are you listening to everything we say?' It gave a long answer about how it was concerned about our privacy and security, but it didn't say no. A couple of days later, we were sitting on the lounge chilling out, and I shouted out, 'Hey Google!' for some random request. When the Mini didn't respond, I said to Julia rhetorically, 'What is it doing back there?' The Mini replied: 'When I'm not responding to your requests, I mostly write poetry.' Suitably creeped out, we unplugged the device and put it back in its box, never to be reactivated again.

That damn Mini is a sign of things to come. By 2020, it's estimated, some 200 billion devices will be hooked up to the internet across the globe.[100] What part of our day won't produce data for someone to make money from?

And these are just the companies that have *legal* access to your private information. There are also, of course, a bunch of nefarious companies and individuals trying to get your data by stealth. In 2019, researchers from the University of Sydney and CSIRO's Data61 Group identified over 2000 counterfeit apps on the Google Play Store impersonating popular games. Some were crappy knock-offs looking to make fast money, but others contained malware or had dangerous data access requests, potentially giving the apps access to SMS records, cameras and microphones.[101] I don't want to be sensationalist: the researchers looked at over a million apps, so the fake hit rate was only about 0.2 per cent. But the example is useful in how it shows the creativity and craftiness of nefarious types online, and the sort of things they'll do to get inside your device.

None of what I've been talking about is theoretical. It's happening now, and has been for years. And these are just the challenges we know about, given the state of tech and the internet in 2020. That's why I think it's like what Jefferson said about having the wolf by the ear: being too lax is a recipe for disaster, but being too strict can drive our boys to hide their behaviour from us, or access tech outside of home.

We might well feel helpless—I certainly do—but we've got to find a way to deal with it.

What to do with the wolf?

Firstly, we've made a big start by acknowledging that these problems exist. Hopefully the dystopian summary I've given in this chapter at least gives you a fighting chance, because you'll know the extent and scale of the influence tech and the internet can play in shaping our boys. Our eyes are wide open.

Secondly, if we can coordinate across households to set common standards and approaches, we should. Our families are at the front line of the next wave of tech transformation, so we might as well try to work together. It's another reason why building better fatherhood support networks is so vital. We can better understand what our boys are doing with tech by talking to one another and swapping stories. Sharing our experiences may also help fathers present a united front in handling access to the latest game or app, and might lead to a consistent approach across families that helps influence the behaviour of a whole friendship circle.

But one of the biggest issues that everybody grapples with is access. Given what we know, it's no wonder that we want to rip the devices out of our kids' hands and just lock them in a box forever, or like Frodo cast them into the fire. And those closest to the furnace, the entrepreneurs of Silicon Valley, are just as worried as us. The CEO of Apple, Tim Cook, has said he doesn't want his nephew on a social network.[102] His predecessor, Steve Jobs, wouldn't let his young kids use iPads.[103] Melinda Gates admitted she wasn't prepared for the effect of technology on her children, even after she and Bill refused phones to their children until they were teenagers.[104] We simply can't give our boys unrestricted access to tech and the internet.

Parents across the country are already trialling different methods to control kids' use of tech in a fair manner. I know parents who ensure that all laptops and devices are charged out in the family room, where they're visible at all times. I know parents who only let their kids online in an open area of the family home, so their activity can be monitored. I know parents who steadfastly refuse to let their kids into their bedrooms with tech, and absolutely not overnight. I know parents who say the price of a social media account is having them as a friend (although kids know ways of getting around this). I've also heard experts suggest that parents change their wi-fi password regularly as a check against unhealthy tech use, or use their leverage as the people who pay bills to cut off their accounts when things get hairy.

I sympathise with the school systems around the country that are considering banning phones during school hours. They're worried about students bullying each other and getting distracted in class. I can't imagine the pressures on a teacher as they deal with all this tech while trying to teach. New South Wales banned phones in public primary schools in 2018, and Victoria is introducing a phone ban in all public primary and secondary schools in 2020.[105] I sympathise with kids who are only using their phones the same way the adults around them do, and those who use them to boost their classroom learning, especially teenagers. I remember being in Year 12 at a school that still treated me like a ten-year-old; it was demeaning and patronising.

I hope that my kids' primary school years will be a fun, amazing time where the physical world will hold as many, if not more incredible experiences than anything online. There is play to be had, adventures to pursue and exploring to be done ahead of streaming TV shows and music, or playing age-appropriate games (ideally with some educational value). I realise I might be being naive, as 81 per cent of Aussie parents say their pre-schoolers use the internet, and of these parents, 94 per cent say their child was using the internet by the age of four.[106] And some of this exposure to tech is vital in the modern world, like primary schools starting to teach computer coding as an important life skill.[107] But such things can be introduced gradually when my kids are young without them dominating their time and attention, and shaping all their life experiences as a result. I'm leaning towards keeping phones out of the possession of Luke and Aila until they're teenagers, when I can have a serious discussion with them about the world they're entering when they step online. Doubly so for social media. Introducing all that tech too early will only sour my sweet, beautiful kids.

If we're at home streaming shows or checking out funny clips on YouTube of monkeys riding pigs or epic dog fails, I want Julia or me there to make sure the 'recommended video' algorithm doesn't throw up something whacky or disturbing, and that there will be no long viewing sessions where my kids just surf YouTube or Twitch while I do the laundry. I'm comfortable with them playing video games when they're of primary school age, as long as the game is appropriate for them and they're not going to see something nasty. But I'll be pretty wary of whoever they're playing with if it's online.

I don't want to just set boundaries for their use of tech, I want to share experiences with them and to help them see the great things that the internet can offer. Screen time can't just be zombie time for my kids while I do something else. Experts say that one of the most constructive ways to engage your kids about tech is to bond with them over it.[108] I want to watch the shows they like alongside them, and talk to them about why they enjoy them so much. I want to encourage them to go outside and play games in the real world, even if they're pretending to be their favourite TV characters. Lord knows how many ideas for games I've got from *Bluey*. And I'd love nothing more than to kick back on a Friday or Saturday night and play some video games with my kids—that sounds like amazing fun. Not only is it fun, but gaming can teach skills like problem-solving and situational analysis. It can also give kids an opportunity to use their literacy, numeracy and even coding skills.[109]

When Luke is a teenager and his interest moves beyond shows and games, and he's mature enough to understand that the tech world can have wide ramifications, he can set foot in it. I'll discuss with him how tech and the internet works. How it can be an amazing place for learning, entertainment and hilarity, but also a place that traces his activities, that actively tries to guide him to sensationalist content to get him hooked, and that offers up a lot of content that is simply false. I'll need to tell him how to watch out for nefarious groups and people that are looking to harm or scam others. Perhaps most of all, he'll need to learn judiciousness about engaging with people's online profiles, knowing that not everything online is what it seems. I don't want him to be a paranoid wreck before he's even had a chance to post his first photo, but equally I don't want him finding out the hard way about how bad the online world can be, or not knowing how to protect his own privacy. There's oodles to enjoy on the internet, but he needs to appreciate that there is both sunshine and shadows.

I can't see how placing hard and fast bans on his use of tech as a teenager will have a positive outcome. Technology is a tool, and our boys won't develop the skills to use it if we keep it out of their reach, especially as they will have already been introduced to some tech from an early age, like content streaming services, computer coding or educational games. Luke has to learn how to regulate his own access to tech, and to better understand the effect using tech can have on his mood, behaviour and mental and emotional wellbeing. That involves giving him access to tech with clear rules and limits, and with clear consequences for breaches of those rules.

It's incumbent on me to be active and engaged in his online life, and to counsel and advise him when things go pear-shaped, or if he encounters bullying behaviour. That means taking further action when necessary, like reporting abuse or fake accounts, giving him access to therapy if he ever needs it, talking to his school about what's going on, even contacting the eSafety Commissioner to make a complaint or an appeal for help. You've gotta use every resource at your disposal to keep this wolf at bay.

It's also up to me to model good tech behaviour. As I've said, I'm by no means the best at that, so it will take a lot of effort for me to shape up as well. I need to learn to put the damn phone out of reach, and not to be a hypocrite by requiring my kids to live up to a standard that I consistently fail to meet.

Crucially, I have to make sure my boy and I have an open, easy dialogue about what he does on the internet and how it shapes his perception of the world. As we've seen, gaming isn't just about playing a game, it's about the community you find and the values it can espouse. Online forums can start out as supportive and then become anything but. Luke might go online to find out more about the world around him, and end up hating it—or himself. It's up to me to make sure he feels he can ask me about what he's seeing, and to help him interrogate it. And it's up to me to keep our relationship in real life close, so he continues to get the love quotient from me, as I nudge him towards being a good man.

MASTERING THE TRAPEZE

ADAM LIAW, ADELAIDE

During his adolescence, Adam Liaw was a real-life Doogie Howser: he enrolled at university at sixteen, and had obtained a double-degree in science and law by twenty-one. After practising law for several years, he won Season 2 of *Masterchef* in 2010, one of the most watched non-sporting events in Australian broadcasting history.[1]

Since being catapulted to national fame, Adam has become an author, TV show host, social commentator and passionate ambassador for the Adelaide Crows Football Club. In August 2019 he and his wife welcomed their third child and second son into the mix too, as if life wasn't busy enough. So Adam is a man who understands the juggle of a working father better than most.

'My work is more similar to blue-collar industries in that I have to go where the work is – it requires me to be physically present,' he says. When I talk to Adam, he has spent most of the past eight weeks travelling for work, only being back for a handful of days. 'I am away a lot more than other dads. I make up for this by being available more when I am home. I use my flexible schedule during the week to spend time with my kids where I can. It's not an ideal solution, but I try to make the most of it.'

Adam thinks there's too much focus on how fathers don't spend enough time with their kids, and too negative a focus on male breadwinners. 'As fathers, we can beat ourselves up about this when we should be giving ourselves a break,' he argues. 'The dad's typical role as breadwinner is underrated in the modern conversation on fatherhood. Providing financial stability is no less important for the functioning and wellbeing of your family. If you looked at the structure of my family, it would fit as neatly in the 1950s as it does now: my wife is at home caring for the kids while I'm the breadwinner. Those roles make sense for us, but that's not the end of the story. I cook and clean. I look after the kids. I'm not absent from household management and domestic duties, but the time I can spend on that is necessarily limited.' In his experience, 'quality time with your kids outweighs quantity any day of the week'.

He sympathises with a lot of younger working fathers trying to manage the expectations of family and work. 'Like in the big law firms,' he says, 'it's often a time when guys are trying to move from junior to more senior ranks at work. It's an engine room phase of your career where you are often one of the hardest-working people in the office and putting in long hours, but these days it's also when you have a young family that needs attention. It creates a crunch of pressures on dads.'

Adam is always conscious of giving his kids space to grow up and be their own person. 'Kids don't need a helicopter parent,' he says, 'they need their independence as well. In fact, the act of growing up as a child is the journey towards independence.' He describes being a parent as offering a safety net for a trapeze artist. 'You're there as a protective measure, aware of the risks they face, but you're not within arm's reach all the time. If they fall, it's not a disaster.'

Rather than trying to force his kids to behave a certain way, Adam focuses on instilling the right values in them. 'If you get the values right, the behaviour falls into place,' he says. Raised a Christian, Adam is not religious these days; the values that really matter to him are family, financial security, and good or moral behaviour. He also says that rather than talk explicitly about values with his kids, he tries to guide their actions on a practical level each day. 'Even something as simple as finding a two-dollar coin on the street can instil values in my kids. Do they look around to find who might have dropped it? Do they pocket the coin? Do they share it with each other? Even decisions like these are an embodiment of values and character.'

With his son Christopher starting school, Adam has thought hard about what masculinity means to him. 'We need to see a more positive masculinity that is inclusive of everyone,' he says. 'For so long masculinity was defined by things men weren't allowed to do – cry, have emotions, show weakness – but the conversation is evolving so that men start dealing with their vulnerabilities and emotions much more openly. I'll definitely be having chats with my sons about their feelings and their mental health, just like I do with my close friends.'

Adam already sees a new approach to masculinity and young men at the Adelaide Crows. 'The young players are away from home for the first time and working hard to just make it into the team at all. It puts a huge physical and emotional pressure on them, which the club is addressing.' Rather than letting young players sink or swim, Adam says, 'they're nurtured through the whole experience. Youngsters are teamed up with an older player for mentoring and the coaches are more hands-on with players' wellbeing and management. It's a big change from what it used to be.'

Adam's having a lot of fun in his fatherhood journey, as he wrote in a piece for the *Sydney Morning Herald* in 2018: 'Christopher and Anna lend me their eyes to see the world from their perspective. The result is that everything I took for granted, that I had become jaded by, or forgotten, or ignored, has meaning once again.'[2]

9

BEING WITH WOMEN

———

Our work as fathers in raising good men culminates when it comes to our sons being with women. Men still have a long way to go to be respectful and considerate boyfriends, ex-boyfriends, husbands, ex-husbands, colleagues, bosses, friends, acquaintances, classmates, even co-passengers on public transport. Fathers need to help their sons see all the different types of amazing, life-changing relationships they can have with women, and to help them also appreciate what a positive relationship looks like from the perspective of the women in their lives.

A major part of this chapter is exploring how men can be better romantic partners. This means with both men and women. Providing the love quotient and being an involved, caring father means helping your son be comfortable with his sexuality whether he is straight, gay, transgender, queer or intersex. Fatherhood, and masculinity, should encompass all love and romance equally. The legalisation of same-sex marriage in Australia is yet another catalyst for dads to help their sons be happy and confident in their unique sexuality. Yet it is also indisputable that with the surge of #MeToo around the world, men have some hard thinking to do about how they relate to women on all levels, and hence the majority of this chapter deals with this aspect of masculinity.

As with tech and the internet, fathers and sons stand on either side of a chasm. Because since the time when we as teenagers were taught about sex, love and romance, the expectations of men have changed enormously. For the better.

As a teenager in the 1990s, my introduction to thinking about women romantically was basic. At the urging of my mum, Dad was forced to sit down with me one night in my bedroom to give me the dreaded talk. Neither of us wanted this to occur. Dad didn't know where to start, and I was old enough not to need what he was about to offer. Nevertheless, he brought out a biology book with an anatomical picture of a woman. I don't remember much apart from him pointing at various parts of the woman's body, and my lungs tightening to the point of breathlessness. I'm pretty sure my brain has mostly erased the memory as a favour to me.

I also recall being in a science lab during Year 10, sitting in a circle with fifteen or twenty classmates, for another tedious period of 'pastoral care'. The teacher probably didn't want to be there either. He was in his sixties at the time, and dressed like he was impersonating Colonel Mustard from *Cluedo*. He was also a bit absentminded, to put it politely.

In this lesson, he all of a sudden began counselling us on how to talk to girls. The awkwardness in the room jumped up several notches. His advice was straightforward: go up to a girl you like, introduce yourself, shake her hand and ask her what her interests are, or tell her about yours. I'm pretty sure he used fishing as an example of a shared interest you could discuss with a girl. He then made us go around the circle and try introducing ourselves, so we weren't going in completely cold if we ever did talk to a real-life human girl.

One boy decided to stir the pot and get a laugh, and told us he thought a good introductory line was: 'Hi there, have you ever tripped over a tree? How about a root?' We all burst into laughter, thinking that was the funniest thing. Our teacher went red in the face, scolded the boy and told him to get out of the classroom.

And that, my friends, was everything I was taught about girls.

In Year 11 pastoral care, the fun continued. It was the beginning of the new school year and our teacher asked us to turn to the boy next to us and have a chat, so we could get to know each other better. Standard ice-breaker stuff.

I was sitting next to a guy who had been held back a year (and who, I remembered, had once punched me so hard in the guts in primary school that I had keeled over for several minutes). I thought we were having a friendly enough chat, and then he asked me about dating. Er, no, I said, I hadn't done any of that. He was astounded: no sex, no dating, not even kissing? Feeling very sheepish, I continued to be honest and said no.

When we regrouped as a class, this guy thought it would be hilarious to tell the whole class about what an inexperienced loser virgin I was. I remember feeling like a tiny, inch-wide cube at that point, and wandered around humiliated for the rest of the day.

At about the same time in my teens, all the original *Star Wars* movies were re-released to celebrate their twentieth anniversary. Now, this was more my thing! Glorious escapism to the galaxy far, far away, rather than being hounded for my lack of prowess with women. Like most fans, my favourite movie of the original trilogy is *The Empire Strikes Back*. I still watch it over and over. As a teen, I loved the scene when Han Solo and Princess Leia begin to fall in love. Han approaches her in the back of the Millennium Falcon, takes her hand and kisses her. One of the best cinematic hook-ups ever, right?

Those three examples were some of the long-lasting impressions I had as a teenage boy of interacting with the opposite sex. These were the lessons in my skull when I left high school. The advice from the dotty old teacher, as well-meaning as it might have been, was shallow, focusing on one small aspect of being with girls: introducing yourself. It came with no advice on how to get to know a girl, or the value of female friendships. My humiliation in pastoral care in Year 11 taught me that you're not a 'real man' unless you've got some notches on your belt. It reinforced how fragile your sense of masculinity could be, and how someone could take it away from you in an instant.

Meanwhile, through my love of pop culture, I was receiving the message that if you like a girl, you shouldn't stop until you get your way. Even if she doesn't seem interested in you, persist. Keep talking to her and trying to get her attention. It's not about what *she* wants, it's about what *you* want. The sub-text to this is yet another reaffirmation of how fragile our sense of masculinity can be, because if you don't ultimately get what you want, then you're a loser and a failure with women.

When I rewatch that scene with Han and Leia these days, I see a decidedly different interaction. I see a man coming up behind a woman, startling her, pushing into her personal space, grabbing her hand without permission, telling her to 'be a little nicer' and backing her into a corner where she can't easily get away. He even notices her trembling, but assumes that's just because she really likes him. Yikes, that wasn't cool. But that was how romance was often portrayed to curious teenagers in the 1980s and '90s, as it was for the men in my grandfather's generation during the 1940s and '50s.

It didn't change much in the 2000s. Leading male characters still forced themselves on the women they liked. One of the favourite movies in my home is *Ratatouille*, released in 2007. A harmless movie about a rat helping a boy, Linguini, cook fancy food, right? Apart from the scene when Linguini kisses Colette without her permission, even as she's holding a can of pepper spray!

Impressionable experiences such as these leave imprints on young men that can last a lifetime. It only gets worse, the more you grow up. Those school-level lessons get magnified in sports clubs, pubs, WhatsApp groups, online gaming and pop culture. Your impressionable mind hardens and your attitude to women can become reductive and hollow. Tropes that look so obsolete now, with the light of #MeToo exposing them, get viewed by young men as conventional wisdom, simply 'the way things are'. Men can't be friends with women because they only ever want to sleep with them . . . women like being pursued by men . . . women want arrogant guys with confidence who know what they want . . . a 'real man' is a player who gets around and can't be tied down . . . if you're inexperienced in the bedroom, you're less of a man than your mates.

Ditching bad romance lessons after #MeToo

#MeToo shone a bright, hot spotlight on these attitudes and the behaviours that go with them. It's fritzing out the male operating system by exposing something we couldn't or wouldn't recognise: there is a big power imbalance between men and women when it comes to romance, sex, love and, well, life and relationships generally.

Ground zero for #MeToo was the sexual assault and harassment lurking offstage in Hollywood studios, but the movement gained momentum because its messages apply in almost every setting. In Australia, 85 per cent of women report being sexually harassed at least once, the most prevalent forms being sexually suggestive comments or jokes.[1] For many men, women remain objects, and women fear what will happen to them if a man feels embarrassed because his advances are rejected, whether it's in the workplace, at a bar, on a dating app or on the street. Men either seem to know this and exploit it, or they are so self-interested that they are oblivious to women's fear. Our romantic interests in women are so driven by our desires that we don't think about what women want or whether they're feeling uncomfortable or harassed.

#MeToo has also exposed how poorly men can take rejection by a woman, and how even the most polite of knockbacks can send a man down a path of retribution. He didn't get her attention. He didn't get a response to his DM. He didn't get her number. He didn't get a date. He didn't get a dance. He didn't get a kiss. He didn't get her home. He didn't win her back after a fight or break-up. Women live with the fear of what might happen next. Any interaction with a man that goes badly might mean damage to a women's career or reputation, verbal or physical abuse, online bullying or even the distribution of revenge porn. Men still hold most of the cards, and can play them against women as they wish. The power element in this harassment and abuse is undeniable.

It is worth noting that men can be the victims as well as the perpetrators. Kevin Spacey's career came to a grinding halt when multiple men accused him of unwanted sexual advances, including men who were at the time underage.[2] In 2017, American actor and former NFL player Terry Crews, a man who is built like a mountain and looks like one of the strongest, toughest men on the planet, confessed that he had been sexually assaulted by a Hollywood executive but did not speak out for fear of retaliation by the perpetrator.[3] In Australia, 57 per cent of men report being sexually harassed at least once (myself included) and about one in twenty will experience sexual assault in their lifetime.[4]

When it comes to heterosexual incidents, as a society we still tend to believe the man's side of the story more than the woman's. One in eight women in Australia is incorrectly identified as the aggressor in a domestic violence situation.[5] Rejection means a man's masculinity—that delicate Fabergé egg—has been shattered because he didn't get what he wanted. It can be verbal abuse, a nasty stream of text messages or photos threatening retaliation, or physical violence.

Canadian author Margaret Atwood, author of *The Handmaid's Tale*, once commented that women most fear being killed by a man, and men most fear being laughed at by a woman.[6] Her observation is not hyperbole. Every three hours a woman is hospitalised in Australia as a result of violence by a partner, carer or family member.[7] One in three young Australian men believes that a woman who says she was raped had consensual sex and regretted it later; one in five thinks domestic violence is a normal reaction to stress; almost one in four think women find it flattering to be pursued.[8]

For the first time in living memory, the conversation about what is acceptable and consensual behaviour between men and women is being led by women. It's not that there is a new standard coming into force that men must learn. It's that women have decided to call out crap behaviour by men more vocally and vehemently. They're not going to let male whims and insecurities dominate their lives and make them live in fear. For men, it's the mother of all wake-up calls.

Luke is a member of the first generation to be born and raised in the #MeToo era. The ground is still shaking from this movement, just as he is trying to take his first steps. As we're trying to eliminate 'mansplaining', he's taking his first words and trying to communicate. What will the world look like when he is a young man? How can I raise my boy to know how to behave and what is expected of him, if we are in a prolonged period of changing male behaviour in order to set a higher standard?

Learning by leaning in to #MeToo

A lot of men seem scared about what #MeToo is throwing our way. The chorus reply from women everywhere is piercingly clear: 'Good! You should be!' Even Superman admitted to second-guessing himself. In 2018, actor Henry Cavill gave an interview to *GQ* in which he expressed his support for #MeToo. 'Stuff has to change, absolutely,' he said, but he went on to say that he thinks '[t]here's something wonderful about a man chasing a woman', and that '[i]t's important to also retain the good things, which were a quality of the past, and get rid of the bad things'. Cavill discussed how hard he felt it was now to woo a woman because of changing standards:[9]

It's very difficult to do that if there are certain rules in place. Because then it's like: 'Well, I don't want to go up and talk to her, because I'm going to be called a rapist or something.' So you're like, 'Forget it, I'm going to call an ex-girlfriend instead, and then just go back to a relationship, which never really worked.' But it's way safer than casting myself into the fires of hell, because I'm someone in the public eye, and if I go and flirt with someone, then who knows what's going to happen?

People online were divided (just for a change) about what Cavill said. Some men and women sympathised with what they saw as a clumsy choice of words. Some men expressed their own fear that any interaction with a woman risks him being labelled a perpetrator of sexual harassment or abuse.[10] Many others said Cavill showed what was wrong with the male response to #MeToo: that it reverted to men being worried about themselves instead of thinking about what women experience.

In a statement, Superman apologised for any 'confusion and misunderstanding' his comments caused, and reiterated that he holds women 'in the highest regard'. Cavill's initial words, the online response and the need to issue a clarification speak volumes of where men's heads are at with #MeToo. While men might be acknowledging that they are expected to behave differently, they remain confused as to what that means, and jump to a place of myopic self-interest, even resentment, worried that even their mildest-mannered interaction with a woman may see them accused of something horrible.

I'll admit that my first reactions went to a similar place. It took a few long, hard conversations with Julia to understand the real point and messages from #MeToo. It took me actively reassessing my own attitudes, assumptions, biases and behaviours. It took me talking less and listening more to other people's perspectives. It took me admitting I was clueless and needed help.

Men can lean in to #MeToo with empathy, open minds and open hearts. We can learn from it and determine for ourselves what needs to change in our lives. If our conversations about #MeToo revolve around, 'Well, how do you pick up women now?' then we're missing the point entirely. It's our chance to reflect on how men interact with women on all levels in daily life, not just romantically or physically. It's healthy and positive for men to feel vulnerable because of #MeToo, if it leads to greater self-examination and a conscious effort to better understand how women feel and what they expect from us.

As fathers, we should take the opportunity to examine our own past. Firstly, we'll have to shed the baggage of what we were taught, the obsolete lessons from our teenage and young adult years. We will then need to talk through with our boys what it means for a good man to be with a woman. This will include being honest with our sons about our own journey to reassessing our attitudes and standards, and to educating ourselves for a new era. We can be open with them that we are reconsidering what we thought was acceptable, that we don't have all the answers, and that we may feel inadequate and uncomfortable about this subject, but that we're working on it and, importantly, learning from our past mistakes. Hand in hand with our boys, we can learn together.

As I said at the outset of this chapter, when I say 'being with a woman', I mean everything. We need to teach our sons a healthy and respectful view of sex, which includes making sure our boys are not so wired on porn that they develop a warped view of what the real thing involves. But teaching our sons about sex means helping them understand how to ask someone out, how to have a relationship, how to handle intimacy, as well as how to deal with rejection and heartache without flying off the handle and hurting others. Our boys should conduct all their relationships with respect and resilience, and we as dads can show them how to do that maturely, reflecting on our own experiences, good and bad. But it also means teaching our sons about more than just sex and love. This is the time to show them that there is depth and enjoyment in seeking holistic relationships with women, and especially in having female friendships that are based on mutual interest, respect and admiration.

Every father can choose for himself whether to embrace the lessons from #MeToo or to bypass them. I'm not here to lecture others on a challenge I'm still getting my head around. However, even as the ramifications from #MeToo continue to unfold, even at Luke's young age I already have a set of things I want to teach him. My hope is that if I get it right, then by the time he's a teenager on the cusp of manhood, Luke will have a much more sophisticated and meaningful approach to being with women than I did when I left school, one that, if he is straight, goes way beyond sex, love and romance. More than that, he'll be more confident and comfortable in his own skin, not feeling any pressure to prove his masculinity to anyone, including himself. If he identifies as gay, bisexual, queer, transgender or intersex, my love and desire to support him will be undiminished and the lessons on having women in his life will still be useful to him as he makes meaningful connections with others.

Regardless of what Luke's future holds, I want him to be able to learn from my previous actions and behaviour. #MeToo has led me to look at my own past in a bid to understand where I fucked up, where my attitudes were wrong, and where I needed to change. How can I raise my son to be a good man if I won't also look at myself as well?

Porn is not paradise

The first thing I probably need to talk to Luke about is porn. My experiences as a teenager were stone-age compared to today's pornography. I once viewed some still images on a friend's computer after school that were so pixellated I couldn't really work out what the people were doing, and occasionally I would sneak a peek at a magazine when walking past a newsagent. These days, thanks once again to the internet, it's never been easier for boys to access free porn on almost any device.

The most popular porn website at the time I'm writing this book is PornHub, which is the eighth-most popular website in the world, attracting over 3 billion visits *per month*.[11] That represents almost one visit for every second person on the planet, and that's just one website. Young Aussie men are checking out PornHub and similar sites at a high rate. In a 2017 study by a medical institute of young Aussies aged fifteen to 29, 100 per cent of young men had viewed porn, with over two-thirds starting at the age of thirteen or younger.[12] Some 84 per cent of the young men surveyed watched porn on a weekly basis, compared to 19 per cent of young women.[13]

Having that chat has got to happen early. AIFS estimates that 44 per cent of Aussie children aged between nine and sixteen are regularly exposed to sexual images, with kids aged nine to twelve much more likely to be distressed by what they see.[14] So as a dad, I can't wait until my boy hits puberty before awkwardly chatting to him about porn, because he will very likely already have seen some. I've got to get in early, while he is still at primary school. That may seem really young, but if I don't, the internet will beat me to it and really freak him out.

I want Luke to know that if he has viewed something explicit, even inadvertently, he can come and talk to me about what he's seen—and he won't be in trouble. He might feel embarrassed by what he's seen, or he might feel really disturbed. I want him to know that my priority will be making sure he's okay, and that I'm happy to talk through whatever issues he may have in processing what he saw. Just as with tech generally, I don't want to make him feel he must hide his activities from me, as then I definitely can't help. I want to be a source of comfort and advice, not a threat hanging over his head every time he goes online.

Next, I'll talk to him about how most porn gives a totally unrealistic impression of what sex is like, and very often a twisted view of how men should treat women. We'll have internet filters in our home, and we'll monitor his device use as best we can, but I'm not an idiot—I know my boy is going to watch porn, as a teenager and as a young man. I'm not going to threaten him never to watch porn, as I think that'd be counter-productive and hypocritical. But I want him to develop a healthy attitude about sex, and a resilience to what he'll see on PornHub and other sites.

Firstly, he needs to understand that porn stars are like sex Olympians—they're super-fit and athletic and the stuff they do for camera is beyond the abilities of most ordinary people. He'll need to understand that porn is fantasy—he can't expect to do the same things in bed, or expect his partner to. He also shouldn't feel bad about his body or abilities just because he's watched a couple of buff hotties do gravity-defying stunts for ten minutes online—and nor should he shame his partner on similar grounds.

We'll also have to discuss how a lot of heterosexual porn portrays women being subjugated or aggressively used or abused by men for their own desires, and that it perpetuates incredibly negative stereotypes that women are objects to be enjoyed by men. He needs to understand, too, that there are well-documented allegations of unethical work practices in the porn industry, and that many producers of porn are linked to illegal exploitation and trafficking. It's not all as hot and amazing as it looks. There is next to zero focus on women having a good time and getting off in a way that they find enjoyable. Australian researchers of gay porn have also identified similarly troubling issues with the way sex is presented on particular sites, including unprotected sex, exploitative scenarios and rape simulation, not to mention studies showing greater body-related stress for gay and bisexual men.[15] Regardless of what type of porn my son may be viewing, it isn't some instruction manual for his own sex life—it's a distorted image that should be viewed with extreme scepticism.

I want Luke to know that good men don't treat women or men badly in the bedroom. If he wants to be a good man in bed as well as out of it, he should spend as much time finding out what his partner likes and providing that, as well as taking care of himself, and he should not try to play out some porn fantasy unless both he and his partner are super into it. (It's worth noting that there's an emerging movement in the porn industry to show normal people making love and filming it consensually, on sites like Make Love Not Porn, as well as websites that focus on creative storytelling and women's pleasure, such as Joybear, Bright Desire and Four Chambers.)[16]

I'll advise him to be wary of the different types of porn he can find online. As a teenager or a young bloke in his twenties, he may think he's hit the jackpot with the volumes of niche porn out on the web, but some of it is extremely fucked up, and some of it illegal. I want him to understand that he should exercise caution in what he chooses to watch, otherwise he risks ending up with some perverted tastes that few people are going to be interested in exploring with him.

Finally, I really want my boy to understand that having sex with people you think are amazing is great, and way better than anything the porn world, ethical or not, can toss up. First sexual encounters are always awkward and bumbling, but I want his to be sweet, affectionate and satisfying as well. If he has too much porn on the brain, he may already be jaded about regular sex before he's lost his virginity. That would be a real tragedy, as those first few times should be exhilarating as a whole new world opens up, not disillusioning because it didn't match up to the sex Olympians online. As best I can, and without causing too much embarrassment for him, I want to make sure he's got his priorities sorted.

Recently there has been a growing public discussion about whether the frequency with which young men watch porn is having an impact on their ability to have real-life sex. Some parenting experts are telling mums and dads to be wary of porn addiction, because it may mean your son won't be able to get it up with his girlfriend or boyfriend. There is no definitive research on whether there's a link for young men between watching lots of porn and suffering erectile dysfunction. One European study concluded that, 'contrary to raising public concerns, pornography does not seem to be a significant risk factor for younger men's desire, erectile, or orgasmic difficulties.'[17] An American study showed that men who watched porn had 'greater sexual responsiveness, not erectile dysfunction'.[18] The public discussion goes on, but treat the dire warnings with a note of caution. It seems like boys are still pretty horny with porn—go figure.

Female friends are awesome

I want to encourage my boy to have meaningful, platonic female friendships all through his life. Some of my closest relationships as an adult are with women I've known for ages, others I've met through various jobs I've had and we're still close, others still started as the partners of friends but over time become close friends in their own right. My female friendships have enriched my life incredibly and made me a better person, and I want that for Luke as well.

Even in my nerdy teenage years, which were largely devoid of romantic experiences, I had friends who were girls, despite being at an all-male high school. I want my boy to know that women can be his friends, confidantes, consiglieres, teammates, colleagues, drinking buddies, flatmates, whatever. It might seem a basic place to start, but I genuinely feel that, as a father, I should make sure Luke appreciates that having close female friends is part of being a well-rounded man.

From the time he's a toddler, I want him to know that it's great to have girls and boys as your closest friends. I want him to be comfortable enjoying the company of girls and young women, without always thinking there's a suggestion that having a female friend somehow makes him less of a boy (back off, 'real man'), or feeling any social pressure to convert such a friendship into something romantic or physical. I want him to know he can invite girls over for playdates when he is a little guy, or go down to the oval for a kick with them, and then, when he's a little older, I want him to know he can invite girls over for study, gaming or movie sessions. I think having female friendships will help Luke learn empathy and respect for others. In 2016, Australian academics studied 2000 Year 10 students across sixteen schools to understand how they developed friendships. The study revealed that boys who were more empathetic had more close female friends than boys who were low on empathy.[19]

As my son becomes a teenager, I don't want him to feel any pressure to start viewing the girls in his life exclusively as potential romantic partners. In our community, we still tend to frame teenage boys' interactions with girls in romantic terms, and the advice of adults is similarly tailored (like the stuff I was taught). The amazing friendships young boys have with girls can fall away so easily once their hormones start raging and the social pressure to be a Lothario builds. It would be a shame, and a huge missed opportunity, if Luke was straight and went out into the world as a young man after school with a bunch of male friends, and only tried to meet women when he was interested in dating them.

Romancing someone without being a dick

Of course, my son will spend a big part of his teenage years contemplating dating and sex—hopefully the real-world stuff, not the mirages put forward by the porn or gaming industries. When he turns thirteen years old, I'll be turning 50, so my advice will be about as contemporary as my pop culture references. I'll need to be honest with myself, as there will be so many things in the daily interactions between teenage boys and girls that I will simply not understand, and I shouldn't pretend otherwise.

Cards on the table: I lost my virginity when I was 21, which Julia still finds kind of hilarious. When I was a single bloke in my mid-twenties, online dating was just becoming a normal way to meet people, and not the exclusive domain of the socially inept. I never used a dating app because they didn't exist. When I met

Julia in 2010, Tinder was still two years away. At that point I had barely started using WhatsApp.

Even though I might seem like an annoying, old relic when Luke hits his adolescence years and starts getting romantically keen on people, I hope I'll still be able to give him some advice, and the lessons I learnt from when I was young.

For starters, I want Luke to know he can be sweet and considerate when asking someone out, and that he doesn't need to put on some display of bravado to show he's a tough guy who doesn't feel anything. Being the nice guy doesn't mean he'll get walked all over, just that he treats people with respect and kindness. He should feel comfortable and confident in himself and what he has to offer as a person.

Also, he shouldn't pester his romantic interest, and shouldn't make them feel pressured to say yes. Remember, we're learning from Han Solo's mistakes here—he definitely shouldn't be creeping on them, making them feel uneasy or intimidated. He has to ask someone out and give them space to say no.

Which brings me to the second big piece of advice I'll have for my boy: if he is knocked back and feels dejected, embarrassed or heartbroken, he shouldn't act like a dick towards the person. They shouldn't feel worried about the consequences of not being interested in my son. They shouldn't fear what he'll say about them at school, or in a chat group, or on a blog, or that he'll spread rumours behind their back. They shouldn't worry that they'll get sent some awful meme, gif or image on their phone, or explicit material from him or his mates. The person should be able to say, 'No thanks,' and get on with their life, unfazed by the encounter.

Of course, it's okay for a boy to want to debrief with his friends and seek solace, and he'll know he can always come and cry on my shoulder and talk to me. I'll always be happy to listen, cuddle him and let my love radiate onto him, advising him that the person he asked out doesn't know what they're missing.

If things go the other way, and the person says yes—amazing! I'll be so happy for him. Probably the last thing my boy will want at the start of a budding romance is advice from his old man. Yet I hope he'd make sure the relationship goes at a pace that he and his partner are both comfortable with. He'll likely be using tech to show his feelings for his partner—and in a way that will likely baffle me. Sexting is a widespread activity among teens, but it tends to be done inside relationships as a way of flirting and showing affection.[20] Youngsters today seem to have more relaxed standards about what is considered explicit than us old fogeys. All I can say is that if he wants to share intimate material with a partner, he should make sure they consent to what they're doing, and they both keep everything private. And if the relationship ends, that stuff needs to get deleted pronto from all his devices, not distributed as reprisal. A 2018 study found that one in five Aussies have been the victim of revenge porn, which can cause long-lasting mental health problems like anxiety, fear and depression.[21] Distributing such material is now against the law in Australia: it's classified as a form of harassment, cyberbullying and a sexual crime.[22]

If my son is in the throes of a passionate relationship and starting to have sex, he'll need to remember that consent must be clear to both partners at all times. One of the big discussions to come out of #MeToo is what the definition of consent should be, and whether it's possible to make it more explicit. Every jurisdiction has its own interpretation. New South Wales is currently reviewing its consent laws, so it could be an entirely different standard by the time my boy is a teenager. Regardless,

I want him to make sure consent is verbal and enthusiastic, and he's sure his partner is into it, is having a good time and is getting as much satisfaction and pleasure as he is.

If the relationship ends—well or badly, on his terms or someone else's—I'll be there to help my son handle it with resilience and decency. It's a scientific fact that break-ups suck, and being dumped is the worst. I've been on both sides of a break-up and can certainly advise Luke on how to handle them better than I did.

The first time I wanted to break up with someone I was in my early twenties, and I didn't know what to do or how to handle it. I avoided the subject for a long time until they eventually asked me whether I wanted to end the relationship. The time I was dumped after a four-year relationship ripped a hole in my heart that took two years to repair. The day it happened I slumped in a ball on the carpet and cried most of the afternoon. I was shocked, sad, anxious and confused for a long time. I took to socialising after work every night and partying all weekend in an effort not to be alone, so I wouldn't have to deal with my emotions. I drank too much. I felt competitive in the break-up, and wanted to show my ex how amazingly I was doing—although no one other than me was interested, of course.

I thought I had been a pretty good boyfriend (although not without my moments), and hadn't deserved to be dumped. It was a typical, self-centred male response to heartache. I was fixated on myself and never really considered that my ex didn't owe me an explanation. It was wrong of me to expect more than 'I don't want to be with you anymore'.

My boy will be able to learn a lot from my cowardice in ending a relationship, and from the mistakes I made while trying to repair my broken heart, if he is willing to listen to his old man and his stories from yesteryear.

Caution being casual

If my boy decides he's going to be single for a while, pursue casual flings and try his hand at being a player with lots of Netflix and chill, I'm sure I'll get in his ear once or twice and offer some advice. As someone who tried the same thing in his twenties, I'll tell him to proceed with caution. Flirting, dancing with and dating lots of women may make you feel like a big man momentarily, but it can end up diminishing you as well. You risk becoming solely focused on your own gratification and self-interest, and other people can feel hurt or used by your actions.

I remember being single, going out to flirt and meet women, and having flings as well as one-night stands. I was an active participant in a toxic hook-up culture that sucks in so many young men and women. I remember thinking for a time how far I'd come from my lovelorn days at high school, where I was the brunt of classmates' jokes. I now had notches on my belt. But eventually it became clear to me that behaving in this way was almost always solely about *my* needs and desires, and proving to myself that I was a 'real man'. It left me feeling hollow, unfulfilled and more than a bit sleazy. I don't want Luke to feel that way.

Casual relationships can be lots of fun, and you can have some thrilling times that both people enjoy. But it requires both parties knowing clearly what it is they're doing; it's dishonest if one person believes it's the start of a deeper emotional relationship when it's not.

I also want him to know that dating isn't black and white, and people's feelings can change over time. I met Julia when we stayed in the same dorm for graduate students at the London School of Economics and Political Science. We were both single and avoiding serious relationships. We laughed at our fellow international students who maintained long-distance relationships with partners back home, wondering why on earth they wouldn't untether themselves to enjoy being single in one of the world's great cities. We started a casual fling one night, determined not to fall for one another for many weeks, but it happened anyway. Luke needs to know that it's not anyone's fault if one person starts falling hard, but it's equally important to talk things over with them, make sure they're happy with what's going on, and respect their wishes if they want to step things up or break it off altogether.

I don't want my boy to think I'm an old nag trying to ruin his good time; if he does, he's not likely to listen to me. I had many amazing experiences when I was single, romantic and otherwise. Being single in your twenties with a little bit of worldliness and your own money to spend is awesome, and there are lots of ways to have fun and make lifelong memories that don't end in someone feeling bad about themselves. I hope he will learn from the mistakes I made, and be the better for it.

Good guy even without the good time

My last piece of advice for Luke will be to encourage him to just be a good man with the women in his life, and to be willing to call out the bullshit of others. Whether it's as romantic partners, friends or colleagues, I want him to show respect, fairness, kindness and empathy in all situations with the women in his life.

That may sound warm and fuzzy, but it can actually be bloody tough. Calling out a mate for a sexist joke at the pub is hard, as is calling out a colleague for talking over the top of a female co-worker or stealing her idea in a meeting. It can put people's noses out of joint and see you ostracised. But I want Luke to be better than me. I've told sexist jokes to get a laugh out of my mates. I've turned a blind eye when a mate said something really offensive. I've looked at my shoes, shuffled awkwardly and laughed nervously when a boss or client has said something sexist or inappropriate. Too many times I went with the crowd and was a wimp. I want Luke to be brave, even if it means he must draw on the love quotient to find the strength to take on adversity. He'll emerge better for it.

I've not got all the answers. I'm far from perfect. I just hope that my experiences as a teenager, young man and father give my boy the knowledge that I lacked on my journey. I also want the weakness of character I showed as a younger man to inform him as he builds his own core strengths and values.

At that point, when he's grown up and has become a good man, I'll be the one asking him for advice.

BONDING AND LISTENING

DARREN CHESTER MP, LAKES ENTRANCE

For over a decade, Darren Chester has been a member of the federal parliament, and he's been a minister since 2013. While Tim Hammond left politics altogether to raise his young family, Darren, who commutes from coastal Victoria to the nation's capital, has seen his four children grow up a lot in that time. His young boys are now on the cusp of manhood.

Before entering politics, Darren worked from home for a few years, a time when he was able to include his kids in his life more easily. One of the biggest adjustments to his new job was working out how to be back home with the family. 'At first I was always catching up on news and checking my emails, so I was home but not present,' he recalls. 'I'm getting better at putting my devices away and just being there with everyone. But just because I am home doesn't mean that my kids want to talk to me. They're all busy living their own lives on their own schedules, so another adjustment was learning to fit back in with them. You can't force yourself on them.'

Darren puts a big emphasis on forging close relationships with his kids through mutual interests. 'As a family we did a lot of activities together, like being members of the surf life saving club,' he says. 'We had lots of time outdoors together just interacting with each other rather than being on our phones. It meant we created a lot of great memories and shared history with each other which helped keep us close.' Darren is conscious about pulling his own weight at home too, making sure he does the cooking most of the week when he's home from Canberra, and getting his boys to help him as well.

Darren works hard to find one-on-one time for his kids whenever he can. 'If I am coming through Melbourne for work I'll let my daughter know, who is at uni down there, and we catch up for dinner,' he says. 'My son and I recently organised a trip away together to South-East Asia, which was a terrific experience for both of us. I also went on a long road trip to South Australia with my other son, where we just had time with each other as we stayed at country pubs along the way.'

Darren makes a point of respecting his kids as individuals, and listens carefully to their opinions and perspectives on the world. 'Their viewpoints can be challenging for me, but they help educate me about what is important to younger people,' he observes. 'For example, they chatted to me here and there about same-sex marriage, and I ended up taking a more supportive position because of my discussions with them.'

Darren says he is 'deeply troubled' by the challenges boys face in the current era, especially how easily they can access porn and the effect it can have on them. 'Porn is not normal and not what women want,' he notes, 'but they're bombarded with these negative images. We've got to get boys to see that if they're going to treat women with respect. It's not enough to just raise strong women who won't put up with bad behaviour – we have to help our boys as well.' He says he tries to model what an equal relationship looks like and how a good man acts. 'I try to show my boys how to treat a partner with respect by how I interact with my wife. I also get the boys to do domestics around the home so they know that's expected of them as well, not just their sisters.'

Given his national and local prominence, Darren does not want to pressure his boys to follow in his footsteps or feel they have to match his career success. 'With my seventeen-year-old son, we'll soon start having a conversation about what he wants to do next,' he says. 'It's not about being judged by others, only what he is happy with as an individual. I want to help him find his own pathway when he's ready, and to take any pressure he may be feeling off him.'

The only advice Darren would impart is this: 'The time goes by very quickly. Trust yourself as parents, and be kind to yourselves along the way.' With a bunch of kids making the transition to adulthood, he's pleased that those who have already flown the coop still want to spend time with their parents. 'Both our girls are at uni, but found time to come down for a family holiday when they didn't have to and could have just hung out with their friends,' he recalls fondly.

That sounds like pretty successful parenting to me.

10

A FINAL RIDE IN THE DELOREAN

———

In August 2019, I started my second stint of paid paternity leave, so I could care for Luke while he was still a sweet little baby. In my second week with him, I took him to a concert at the Opera House that was specifically designed for bubs up to eighteen months old. An Indigenous dance troupe from South Australia designed the show to allow babies to interact with the performers as they sang and danced. In the Jørn Utzon Room, all the parents sat with their babies on a large, colourful mat.

From the moment the singing began, the babies were transfixed by the sounds of the instruments and the movement of the dancers. I've never seen a room of kids so young being so engaged—it was marvellous. My little boy was mesmerised by the performer with the clapping sticks, and crawled closer to her for a better look. She let him hold the sticks and tap them for himself—his first go at the music of our First Nations.

The show was just over half an hour long, but it was one of those special events that I'll remember for the rest of my life, and one of my earliest bonding experiences with my son. It was also one of those magical Sydney days when the ocean sparkled under a big blue sky, and the waves lapped against the stone walls of the Opera House and the nearby Botanical Gardens.

Of the 35 parents sharing this special experience with their kids, I was the only dad. I don't feel smug or superior about that, I just feel sad. Sad that all the fathers of all the other kids in the room missed a unique experience with their kids. About 500 metres from the concert, on the other side of the Circular Quay train station, tens of thousands of fathers sat in office towers, busily working away, sending emails, writing project proposals, attending meetings, shuffling papers and brainstorming on videoconferences. Doing tasks they'd done a thousand times over, and missing out on an event happening just down the road that might come along only once or twice in a lifetime. So it goes, every day, for the fathers around the country who are earning a living while their young sons explore the world.

Tragic epiphanies

Early in this book I mentioned that if I got in the Doc's DeLorean and headed back a decade, to around 2009, Past Me would be more than a little terrified by how my life had unfolded. But what if Future Me, from 2029 or 2039, got into the DeLorean and visited me today? I know I wouldn't flee the scene. Instead I'd listen carefully to each word he said. If he came with sadness, telling me that somewhere on the journey I lost my way, lamenting that my kids were disappointed by their father's priorities, I would be torn up with anguish, but relieved that he'd warned me. What I hope he'd tell me is that both of them are well-adjusted young adults who still love spending time with their parents.

Over twenty years ago, a working dad called Daniel Petre wrote a book called *Father Time*.[1] Petre had climbed further up the corporate ladder than most breadwinners will ever do: at one stage he ran Microsoft in Australia, and for a time he worked at the company's Seattle headquarters. His book urged dads to create and then protect time with their families before life completely passed them by. It's filled with examples of fathers who had slogged their guts out for decades, building a big, successful career, staying late at the office and attending to every whim of every client. Then, in their fifties or sixties, these men were faced with major health scares, or tragedies for themselves or a loved one, and had an epiphany. They suddenly discovered that they were mortal, that life was fragile and time scarce. These men who had revelled in being the breadwinner suddenly rejected the long hours and the unreasonable sacrifices, realised that their family was the one thing that ultimately mattered to them, and committed themselves to renewing their frayed bonds with their partners and children. However, it was too late for a lot of them. Their kids, now teenagers and adults, had endured too much absence from dad, and wanted little to do with the stranger who was their father. And he, filled with excitement about spending more time with his family, was heartbroken, burning with regret for the lost years and even more aware of his own vulnerabilities.

Even the most meaningful, purposeful career cannot fill the part of the soul where fatherhood belongs. Petre reminds his male readers that at the end of the day a job is just a job, while family is so much more. His book may have been written in the 1990s but its advice on how to pre-empt late-in-life epiphanies resonates even more strongly in today's overworked society, where our mischievous devices mean the office is accessible at all hours. I have close friends and colleagues who have plunged headlong down the path Petre and his cadre of older fathers are begging younger men to avoid. I often wonder whether they will heed the advice of those who came before them, or whether only an epiphany of their own will make them change.

Across our community, we're strangely comfortable with the idea that older dads will regret the time lost—as if it is unavoidable. In 2019 I took part in a talkback segment for *Life Matters* on ABC Radio, talking about what it's like for fathers to actively care for their kids. The first caller was Bob from the Blue Mountains, in New South Wales. Bob was a sobering reminder of what we're up against in unlocking the future of fatherhood. He was convinced that dads taking parental leave was an 'indulgence', that it was 'going against the DNA of any bloke' for men to care for kids, and that men were there 'to pull the plough, not sit in the buggy'. But he also said the way of men is to discover that their kids are fascinating people only after they've worked their tails off their whole lives.

For all their toil and sacrifice, our fathers deserve more than a retirement filled with such discoveries. They shouldn't have to look back on their lives with sadness because they can't recall whether they were actually on that family holiday, or at that recital or match, or at that parent/teacher night, or whether they saw their son's first steps or heard his first words. They don't deserve to have a family life that is so fleeting. And their sons don't deserve it either.

Legacy

My son is only one year old, and already I can tell he's a sweet boy. He loves sharing his accomplishments with his family. When he bangs two blocks together, finds a new object that excites him, sees a bird or a dog, or meets another baby to play with, he turns to us and smiles, chitter-chattering as if to say, 'Oh my god! Are you seeing what I'm seeing? Isn't this incredible!' He adores his big sister, who is one of the best people at getting him to calm down when he's upset. When I pick him up for a cuddle, he grabs my chest tightly and nestles into my neck. When he goes exploring, he looks around to check that I'm still there and that everything is okay. Every day I'm reminded how precious his sweet nature is, and how vulnerable.

Every generation wants to leave their kids better off than they were. I want to leave Luke with a better version of masculinity than the one I inherited. I want to take this misshapen, weathered rump we currently call modern manhood and turn it into something grander for him. I want to take those words associated with the 'real man' and reclaim them for all men in my son's era.

When we say men are strong, it can be that they are strong in their care for people, strong in their respect for others, strong in their values and integrity. When we say men should be in control, it can be that they are in control of their own identity, which they freely choose for themselves, in control of their lives, and in control of their insecurities and vulnerabilities. When we say men should be stoic, it can be that men demonstrate grace under pressure in balancing their career ambitions with their devotion to their family. When we say men are intelligent, it can include emotional intelligence and a softness that puts others around them at ease. I want to make it that all men are real men, and that part of masculinity's inherent virtue is being accepting and inclusive, and finding solidarity in diversity.

For the sake of my sweet son, when he's older I don't want him holding manhood in his hands like it's a delicate Fabergé egg that will break or damage easily. I don't want him thinking he's clinging to his manhood by a thread at all times. I want him to be wrapped in masculinity like an armour, forged from a love that sends him into the world powered by unending self-belief and purpose, ready for and resilient to the blowback he will inevitably face throughout his life. I want him to be able to share his masculinity with other men who may feel lost or trapped, and who want help to be the men they really want to be.

I owe it to Luke to give him this better masculinity, and I owe it to myself to pass on something valuable, born of the mistakes and experiences of my past. I will do my best to live up to the opportunity that being his dad has given me.

A new roar

One of my favourite fatherhood moments of all time is the death of Darth Vader in *Return of the Jedi*. I know that seems ridiculous, but hear me out. With the second Death Star being destroyed, the Emperor dead, Stormtroopers panicking in the chaos, Luke strains to drag his dying father to his ship to escape. Vader stops him, telling him that his death is inevitable, and that all he wants before he goes is to take his mask off and 'look on you with my own eyes'. And so, moments before he passes away, the two men have their first and only genuine interaction as father and son. Vader asks Luke to leave him behind, and Luke replies, 'I'll not leave you here—I've got to save you.' Vader, with death closing in, says, 'You already have, Luke.' It may sound trite, but I've watched that scene countless times because it really speaks to me. Because fatherhood saved me.

At a dinner at a fancy seafood restaurant in Pyrmont with my parents in 2006, with Sydney Harbour glittering behind us, I remember boasting that I would never get married or have children. I recall arguing that there were too many exciting things to do in life, too many places to travel to and too many adventures to be had. I would allow nothing and no one to tie me down.

Against my expectations, fatherhood brought my better qualities to the fore, and expanded my heart more than I thought possible. I hear my children's voices wherever I go, and daydream about the things we've done together and will do in the future. Their spirits nourish my soul. Because of them, I've been forced to recast my own manhood and what I value. I'm forever grateful that they did something so generous for me.

Through my children, I can faintly glimpse the future. One winter's Sunday in 2019, my family and I were taking a stroll through our neighbourhood, heading towards a creek that meanders behind a nearby park. As we were walking down one hilly street, Aila kept finding small rocky outcrops sticking out of the pavement to jump off. She came across a particularly large one with a big drop. She walked to the edge of the outcrop, dressed in her bumblebee parker and fluffy beanie, and paused. She took a deep breath, exhaled and said to herself, 'Strong and brave,' and then jumped. It's already one of my fondest moments with her.

I'm thrilled to grow up in an era, and in a country, that tells girls they can truly be anything. I said at the start of this book that I hear a stampede of women roaring, *The future is female* as they prepare the way for millions more girls. I realised on that Sunday afternoon, as I watched Aila remind herself that she is strong and brave before taking the biggest leap of her young life, that she is already part of that stampede. With each step she takes, with each jump she makes, she creates that future for herself and other women. Long may she do so.

Now I think I hear a new roar building, a stampede beginning to gather strength. A collection of men determinedly pushing prams, purposefully stepping forward with baby carriers, tenderly holding the hands of their boys, and raising them up high on their shoulders to feel the warmth of the sun. Perhaps I even hear it in the pitter-patter of Luke's hands as he crawls over to smile lovingly at me. The roar gradually becomes louder, and I can make out their cry: *There's more to being a man.*

ACKNOWLEDGEMENTS

My first acknowledgement is to Julia. We've been together for nine years and married for five years, and more than ever I believe we're equal partners in all we do. It was a miraculous chance that we met in London in 2010, and I remain eternally grateful to the universe that we did. The ideas and values in this book belong as much to Julia as they do to me. She also came up with the idea for the front cover, an example of her creative flair. She helped create the time and space for me to write and greatly assisted me in completing the book. More times than I can remember, I came to Julia—often stressed and needy—to bounce ideas, test lines and seek emotional support when I doubted myself. Frequently throughout the writing of this book, Julia loaned me her bullish optimism and confidence when my anxieties and fears had a hold of me. I'm indebted to Julia for her enormous help and her advice.

I'd like to acknowledge my very close friend Brendon McKeon. I'm an only child, but Brendon is the closest thing I have to a brother. He has been an incredibly supportive friend throughout this journey, always genuinely interested to know how the book was progressing and forever supporting me in what I was doing. Like with Julia, Brendon would often help me find my own confidence when things were particularly hard. He was also a sympathetic ear when I wanted to share my frustrations or my excitement. Brendon is also the type of man the world sorely needs in spades—intelligent, loving, compassionate, empathetic, respectful and funny. My son will be lucky to know Uncle Brendon as he grows up.

I'd also like to acknowledge my parents who have always been encouraging and positive about my writing, well before there was any book on the horizon. My mum was an English teacher for most of her career, and her passion for the English language had a big influence on my writing. My mum and dad have also been incredibly supportive of Julia, myself and our family as we muddle through the challenging times of raising two small children and maintaining our careers. We enjoy a lovely family life in large part because of their enormous generosity.

I'll also take this chance to thank the terrific team at Allen & Unwin, my publisher Kelly Fagan, who has been instrumental on this journey, along with Tom Bailey-Smith, Senior Editor, and Julian Welch, my copyeditor. As a first-time author their expertise and advice was crucial. Kelly was at all times understanding as I tried to juggle family and professional life with writing the book. I am immensely grateful as well for the stunning creative work of Christa Moffitt who designed the front cover (which I love). Thank you to you all.

ACKNOWLEDGEMENTS

Finally, I must thank my good friend, Lauren Sams, a terrific author and editor in her own right, for introducing me to Kelly Fagan. Lauren was the person who first saw that my short pieces perhaps held bigger promise. Without Lauren introducing me to Kelly, there is no book!

ENDNOTES

_____

Prologue

1 Molloy, Shannon, 'The men's mental health crisis Australia can no longer ignore—six male suicides a day', *News.com.au*, 10 October 2018, <https://www.news.com.au/lifestyle/health/mind/the-mens-mental-health-crisis-australia-can-no-longer-ignore-six-male-suicides-a-day/news-story/cc77b01572676c8b140424777c3ff642>

1 A little help?

1 Krazit, Tom, 'The Backstory Of Steve Jobs' Quote About Parenthood', Gigaom, 11 October 2011, <https://gigaom.com/2011/10/11/419-the-long-backstory-of-steve-jobs-quote-about-parenthood/>

2 Australian Bureau of Statistics, 'Dad's the word', ABS, 2 September 2016, <http://www.abs.gov.au/ausstats/abs@.nsf/Lookup/by%20Subject/4125.0~August%202016~Media%20Release~Dad's%20the%20word%20(Media%20Release)~2>

3 Shepherd, Briana, 'The generation who won't be grandparents is grappling with a sense of family emptiness', *ABC News*, 22 September 2019,

<https://www.abc.net.au/news/2019-09-22/the-generation-who-wont-be-grandparents/11532734>

4   Fletcher, Richard, 'Dads get postnatal depression too', *The Conversation*, 2 May 2016, <http://theconversation.com/dads-get-postnatal-depression-too-55829>

5   Fletcher, Richard, 'Dads get postnatal depression too', *The Conversation*, 2 May 2016, <http://theconversation.com/dads-get-postnatal-depression-too-55829>

6   Taylor, Elly, 'Dad's mental health: good news, bad news', Australian Men's Health Forum, 2019, <https://www.amhf.org.au/dads_mental_health_good_news_bad_news>

7   Murkoff, Heidi and Mazel, Sharon, *What to expect: The First Year*, Workman Publishing, New York, 2014.

8   Australian Bureau of Statistics, 'Same-sex Couples in Australia, 2016', ABS, 18 January 2018, <https://www.abs.gov.au/ausstats/abs@.nsf/Lookup/by%20 Subject/2071.0~2016~Main%20Features~Same-Sex%20Couples~85>

9   Henriques-Gomes, Luke, '"It's soul destroying": the stress and stigma of being a single parent on welfare', *The Guardian*, 19 April 2019, https:// www.theguardian.com/australia-news/2019/apr/19/its-soul-destroying-the-stress-and-stigma-of-being-a-single-parent-on-welfare>

10 Australian Institute of Family Studies, 'Divorce rates in Australia', AIFS, 2017, <https://aifs.gov.au/facts-and-figures/divorce-rates-australia>

2   Beyond the breadwinner

1   Shad, Simon, 'A "free" public school education can cost $1,300 a year—and it's getting harder for parents to say no', *ABC News*, 20 March 2019, <https://www.abc.net.au/news/2019-03-20/parents-pitch-in-for-the-high-cost-of-public-schooling/10917358>

2   Phillips, Ben et al, *Cost of Kids: The Cost of Raising Children in Australia*, Income and Wealth Report, Issue 33, National Centre for Social and Economic Modelling at the University of Canberra, AMP, Sydney, 2013, p 3, <https://www.natsem.canberra.edu.au/storage/AMP_NATSEM_33. pdf>; Australian Securities and Investments Commission, 'Australian spending habits', Moneysmart, 2 August 2019, <https://www.moneysmart. gov.au/managing-your-money/budgeting/australian-spending-habits>

3   Australian Bureau of Statistics, '6224.0.55.001—Labour Force, Australia: Labour Force Status and Other Characteristics of Families', ABS, 3 October 2019, <https://www.abs.gov.au/ausstats/abs@.nsf/Latestproducts/ 6224.0.55.001Main%20Features4June%202019?opendocument&

tabname=Summary&prodno=6224.0.55.001&issue=June%202019&
num=&view=>

4   Krznaric, Roman, 'Man about the house', *The Guardian*, 14 January 2012,
    <https://www.theguardian.com/lifeandstyle/2012/jan/14/roman-krznaric-
    househusband-father>

5   Wilton, Dave, 'Husband', *Word Origins*, 31 May 2007, <http://www.
    wordorigins.org/index.php/index/2007/05/>; Krznaric, Roman, 'Man about
    the house', *The Guardian*, 14 January 2012, <https://www.theguardian.com/
    lifeandstyle/2012/jan/14/roman-krznaric-househusband-father>

6   Burgess, Adrienne, *Fatherhood Reclaimed: The making of the modern father*,
    Ebury Publishing, London, 1998, pp 43–44; Krznaric, Roman, 'Man about
    the house', *The Guardian*, 14 January 2012, <https://www.theguardian.
    com/lifeandstyle/2012/jan/14/roman-krznaric-househusband-father>

7   Kirkus Review, 'The politics of parenthood: Child Care, Women's Rights,
    and the Myth of the Good Mother', *Kirkus Reviews*, 20 May 2010,
    <https://www.kirkusreviews.com/book-reviews/mary-frances-berry/the-
    politics-of-parenthood/>

8   Burgess, Adrienne, *Fatherhood Reclaimed: The making of the modern father*,
    Ebury Publishing, London, 1998, p 36.

9   Burgess, Adrienne, *Fatherhood Reclaimed: The making of the modern father*,
    Ebury Publishing, London, 1998, pp 36–37.

10 Burgess, Adrienne, *Fatherhood Reclaimed: The making of the modern father*,
    Ebury Publishing, London, 1998, p 38.

11 Burgess, Adrienne, *Fatherhood Reclaimed: The making of the modern father*,
    Ebury Publishing, London, 1998, p 46.

12 Burgess, Adrienne, *Fatherhood Reclaimed: The making of the modern father*,
    Ebury Publishing, London, 1998, p 38.

13 Burgess, Adrienne, *Fatherhood Reclaimed: The making of the modern father*,
    Ebury Publishing, London, 1998, p 39.

14 Burgess, Adrienne, *Fatherhood Reclaimed: The making of the modern father*,
    Ebury Publishing, London, 1998, p 39.

15 Burgess, Adrienne, *Fatherhood Reclaimed: The making of the modern father*,
    Ebury Publishing, London, 1998, p 39.

16 Burgess, Adrienne, *Fatherhood Reclaimed: The making of the modern father*,
    Ebury Publishing, London, 1998, p 39.

17 Burgess, Adrienne, *Fatherhood Reclaimed: The making of the modern father*,
    Ebury Publishing, London, 1998, p 46.

18 Burgess, Adrienne, *Fatherhood Reclaimed: The making of the modern father*,
    Ebury Publishing, London, 1998, p 42.

19 Aboriginal and Torres Strait Islander Healing Foundation, *A Resource for Collective Healing for Members of the Stolen Generation: Planning, implementing and evaluating effective local response*, Muru Marri, November 2014, p10, <https://healingfoundation.org.au/app/uploads/2017/02/Muru-Marri-SCREEN-singles-sml.pdf>

20 Khazan, Olga, 'Inherited Trauma Shapes Your Health', *The Atlantic*, 16 October 2018, <https://www.theatlantic.com/health/archive/2018/10/trauma-inherited-generations/573055/>

21 Higgins, Isabella, 'Stolen Generations study reveals impact of intergenerational trauma', *ABC News*, 15 August 2018, <https://www.abc.net.au/news/2018-08-15/stolen-generations-study-impact-of-intergenerational-trauma/10118132>; Australian Institute of Health and Welfare, *Aboriginal and Torres Strait Islander Stolen Generations and descendants: Numbers, demographic characteristics and selected outcomes*, AIHW, Canberra, 2018, pp vii–viii, <https://healingfoundation.org.au/stolen-generations/stolengenerationsreport/>

22 Daley, Paul, 'The killing times: As the toll of Australia's frontier brutality keeps climbing, truth telling is long overdue' *The Guardian*, 4 March 2019, <https://www.theguardian.com/australia-news/2019/mar/04/as-the-toll-of-australias-frontier-brutality-keeps-climbing-truth-telling-is-long-overdue>

23 Reilly, Lyndall and Rees, Susan, 'Fatherhood in Australian Aboriginal and Torres Strait Islander communities: An Examination of Barriers and Opportunities to Strengthen the Male Parenting Role', *The American Journal of Men's Health*, Volume 12, Issue 2, March 2018, pp 420–430, <https://www.ncbi.nlm.nih.gov/pmc/articles/PMC5818118/>

24 Russell, Sophie and Cunneen, Chris, 'As Indigenous incarceration rates keep rising, justice reinvestment offers a solution, *The Conversation*, 11 December 2018, <https://theconversation.com/as-indigenous-incarceration-rates-keep-rising-justice-reinvestment-offers-a-solution-107610>

25 Biddulph, Stephen, *Raising Boys in the 21st Century*, Finch Publishing, Sydney, 2018, p 72.

26 Australian Bureau of Statistics, '4102.0—Australian Social Trends, 1996: Family Functioning: War Veterans and their Carers', ABS, 24 June 1996, <http://www.abs.gov.au/AUSSTATS/abs@.nsf/Previousproducts/A99F9680BAF24C4FCA2570EC0073D3B5?opendocument>

27 Australian War Memorial, 'First World War 1914–18', Australian War Memorial, <https://www.awm.gov.au/articles/atwar/first-world-war>

28 Australian War Memorial, '"God Bless Daddy" 45,000 Australian fathers are fighting, Will you help?', Australian War Memorial, <https://www.awm.gov.au/collection/C95653>

29 Australian War Memorial, '"Daddy, what did you do in the Great War?"', Australian War Memorial, <https://www.awm.gov.au/collection/ARTV00433/>

30 National Museum Australia, 'Defining moments: Great Depression', National Museum of Australia, <https://www.nma.gov.au/defining-moments/resources/great-depression>

31 National Museum Australia, 'Defining moments: Great Depression', National Museum of Australia, <https://www.nma.gov.au/defining-moments/resources/great-depression>

32 Australian Bureau of Statistics, 'ANZAC facts and figures from the ABS', ABS, 24 April 2008, <http://www.abs.gov.au/ausstats/abs@.nsf/products/2C82DF602726FDECCA257434007E85EF?OpenDocument>

33 Australian Bureau of Statistics, '4102.0—Australian Social Trends, 1996: Family Functioning: War Veterans and their Carers', ABS, 24 June 1996, <http://www.abs.gov.au/AUSSTATS/abs@.nsf/Previousproducts/A99F9680BAF24C4FCA2570EC0073D3B5?opendocument>

34 *Saturday Extra*, 'Children in World War 2', ABC Radio National, 21 January 2006, <https://www.abc.net.au/radionational/programs/saturdayextra/children-in-world-war-2/3311396>

35 James, Karl, 'Wartime 45—Feature Article: Soldiers to citizens', Australian War Memorial, <https://www.awm.gov.au/wartime/45/article>.

36 Biddulph, Stephen, *Raising Boys in the 21st Century*, Finch Publishing, Sydney, 2018, p 72.

3 Getting stuck in

1 Chilton, Howard, *Baby on Board: Understanding your baby's needs in the first twelve months*, Nascor Publishing, Sydney, 2013.

2 BabyCentre, 'Five myths of fatherhood', BabyCentre, June 2017, <https://www.babycentre.co.uk/a539837/five-myths-of-fatherhood>

3 Frameworks Institute, *Perceptions of Parenting: Mapping the Gaps between Expert and Public Understandings of Effective Parenting in Australia*, Parenting Research Centre, May 2016, p 7, <https://www.parentingrc.org.au/publications/perceptions/>; BabyCentre, 'Five myths of fatherhood', BabyCentre, June 2017, <https://www.babycentre.co.uk/a539837/five-myths-of-fatherhood>

4 50/50 by 2030 Foundation, *From Girls to Men: Social Attitudes to Gender Equality in Australia*, University of Canberra, September 2018, p 36, <https://www.5050foundation.edu.au/assets/reports/documents/From-Girls-to-Men.pdf>.

5   Baxter, Jennifer, 'Stay-at-home dads: Research Summary', Australian
    Institute of Family Studies, May 2017, <https://aifs.gov.au/publications/
    stay-home-dads>

6   50/50 by 2030 Foundation, *From Girls to Men: Social Attitudes to Gender
    Equality in Australia*, University of Canberra, September 2018, p 34,
    <https://www.5050foundation.edu.au/assets/reports/documents/From-
    Girls-to-Men.pdf>

7   50/50 by 2030 Foundation, *From Girls to Men: Social Attitudes to Gender
    Equality in Australia*, University of Canberra, September 2018, p 36,
    <https://www.5050foundation.edu.au/assets/reports/documents/From-
    Girls-to-Men.pdf>

8   Australian Institute of Family Studies, 'Work and Family', AIFS, 2017,
    <https://aifs.gov.au/facts-and-figures/work-and-family>

9   Australian Institute of Family Studies, 'Work and Family', AIFS, 2017,
    <https://aifs.gov.au/facts-and-figures/work-and-family>

10 Strazdins, Lyndall, 'Gender, work, care, time: Why father's care
    matters', presentation given to the Father's Forum at ANU, Canberra,
    9 August 2018, slide 2, <http://genderinstitute.anu.edu.au/why-
    fathers%E2%80%99-care-matters-enabling-gender-equity-care-and-work>

11 Baxter, Jennifer, 'Stay-at-home dads: Research Summary', Australian
    Institute of Family Studies, May 2017, <https://aifs.gov.au/publications/
    stay-home-dads>; Dent, Georgie, 'One in four Australian men do no
    housework. Not a single thing. Nada. Nothing', *Women's Agenda*, 28 June
    2017, <https://womensagenda.com.au/latest/eds-blog/one-in-four-
    australian-men-do-no-housework/>

12 Gluyas, Alexander and Mannix, Liam, 'Men are doing more housework.
    Women are still doing a lot more', *Sydney Morning Herald*, 30 June 2018,
    <https://www.smh.com.au/national/men-are-doing-more-housework-
    women-still-do-a-lot-more-20180730-p4zuh1.html>

13 Cowie, Tom and Grieve, Charlotte, 'Women breadwinners still doing most
    of the housework: survey', *Sydney Morning Herald*, 30 June 2019, <https://
    www.smh.com.au/national/women-breadwinners-still-doing-most-of-the-
    housework-survey-20190729-p52bti.html?__twitter_impression=true>

14 Melbourne Institute: Applied Economic and Social Research, *The
    Household, Income and Labour Dynamics in Australia Survey: Selected
    Findings from Waves 1 to 17*, University of Melbourne, 2019, p 98, <https://
    melbourneinstitute.unimelb.edu.au/__data/assets/pdf_file/0011/3127664/
    HILDA-Statistical-Report-2019.pdf>

15 Australian Bureau of Statistics 'ABS reveals new Census insights into Australia's same-sex couples', ABS, 13 December 2017, <https://www.abs.gov.au/AUSSTATS/abs@.nsf/mediareleasesbyReleaseDate/9AEDED8E8FB6CB56CA2581F4007A9C06?OpenDocument>

16 Reilly, Natalie, 'The increased stress felt by working mothers has finally been measured', *Sydney Morning Herald*, 6 February 2019, <https://www.smh.com.au/lifestyle/life-and-relationships/the-increased-stress-felt-by-working-mothers-has-finally-been-measured-20190205-p50vrw.html>; Institute for Social and Economic Research, 'Chronic stress levels 40% higher in full-time working women with children, but flexible work reduces stress', University of Essex, 26 January 2019, <https://www.iser.essex.ac.uk/2019/01/26/chronic-stress-levels-40-higher-in-full-time-working-women-with-children-but-flexible-work-reduces-stress>

17 Frameworks Institute, *Perceptions of Parenting: Mapping the Gaps between Expert and Public Understandings of Effective Parenting in Australia*, Parenting Research Centre, May 2016, p 8, <https://www.parentingrc.org.au/publications/perceptions/>

18 Yavorsky, Jill, 'Searching for an Equal Co-Parent: Six Factors That Influence Whether Dad Pulls His Weight at Home', *Slate*, 11 October 2017, <https://slate.com/human-interest/2017/10/searching-for-an-equal-co-parent.html>; Hook, Jennifer and Wolfe, Christina, 'Parental Involvement and Work Schedules: Time with Children in the United States, Germany, Norway, and the United Kingdom', *European Sociological Review*, Volume 29, Issue 3, June 2013, pp 411–425, <https://www.ncbi.nlm.nih.gov/pmc/articles/PMC3685587/>

19 Aitkenhead, Decca, 'The Interview: Russell Brand on his hedonistic past, marriages, and becoming a father', *The Sunday Times*, 20 January 2019, <https://www.thetimes.co.uk/article/the-interview-russell-brand-on-his-hedonistic-past-marriages-and-becoming-a-father-wn6gjkwzd>

20 Peoplestaff225, 'Eddie Murphy Doesn't Change Diapers Because It's "Not Fair to the Child": "I Would Be Horrible At It"', *People*, 17 August 2016, <https://people.com/parents/eddie-murphy-says-he-doesnt-change-diapers/>

21 Australian Bureau of Statistics, 'Australian Women are now having children older than ever', 11 December 2018, ABS, <http://www.abs.gov.au/ausstats%5Cabs@.nsf/0/8668A9A0D4B0156CCA25792F0016186A?Opendocument>; United Nations Children's Fund, 'Measles deaths plummet', UNICEF, 4 March 2005, <https://www.unicef.org/immunization/index_25339.html>

22 Plas-plooij, Xaviera, Plooj, Frans and Van De Rijt, Hetty, *The Wonder Weeks: A Stress-Free Guide to Your Baby's Behaviour*, Countryman Press, New York, 2019.

23 De Geyn, Lisa, 'What is all the fuss about the Wonder Weeks?', *Today's Parent*, 16 January 2019, <https://www.todaysparent.com/baby/baby-development/what-is-all-the-fuss-about-the-wonder-weeks/>

24 De Geyn, Lisa, 'What is all the fuss about the Wonder Weeks?', *Today's Parent*, 16 January 2019, <https://www.todaysparent.com/baby/baby-development/what-is-all-the-fuss-about-the-wonder-weeks/>

25 The Wonder Weeks, 'Scientific History The Wonder Weeks', *The Wonder Weeks*, <https://www.thewonderweeks.com/scientific-history/>

26 The Wonder Weeks, 'Scientific History The Wonder Weeks', *The Wonder Weeks*, <https://www.thewonderweeks.com/scientific-history/>

27 de Weerth, C and van Geert, P, 'Emotional instability as an indicator of strictly timed infantile developmental transitions', *British Journal of Developmental Psychology*, Volume 16, Issue 1, 12 March 1998, p 15-44, <https://onlinelibrary.wiley.com/doi/abs/10.1111/j.2044-835X.1998.tb00748.x>

28 Burkeman, Oliver, 'The diabolical genius of the baby advice industry', *The Guardian*, 16 January 2018, <https://www.theguardian.com/news/2018/jan/16/baby-advice-books-industry-attachment-parenting>; De Geyn, Lisa, 'What is all the fuss about the Wonder Weeks?', *Today's Parent*, 16 January 2019, <https://www.todaysparent.com/baby/baby-development/what-is-all-the-fuss-about-the-wonder-weeks/>

29 Burkeman, Oliver, 'The diabolical genius of the baby advice industry', *The Guardian*, 16 January 2018, <https://www.theguardian.com/news/2018/jan/16/baby-advice-books-industry-attachment-parenting>; De Geyn, Lisa, 'What is all the fuss about the Wonder Weeks?', *Today's Parent*, 16 January 2019, <https://www.todaysparent.com/baby/baby-development/what-is-all-the-fuss-about-the-wonder-weeks/>

30 The Wonder Weeks, 'Scientific History The Wonder Weeks', *The Wonder Weeks*, <https://www.thewonderweeks.com/scientific-history/>

31 Burkeman, Oliver, 'The diabolical genius of the baby advice industry', *The Guardian*, 16 January 2018, <https://www.theguardian.com/news/2018/jan/16/baby-advice-books-industry-attachment-parenting>

32 Gopnik, Alison, *The Gardener and the Carpenter: What the New Science of Child Development Tells Us about the Relationship Between Parents and Children*, The Bodley Head, London, 2016, p 25.

33 Center on the Developing Child, *The Science of Early Childhood Development* (InBrief), Harvard University, 2007, <https://developingchild.harvard.edu/resources/inbrief-science-of-ecd/>; Centre for Community Child Health, *The First Thousand Days—Our Greatest Opportunity*, Policy

Brief, Edition Number 28, The Royal Children's Hospital Melbourne, p 2, <https://www.rch.org.au/uploadedFiles/Main/Content/ccchdev/1803-CCCH-Policy-Brief-28.pdf>

34   Chen, Er-Mei et al, 'Effects of Father-Neonate Skin-to-Skin Contact in Attachment: A Randomized Controlled Trial', *Nursing Research and Practice*, 2017, <https://www.ncbi.nlm.nih.gov/pmc/articles/PMC5282438/>; Kuo, P et al, 'Fathers' cortisol and testosterone in the days around the infants' births predict later paternal involvement', *Hormones and Behaviour*, Volume 106, November 2018, pp 28–34, <https://www.ncbi.nlm.nih.gov/pubmed/30165061>

35   Fatherhood Institute, 'FI Research Summary: Dads and Hormones', The Fatherhood Institute, 7 November 2014, <http://www.fatherhoodinstitute.org/2014/fi-research-summary-dads-and-hormones/>; Kuo, P et al, 'Fathers' cortisol and testosterone in the days around the infants' births predict later paternal involvement', *Hormones and Behaviour*, Volume 106, November 2018, pp 28–34, <https://www.ncbi.nlm.nih.gov/pubmed/30165061>

36   Fatherhood Institute, 'FI Research Summary: Dads and Hormones', The Fatherhood Institute, 7 November 2014, <http://www.fatherhoodinstitute.org/2014/fi-research-summary-dads-and-hormones/>

37   Brennan, Deborah and Pascoe, Susan, *Lifting Our Game: Report of the Review To Achieve Educational Excellence in Australian Schools Through Early Childhood Interventions*, Victorian Government, December 2017, p 15, <https://education.nsw.gov.au/early-childhood-education/whats-happening-in-the-early-childhood-education-sector/lifting-our-game-report/Lifting-Our-Game-Final-Report.pdf>

38   Centre for Community Child Health, *The First Thousand Days: An Evidence Paper—Summary*, The Royal Children's Hospital Melbourne, September 2017, pp 1–3, <https://www.rch.org.au/uploadedFiles/Main/Content/ccchdev/CCCH-The-First-Thousand-Days-An-Evidence-Paper-Summary-September-2017.pdf>

39   Brennan, Deborah and Pascoe, Susan, *Lifting Our Game: Report of the Review To Achieve Educational Excellence in Australian Schools Through Early Childhood Interventions*, Victorian Government, December 2017, p 7, <https://education.nsw.gov.au/early-childhood-education/whats-happening-in-the-early-childhood-education-sector/lifting-our-game-report/Lifting-Our-Game-Final-Report.pdf>

40   Brennan, Deborah and Pascoe, Susan, *Lifting Our Game: Report of the Review To Achieve Educational Excellence in Australian Schools Through Early Childhood Interventions*, Victorian Government, December 2017,

p 7, <https://education.nsw.gov.au/early-childhood-education/whats-happening-in-the-early-childhood-education-sector/lifting-our-game-report/Lifting-Our-Game-Final-Report.pdf>

41 Sarkadi, Anna, et al, 'Fathers' involvement and children's developmental outcomes: a systematic review of longitudinal studies', *Acta Paediatrica*, Volume 97, Issue 2, February 2008, pp 153–158, <https://www.ncbi.nlm.nih.gov/pubmed/18052995>; Centre for Community Child Health, *The First Thousand Days: An Evidence Paper*, The Royal Children's Hospital Melbourne, September 2017, p 32, <https://www.rch.org.au/uploadedFiles/Main/Content/ccchdev/CCCH-The-First-Thousand-Days-An-Evidence-Paper-September-2017.pdf>

42 Wilson, Katherine, 'Father involvement and child well-being', *Journal of Paediatrics and Child Health*, Volume 47, Issue 7, July 2011, pp 405–407, <https://onlinelibrary.wiley.com/doi/abs/10.1111/j.1440-1754.2010.01770.x>; Centre for Community Child Health, *The First Thousand Days: An Evidence Paper*, The Royal Children's Hospital Melbourne, September 2017, p 32, <https://www.rch.org.au/uploadedFiles/Main/Content/ccchdev/CCCH-The-First-Thousand-Days-An-Evidence-Paper-September-2017.pdf>

43 Wood, Lisa and Lambin, Estée, *How fathers and father figures can shape child health and wellbeing*, The University of Western Australia, June 2013, pp 1–14, <http://thefatheringproject.org/fpwp/wp-content/uploads/2015/11/New-Fathering-Research.pdf>

44 Feldman, Ruth, et al, 'Father's brain is sensitive to childcare experiences', Proceedings of the National Academy of Sciences of the United States of America, Volume 111, Number 27, pp 9792–9797, <https://www.pnas.org/content/111/27/9792>; Norton, Elizabeth, 'Parenting Rewires the Male Brain', *Science Magazine*, 27 May 2014, <https://www.sciencemag.org/news/2014/05/parenting-rewires-male-brain>

45 Kim, Pilyoung, et al, 'Neural Plasticity in Fathers of Human Infants', *Social Neuroscience*, Volume 9, Number 5, pp 522–535, October 2014, <https://www.ncbi.nlm.nih.gov/pmc/articles/PMC4144350/>; Boren Zachary Davies, 'New Fathers Experience Brain Change to Bond With Their Child', *The Independent*, 22 December 2014, <https://www.independent.co.uk/life-style/health-and-families/health-news/new-fathers-experience-brain-change-to-bond-with-their-child-9940117.html>

46 Carlson, Daniel et al, 'The Division of Child Care, Sexual Intimacy, and Relationship Quality in Couples', *Gender & Society*, Volume 30, Issue 3, June 2016, pp 442–466, <https://journals.sagepub.com/doi/abs/10.1177/0891243215626709>

ENDNOTES

4 Time to be a dad

1. Leach, Liana, 'Gaps in Australia's PPL System—inequities and opportunities', presentation to *Next Steps for Paid Parental Leave: Advancing leave policy in Australia*, Australian National University, Canberra, 22 August 2019, <https://www.anu.edu.au/events/next-steps-for-paid-parental-leave-advancing-leave-policy-in-australia>

2. Yeo, Natalie, 'The New and Improved Aussie Dad: Fashionable, Financially Secure and Family-Oriented', Nielsen Insights, 29 August 2017, <https://www.nielsen.com/au/en/insights/article/2017/the-new-and-improved-aussie-dad-fashionable-financially-secure-and-family-oriented/>

3. Diversity Council of Australia, 'This Father's Day, let's encourage men to work flexibly!', DCA, 30 August 2015, <https://www.dca.org.au/media-releases/fathers-day-lets-encourage-men-work-flexibly>; Nickless, Rachel, 'What men want: flexible work', *Australian Financial Review*, 29 August 2012, <https://www.afr.com/policy/economy/what-men-want-flexible-work-20120829-j1x8p>

4. Diversity Council of Australia, 'This Father's Day, let's encourage men to work flexibly!', DCA, 30 August 2015, <https://www.dca.org.au/media-releases/fathers-day-lets-encourage-men-work-flexibly>; Workplace Gender Equality Agency, *The Business Case for Gender Equality*, WGEA, November 2018, p 3, <https://www.wgea.gov.au/sites/default/files/documents/wgea-business-case-for-gender-equality_0.pdf>

5. Daddilife, *The Millennial Dad at Work*, May 2019, Daddilife, p 11 <https://www.daddilife.com/wp-content/uploads/2019/05/The-Millenial-Dad-at-Work-Report-2019.pdf>

6. Baxter, Jennifer, *Stay-at-home fathers in Australia: Research Report 2018*, Australian Institute of Family Studies, 2018, p 23, <https://aifs.gov.au/sites/default/files/publication-documents/stay-at-home_fathers_in_australia_0.pdf>

7. Priestley, Angela, '"Not doing it would be silly": ING to offer paid parental leave equality removing "primary"/"secondary" labels', *Women's Agenda*, August 2019, <https://womensagenda.com.au/latest/ing-first-bank-paid-parental-leave-equality/>

8. Perraudin, Frances, 'Men less likely than women to cite impact of parental leave on career', *The Guardian*, 5 August 2019, <https://www.theguardian.com/lifeandstyle/2019/aug/04/men-women-parental-leave-impact-career>

9. Australian Bureau of Statistics, 'Dad's the word', ABS, 2 September 2016, <http://www.abs.gov.au/ausstats/abs@.nsf/Lookup/by%20Subject/4125.0~August%202016~Media%20Release~Dad's%20the%20word%20(Media%20Release)~2>

10 Australian Bureau of Statistics, 'Dad's the word', ABS, 2 September 2016, <http://www.abs.gov.au/ausstats/abs@.nsf/Lookup/by%20 Subject/4125.0~August%202016~Media%20Release~Dad's%20the%20 word%20(Media%20Release)~2>

11 Cooklin, Amanda, 'Conflicts between work and family and fathers' mental health: research summary', Australian Institute of Family Studies, June 2019, <https://aifs.gov.au/aifs-conference/conflicts-between-work-and-family-and-fathers-mental-health>; Australian Institute of Family Studies, 'Work and Family', AIFS, 2017, <https://aifs.gov.au/facts-and-figures/work-and-family>; Workplace Gender Equality Agency, 'Dad's the word', WGEA, 26 June 2019, <https://wgea.gov.au/newsroom/latest-news/dads-the-word>

12 Australian Institute of Family Studies, 'Work and Family', AIFS, 2017, <https://aifs.gov.au/facts-and-figures/work-and-family>

13 Data taken from Paid Parental Leave evaluation survey 2013 as presented by Leach, Liana, 'Gaps in Australia's PPL System—inequities and opportunities', presentation to *Next Steps for Paid Parental Leave: Advancing leave policy in Australia*, Australian National University, Canberra, 22 August 2019, <https://www.anu.edu.au/events/next-steps-for-paid-parental-leave-advancing-leave-policy-in-australia>

14 Australian Bureau of Statistics, 'One in 20 dads take primary parental leave', ABS, 19 September 2017, <http://www.abs.gov.au/ausstats/abs@.nsf/Lookup/by%20Subject/4125.0~Sep%202017~Media%20 Release~One%20in%2020%20dads%20take%20primary%20parental%20 leave%20(Media%20Release)~11>

15 Parents At Work, *Advancing Parental Leave Equality and Introducing Shared Care in Australia: The business case for action*, Parents At Work, 2018, p 4, <http://parentsandcarersatwork.com/wp-content/uploads/2018/08/PAW_ White-Paper-Parental-Leave-Equality.pdf>

16 Workplace Gender Equality Agency, *Towards gender balanced parental leave: Australian and international trends—Insight paper*, WGEA, October 2017, p 8, <https://www.wgea.gov.au/sites/default/files/documents/Parental-leave-and-gender-equality.pdf>

17 Workplace Gender Equality Agency, *Towards gender balanced parental leave: Australian and international trends—Insight paper*, WGEA, October 2017, p 9, <https://www.wgea.gov.au/sites/default/files/documents/Parental-leave-and-gender-equality.pdf>

18 Parents At Work, *Advancing Parental Leave Equality and Introducing Shared Care in Australia: The business case for action*, Parents At Work, 2018, p 4, <http://parentsandcarersatwork.com/wp-content/uploads/2018/08/PAW_ White-Paper-Parental-Leave-Equality.pdf>

19 Parents At Work, *Advancing Parental Leave Equality and Introducing Shared Care in Australia: The business case for action*, Parents At Work, 2018, p 6, <http://parentsandcarersatwork.com/wp-content/uploads/2018/08/PAW_White-Paper-Parental-Leave-Equality.pdf>

20 Australian Bureau of Statistics, 'Pregnancy and Work Transitions', ABS, 20 November 2013, <http://www.abs.gov.au/ausstats/abs@.nsf/Lookup/4102.0Main+Features10Nov+2013>

21 Data extracted from Workplace Gender Equality Agency Data Explorer, WGEA, October 2019, <https://data.wgea.gov.au/home>; see also Workplace Gender Equality Agency, *Towards gender balanced parental leave: Australian and international trends—Insight paper*, WGEA, October 2017, p 6, <https://www.wgea.gov.au/sites/default/files/documents/Parental-leave-and-gender-equality.pdf>

22 Australian Human Rights Commission, *Supporting Working Parents: Pregnancy and Return to Work National Review—Report 2014*, AHRC, 2014, p 48, <https://www.humanrights.gov.au/sites/default/files/document/publication/SWP_Report_2014.pdf>

23 Australian Human Rights Commission, *Supporting Working Parents: Pregnancy and Return to Work National Review—Report 2014*, AHRC, 2014, p 55, <https://www.humanrights.gov.au/sites/default/files/document/publication/SWP_Report_2014.pdf>

24 Australian Human Rights Commission, *Supporting Working Parents: Pregnancy and Return to Work National Review—Report 2014*, AHRC, 2014, p 56, <https://www.humanrights.gov.au/sites/default/files/document/publication/SWP_Report_2014.pdf>

25 Cowie, Tom and Grieve, Charlotte, 'Women breadwinners still doing most of the housework: survey', *Sydney Morning Herald*, 30 June 2019, <https://www.smh.com.au/national/women-breadwinners-still-doing-most-of-the-housework-survey-20190729-p52bti.html>

26 Australian Human Rights Commission, *Supporting Working Parents: Pregnancy and Return to Work National Review—Report 2014*, AHRC, 2014, p 1, <https://www.humanrights.gov.au/sites/default/files/document/publication/SWP_Report_2014.pdf>

27 Australian Human Rights Commission, *Supporting Working Parents: Pregnancy and Return to Work National Review—Report 2014*, AHRC, 2014, p 49, <https://www.humanrights.gov.au/sites/default/files/document/publication/SWP_Report_2014.pdf>

28 Pollard, Kate, 'Why more dads wants better access to parental leave', Circle In, October 2018, <https://www.circlein.com.au/why-more-dads-want-better-access-to-parental-leave/>

29 Australian Institute of Family Studies, 'Work and Family', AIFS, 2017, <https://aifs.gov.au/facts-and-figures/work-and-family>

30 Workplace Gender Equality Agency, 'Employers need to care more about carers', WGEA, 22 November 2018, <https://www.wgea.gov.au/newsroom/latest-news/employers-need-to-care-more-about-carers>

31 Diversity Council of Australia, 'This Father's Day, let's encourage men to work flexibly!', DCA, 30 August 2015, <https://www.dca.org.au/media-releases/fathers-day-lets-encourage-men-work-flexibly>; Nickless, Rachel, 'What men want: flexible work, *Australian Financial Review*, 29 August 2012, <https://www.afr.com/policy/economy/what-men-want-flexible-work-20120829-j1x8p>

32 Baxter, Jennifer, 'Fathers and work: A statistical overview—Research Summary', Australian Institute of Family Studies, May 2019, <https://aifs.gov.au/aifs-conference/fathers-and-work>

33 50/50 by 2030 Foundation, *From Girls to Men: Social Attitudes to Gender Equality in Australia*, University of Canberra, September 2018, p 37, <https://www.5050foundation.edu.au/assets/reports/documents/From-Girls-to-Men.pdf>

34 50/50 by 2030 Foundation, *From Girls to Men: Social Attitudes to Gender Equality in Australia*, University of Canberra, September 2018, p 41, <https://www.5050foundation.edu.au/assets/reports/documents/From-Girls-to-Men.pdf>

35 Pollard, Kate, 'Why more dads wants better access to parental leave', Circle In, October 2018, <https://www.circlein.com.au/why-more-dads-want-better-access-to-parental-leave/>

36 Strazdins, Lyndall, 'Gender, work, care, time: Why father's care matters', presentation given to the Father's Forum at ANU, Canberra, 9 August 2018, slides 3, 10, <http://genderinstitute.anu.edu.au/why-fathers%E2%80%99-care-matters-enabling-gender-equity-care-and-work>

37 Strazdins, Lyndall, 'Gender, work, care, time: Why father's care matters', presentation given to the Father's Forum at ANU, Canberra, 9 August 2018, slides 3, 10, <http://genderinstitute.anu.edu.au/why-fathers%E2%80%99-care-matters-enabling-gender-equity-care-and-work>

38 Baxter, Jennifer et al, 'Long Hours and longings—Research summary', Australian Institute of Family Studies, September 2017, <https://aifs.gov.au/publications/long-hours-and-longings>

39 Baxter, Jennifer et al, 'Long Hours and longings—Research summary', Australian Institute of Family Studies, September 2017, <https://aifs.gov.au/publications/long-hours-and-longings>

40 Cooklin, Amanda, 'Conflicts between work and family and fathers' mental health: research summary', Australian Institute of Family Studies, June 2019, <https://aifs.gov.au/aifs-conference/conflicts-between-work-and-family-and-fathers-mental-health>

41 Fitzsimmons, Caitlin, 'Work–family conflict on the rise for fathers', *Sydney Morning Herald*, 16 June 2019, <https://www.smh.com.au/business/workplace/work-family-conflict-on-the-rise-for-fathers-20190614-p51xr1.html>; Cooklin, Amanda, 'Conflicts between work and family and fathers' mental health: research summary', Australian Institute of Family Studies, June 2019, <https://aifs.gov.au/aifs-conference/conflicts-between-work-and-family-and-fathers-mental-health>

42 Leach, Liana, 'Fathers' work and family conflicts and the outcomes for children's mental health—Research summary', Australian Institute of Family Studies, June 2019, <https://aifs.gov.au/aifs-conference/fathers-work-and-family-conflicts-and-outcomes-childrens-mental-health>

43 Baxter, Jennifer, 'Stay-at-home fathers in Australia—Research report', Australian Institute of Family Studies, April 2018 <https://aifs.gov.au/publications/stay-home-fathers-australia>

44 Australian Institute of Family Studies, 'Stay-at-home dads: Still rare but numbers rising', AIFS, 5 April 2018 <https://aifs.gov.au/media-releases/stay-home-dads-still-rare-numbers-rising>

45 Baxter, Jennifer, *Stay-at-home fathers in Australia: Research Report 2018*, Australian Institute of Family Studies, 2018, p 13, <https://aifs.gov.au/sites/default/files/publication-documents/stay-at-home_fathers_in_australia_0.pdf>

46 Baxter, Jennifer, *Stay-at-home fathers in Australia: Research Report 2018*, Australian Institute of Family Studies, 2018, p 23, <https://aifs.gov.au/sites/default/files/publication-documents/stay-at-home_fathers_in_australia_0.pdf>

47 Australian Institute of Family Studies, 'Work and Family', AIFS, 2017, <https://aifs.gov.au/facts-and-figures/work-and-family>

48 Baxter, Jennifer, *Stay-at-home fathers in Australia: Research Report 2018*, Australian Institute of Family Studies, 2018, pp 8–10, <https://aifs.gov.au/sites/default/files/publication-documents/stay-at-home_fathers_in_australia_0.pdf>

49 Baxter, Jennifer, *Stay-at-home fathers in Australia: Research Report 2018*, Australian Institute of Family Studies, 2018, p 22, <https://aifs.gov.au/sites/default/files/publication-documents/stay-at-home_fathers_in_australia_0.pdf>.

50 Baxter, Jennifer, *Stay-at-home fathers in Australia: Research Report 2018*, Australian Institute of Family Studies, 2018, p 4, <https://aifs.gov.au/sites/default/files/publication-documents/stay-at-home_fathers_in_australia_0.pdf>

51 Baxter, Jennifer, *Stay-at-home fathers in Australia: Research Report 2018*, Australian Institute of Family Studies, 2018, p 25, <https://aifs.gov.au/sites/default/files/publication-documents/stay-at-home_fathers_in_australia_0.pdf>

52 Ortiz, Erik, 'Where Did the 40-Hour Workweek Come from?', *NBC News*, 2 September 2014, <https://www.nbcnews.com/news/us-news/where-did-40-hour-workweek-come-n192276>

53 Roy, Eleanor Ainge, '"No downside": New Zealand Firm adopts four-day week after successful trial', *The Guardian*, 2 October 2018, <https://www.theguardian.com/world/2018/oct/02/no-downside-new-zealand-firm-adopts-four-day-week-after-successful-trial>

54 Jennings-Edquist, Grace, 'New dads can find it hard to access support. This is where other fathers meet mates to talk to', *ABC News*, 2 September 2019 <https://www.abc.net.au/life/where-new-dads-can-find-support-groups/11077854>

Fork in the road

1 Wright, Shane, 'Tim Hammond—the first term MP tipped to be Prime Minister', *The West Australian*, 22 June 2017, <https://thewest.com.au/news/wa/labor-new-boy-tipped-for-pm-ng-b88512016z>

5   Boy biology

1 Chilton, Howard, *Baby on Board: Understanding your baby's needs in the first twelve months*, Nascor Publishing, Sydney, 2013.

2 Biddulph, Stephen, *Raising Boys in the 21st Century*, Finch Publishing, Sydney, 2018, p 38.

3 Henig, Robin Marantz, 'How science is helping us understand gender', *National Geographic*, January 2017, <https://www.nationalgeographic.com/magazine/2017/01/how-science-helps-us-understand-gender-identity/>

4 Henig, Robin Marantz, 'How science is helping us understand gender', *National Geographic*, January 2017, <https://www.nationalgeographic.com/magazine/2017/01/how-science-helps-us-understand-gender-identity/>

5 Henig, Robin Marantz, 'How science is helping us understand gender', *National Geographic*, January 2017, <https://www.nationalgeographic.com/magazine/2017/01/how-science-helps-us-understand-gender-identity/>

6 Australian Human Rights Commission, 'New protection', AHRC, 1 August 2013, <https://www.humanrights.gov.au/our-work/sexual-orientation-gender-identity-intersex-status/projects/new-protection>

7 Oremus, Will, 'Facebook offers greater choice for gender identity', *Sydney Morning Herald*, 14 February 2014, <https://www.smh.com.au/technology/facebook-offers-greater-choice-for-gender-identity-20140214-32q40.html>

8 Sullivan, Rebecca, 'This question about gender identity has 33 possible answers', *News.com.au*, 29 July 2016, <https://www.news.com.au/lifestyle/relationships/sex/this-question-about-gender-identity-has-33-possible-answers/news-story/66b72adfbc566d29453581cc71279d6b>

9 Whyte, Stephen et al, 'Man, Woman, "Other": Factors Associated with Nonbinary Gender Identification', *Archives of Sexual Behavior*, Volume 47, Issue 8, pp 2397–2406, <https://link.springer.com/article/10.1007%2Fs10508-018-1307-3>

10 Australian Bureau of Statistics, 'Sex and Gender Diversity in the 2016 Census', ABS, 6 November 2018, <https://www.abs.gov.au/ausstats/abs@.nsf/Lookup/by%20Subject/2071.0~2016~Main%20Features~Sex%20and%20Gender%20Diversity%20in%20the%202016%20Census~100>

11 Simko-Bednarksi, Evan, 'New York City birth certificates get gender-neutral option', *CNN*, 3 January 2019, <https://edition.cnn.com/2019/01/03/health/new-york-city-gender-neutral-birth-certificate-trnd/index.html>

12 Government of Canada, 'Choose or update the gender identifier on your passport or travel document', Government of Canada, 11 July 2019, <https://www.canada.ca/en/immigration-refugees-citizenship/services/canadian-passports/change-sex.html>

13 Abboud, Patrick, 'Fa'afafine: The boys raised to be girls', *SBS News*, 26 August 2013, <https://www.sbs.com.au/news/fa-afafine-the-boys-raised-to-be-girls>; Henig, Robin Marantz, 'How science is helping us understand gender', *National Geographic*, January 2017, <https://www.nationalgeographic.com/magazine/2017/01/how-science-helps-us-understand-gender-identity/>

14 Abboud, Patrick, 'Fa'afafine: The boys raised to be girls', *SBS News*, 26 August 2013, <https://www.sbs.com.au/news/fa-afafine-the-boys-raised-to-be-girls>; Henig, Robin Marantz, 'How science is helping us understand gender', *National Geographic*, January 2017, <https://www.nationalgeographic.com/magazine/2017/01/how-science-helps-us-understand-gender-identity/>

15 Henig, Robin Marantz, 'How science is helping us understand gender', *National Geographic*, January 2017, <https://www.nationalgeographic.com/magazine/2017/01/how-science-helps-us-understand-gender-identity/>

16 Mosley, Michael, 'The extraordinary case of the Guevedoces', *BBC News*, 20 September 2015, <https://www.bbc.com/news/magazine-34290981>

17 Associated Foreign Press in Stockholm, 'Sweden adds gender neutral pronoun to dictionary', *The Guardian*, 25 March 2015, <https://www.theguardian.com/world/2015/mar/24/sweden-adds-gender-neutral-pronoun-to-dictionary>

18 Barry, Ellen, 'In Sweden's Preschools, Boys Learn to Dance and Girls Learn to Yell', *The New York Times*, 24 March 2018, <https://www.nytimes.com/2018/03/24/world/europe/sweden-gender-neutral-preschools.html>

19 Marsh, Sarah, 'The gender fluid generation: young people on being male, female or non-binary', *The Guardian*, 23 March 2016, <https://www.theguardian.com/commentisfree/2016/mar/23/gender-fluid-generation-young-people-male-female-trans>

20 Wong, Curtis M., '50 Percent of Millennials Believe Gender Is A Spectrum, Fusion's Massive Millennial Poll Finds', 2 February 2016, <https://www.huffingtonpost.com.au/2015/02/05/fusion-millennial-poll-gender_n_6624200.html>

21 Centre for Community Child Health, *The First Thousand Days: An Evidence Paper—Summary*, The Royal Children's Hospital Melbourne, September 2017, p 1, <https://www.rch.org.au/uploadedFiles/Main/Content/ccchdev/CCCH-The-First-Thousand-Days-An-Evidence-Paper-Summary-September-2017.pdf>

22 Centre for Community Child Health, *The First Thousand Days: An Evidence Paper—Summary*, The Royal Children's Hospital Melbourne, September 2017, p 2, <https://www.rch.org.au/uploadedFiles/Main/Content/ccchdev/CCCH-The-First-Thousand-Days-An-Evidence-Paper-Summary-September-2017.pdf>

23 Centre for Community Child Health, *The First Thousand Days: An Evidence Paper—Summary*, The Royal Children's Hospital Melbourne, September 2017, p 7, 12, <https://www.rch.org.au/uploadedFiles/Main/Content/ccchdev/CCCH-The-First-Thousand-Days-An-Evidence-Paper-Summary-September-2017.pdf>

24 Biddulph, Stephen, *Raising Boys in the 21st Century*, Finch Publishing, Sydney, 2018, pp 39–40.

25 Schore, Allan, 'All Our Sons: The Developmental Neurobiology and Neuroendocrinology of Boys At Risk', *Infant Mental Health Journal*,

Volume 38, Issue 1, January/February 2017, pp 15–52, <https://onlinelibrary.wiley.com/doi/abs/10.1002/imhj.21616>; Narvaez, Darcia, 'Be Worried About Boys, Especially Baby Boys', *Psychology Today*, 8 January 2017, <https://www.psychologytoday.com/au/blog/moral-landscapes/201701/be-worried-about-boys-especially-baby-boys>

26 Narvaez, Darcia, 'Be Worried About Boys, Especially Baby Boys', *Psychology Today*, 8 January 2017, <https://www.psychologytoday.com/au/blog/moral-landscapes/201701/be-worried-about-boys-especially-baby-boys>

27 Schore, Allan, 'All Our Sons: The Developmental Neurobiology and Neuroendocrinology of Boys At Risk', *Infant Mental Health Journal*, Volume 38, Issue 1, January/February 2017, pp 15–52, <https://onlinelibrary.wiley.com/doi/abs/10.1002/imhj.21616>

28 Biddulph, Stephen, *Raising Boys in the 21st Century*, Finch Publishing, Sydney, 2018, p 40.

29 Biddulph, Stephen, *Raising Boys in the 21st Century*, Finch Publishing, Sydney, 2018, p 8.

30 Biddulph, Stephen, *Raising Boys in the 21st Century*, Finch Publishing, Sydney, 2018, p 11.

31 Raising Children, 'Child development: the first five years', *Raisingchildren.net.au*, 4 June 2018, <https://raisingchildren.net.au/newborns/development/understanding-development/development-first-five-years>

32 Raising Children, 'Child development: the first five years', *Raisingchildren.net.au*, 4 June 2018, <https://raisingchildren.net.au/newborns/development/understanding-development/development-first-five-years>

33 Centre for Community Child Health, *The First Thousand Days: An Evidence Paper—Summary*, The Royal Children's Hospital Melbourne, September 2017, pp 15–26 <https://www.rch.org.au/uploadedFiles/Main/Content/ccchdev/CCCH-The-First-Thousand-Days-An-Evidence-Paper-Summary-September-2017.pdf>

34 Centre for Community Child Health, *The First Thousand Days: An Evidence Paper—Summary*, The Royal Children's Hospital Melbourne, September 2017, p 18, <https://www.rch.org.au/uploadedFiles/Main/Content/ccchdev/CCCH-The-First-Thousand-Days-An-Evidence-Paper-Summary-September-2017.pdf>

35 Anderson, Shauna, 'You know you have a "threenager" when …' *Mamamia*, 5 May 2016, <https://www.mamamia.com.au/you-know-you-have-a-threenager-when/>

36 Biddulph, Stephen, *Raising Boys in the 21st Century*, Finch Publishing, Sydney, 2018, pp 40–41.

37 Stamell, Demeter, 'David Campbell says he and his wife Lisa were at "war" with their "Threenage" twins', *Mamamia*, 1 April 2018, <https://www.mamamia.com.au/david-campbell-kids/>

38 Roberts, Lindsey M., 'Navigating the choppy waters of life with a "threenager"', *The Washington Post*, 17 August 2016, <https://www.washingtonpost.com/news/parenting/wp/2016/08/17/navigating-the-choppy-waters-of-life-with-a-threenager/?utm_term=.487c12ed7ecb>

39 Fattal, Isabel, 'Why Toddlers Deserve More Respect', *The Atlantic*, 13 December 2017, <https://www.theatlantic.com/education/archive/2017/12/the-myth-of-the-terrible-twos/548282/>

40 Steinbeck, Kate, 'Health Check: do boys really have a testosterone spurt at age four?', *The Conversation*, 23 October 2017, <https://theconversation.com/health-check-do-boys-really-have-a-testosterone-spurt-at-age-four-82587>

41 Steinbeck, Kate, 'Health Check: do boys really have a testosterone spurt at age four?', *The Conversation*, 23 October 2017, <https://theconversation.com/health-check-do-boys-really-have-a-testosterone-spurt-at-age-four-82587>; Biddulph, Stephen, *Raising Boys in the 21st Century*, Finch Publishing, Sydney, 2018, p 43.

42 Organization for Economic Cooperation and Development, *Education at a Glance 2019*, OECD Publishing, B1 2019, p148, <https://read.oecd-ilibrary.org/education/education-at-a-glance-2019_f8d7880d-en#page150>

43 Pressick-Kilborn, Kimberley, 'The "right" age to start school varies for each child', *The Conversation*, 25 June 2018, <https://theconversation.com/the-right-age-to-start-school-varies-for-each-child-98704>; Organization for Economic Cooperation and Development, *Education at a Glance 2019*, OECD Publishing, B1 2019, p148, <https://read.oecd-ilibrary.org/education/education-at-a-glance-2019_f8d7880d-en#page150>

44 Biddulph, Stephen, *Raising Boys in the 21st Century*, Finch Publishing, Sydney, 2018, p40, 222; Knapton, Sarah, 'Girls really do mature quicker than boys, scientists find', *The Telegraph*, 20 December 2013, <https://www.telegraph.co.uk/news/science/science-news/10529134/Girls-really-do-mature-quicker-than-boys-scientists-find.html>

45 9Honey, 'Raising boys: crucial tips for parents raising young men', *9Honey*, 2018, <https://honey.nine.com.au/2018/05/29/11/26/raising-boys>

46 Hanly, Mark et al, 'School starting age and child development in a state-wide, population-level cohort of children in their first year of school in New South Wales, Australia', *Early Childhood Research* Quarterly, Volume 48, 3rd Quarter 2019, pp 325–340, https://www.sciencedirect.

com/science/article/pii/S0885200619300110?via%3Dihub; 9Honey, 'Raising boys: crucial tips for parents raising young men', *9Honey*, 2018, <https://honey.nine.com.au/2018/05/29/11/26/raising-boys>; Baker, Jordan and Keoghan, Sarah, '"A bad idea": the perils of starting school too early then repeating', *Sydney Morning Herald*, 3 February 2019, <https://www.smh.com.au/education/a-bad-idea-the-perils-of-starting-school-too-early-then-repeating-20190131-p50uyc.html>; Sahlberg, Pasi, 'When is the best age to start school? How about 7?', *Sydney Morning Herald*, 12 June 2018, <https://www.smh.com.au/education/when-is-the-best-age-to-start-school-how-about-7-20180610-p4zko8.html>

47 Baker, Jordan, '"A gift of time", Children who start school later fare better, study finds', *Sydney Morning Herald*, 9 April 2019, <https://www.smh.com.au/education/a-gift-of-time-children-who-start-school-later-fare-better-study-finds-20190408-p51bw1.html>

48 Baker, Jordan, '"A gift of time", Children who start school later fare better, study finds', *Sydney Morning Herald*, 9 April 2019, <https://www.smh.com.au/education/a-gift-of-time-children-who-start-school-later-fare-better-study-finds-20190408-p51bw1.html>; Hanly Mark et al, 'School starting age and child development in a state-wide, population-level cohort of children in their first year of school in New South Wales, Australia', *Early Childhood Research* Quarterly, Volume 48, 3rd Quarter 2019, p 325-340, <https://www.sciencedirect.com/science/article/pii/S0885200619300110?via%3Dihub>

49 Biddulph, Stephen, *Raising Boys in the 21st Century*, Finch Publishing, Sydney, 2018, p 15.

50 Australian Scholarships Group, 'Metropolitan Australia: Estimated Schooling Costs: Child born in 2019', ASG, 2019, <https://www.asg.com.au/doc/default-source/2019-ASG-Planning-for-Education-Index/2019-australia--metro---child-born-in-2019.pdf?sfvrsn=0>

51 Dunn, Amanda, 'Something is happening to our kids, and it's time we talked about it', *The Bendigo Advertiser*, 30 July 2017, <https://www.bendigoadvertiser.com.au/story/4820987/something-is-happening-to-our-kids/>

52 Dunn, Amanda, 'Something is happening to our kids, and it's time we talked about it', *The Bendigo Advertiser*, 30 July 2017, <https://www.bendigoadvertiser.com.au/story/4820987/something-is-happening-to-our-kids/>

53 Biddulph, Stephen, *Raising Boys in the 21st Century*, Finch Publishing, Sydney, 2018, pp 45–46.

54 *Life Matters*, 'Talkback—are a child's "middle years" more important than we thought?', ABC Radio National, 12 April 2019, <https://www.abc.net.au/radionational/programs/lifematters/talkback:-childs-middle-years/10987338>

55 Biddulph, Stephen, *Raising Boys in the 21st Century*, Finch Publishing, Sydney, 2018, p 40.

56 Biddulph, Stephen, *Raising Boys in the 21st Century*, Finch Publishing, Sydney, 2018, p 23.

57 Biddulph, Stephen, *Raising Boys in the 21st Century*, Finch Publishing, Sydney, 2018, p 23.

58 Biddulph, Stephen, *Raising Boys in the 21st Century*, Finch Publishing, Sydney, 2018, p 47.

59 Magid, Kesson et al, 'Childhood ecology influences salivary testosterone, pubertal age and stature of Bangladeshi UK migrant men', *Nature Ecology & Evolution*, Volume 2, 2018, pp 1146–1154, <https://www.nature.com/articles/s41559-018-0567-6>; Durham University, 'Men's testosterone levels largely determined by childhood environment', Durham University, 25 June 2018, <https://www.dur.ac.uk/news/newsitem/?itemno=35110>; Biddulph, Stephen, *Raising Boys in the 21st Century*, Finch Publishing, Sydney, 2018, p 54.

60 Biddulph, Stephen, *Raising Boys in the 21st Century*, Finch Publishing, Sydney, 2018, p 47; Pain, Clare, 'Teen brains undergo neural pruning', *ABC Science*, 2 April 2012, <https://www.abc.net.au/science/articles/2012/04/02/3467743.htm>; Campbell, Ian et al, 'Sex, puberty, and the timing of sleep EEG measured adolescent brain maturation', *Proceedings of the National Academy of Sciences of the United States of America*, Volume 109, Issue 15, pp 5740–5743, <https://www.pnas.org/content/109/15/5740>

61 Zhou, Christina, 'More Australian adult children are living at home, census data shows', *Domain*, 13 July 2017, <https://www.domain.com.au/news/more-australian-adult-children-are-living-at-home-census-data-shows-20170711-gx8urj/>

6 Getting real about masculinity

1 The Men's Project and Flood, Michael, *The Man Box: A Study on Being a Young Man in Australia*, Jesuit Social Services, Melbourne, 2018, p 6, <https://jss.org.au/wp-content/uploads/2018/10/The-Man-Box-A-study-on-being-a-young-man-in-Australia.pdf>

2 The Men's Project and Flood, Michael, *The Man Box: A Study on Being a Young Man in Australia*, Jesuit Social Services, Melbourne, 2018, p 15 <https://jss.org.au/wp-content/uploads/2018/10/The-Man-Box-A-study-on-being-a-young-man-in-Australia.pdf>

3 The Men's Project and Flood, Michael, *The Man Box: A Study on Being a Young Man in Australia*, Jesuit Social Services, Melbourne, 2018, p 19, <https://jss.org.au/wp-content/uploads/2018/10/The-Man-Box-A-study-on-being-a-young-man-in-Australia.pdf>

4 The Men's Project and Flood, Michael, *The Man Box: A Study on Being a Young Man in Australia*, Jesuit Social Services, Melbourne, 2018, p 15 <https://jss.org.au/wp-content/uploads/2018/10/The-Man-Box-A-study-on-being-a-young-man-in-Australia.pdf>

5 The Men's Project and Flood, Michael, *The Man Box: A Study on Being a Young Man in Australia*, Jesuit Social Services, Melbourne, 2018, p 21, <https://jss.org.au/wp-content/uploads/2018/10/The-Man-Box-A-study-on-being-a-young-man-in-Australia.pdf>

6 The Men's Project and Flood, Michael, *The Man Box: A Study on Being a Young Man in Australia*, Jesuit Social Services, Melbourne, 2018, p 8, <https://jss.org.au/wp-content/uploads/2018/10/The-Man-Box-A-study-on-being-a-young-man-in-Australia.pdf>

7 50/50 by 2030 Foundation, *From Girls to Men: Social Attitudes to Gender Equality in Australia*, University of Canberra, September 2018, p 7, <https://www.5050foundation.edu.au/assets/reports/documents/From-Girls-to-Men.pdf>

8 50/50 by 2030 Foundation, *From Girls to Men: Social Attitudes to Gender Equality in Australia*, University of Canberra, September 2018, p 36, <https://www.5050foundation.edu.au/assets/reports/documents/From-Girls-to-Men.pdf>

9 50/50 by 2030 Foundation, *From Girls to Men: Social Attitudes to Gender Equality in Australia*, University of Canberra, September 2018, p 35, <https://www.5050foundation.edu.au/assets/reports/documents/From-Girls-to-Men.pdf>

10 Australia's National Resource Organisation for Women's Safety Limited, *National Community Attitudes towards Violence Against Women Survey (NCAS)*, ANROWS, 2017, <https://www.anrows.org.au/research-program/ncas/>

11 Australia's National Resource Organisation for Women's Safety Limited, *Young Australians' attitudes to violence against women and gender equality: Findings from the 2017 National Community Attitudes towards Violence Against Women Survey (NCAS)*, ANROWS Insights, Issue 01, 2019, p 24, 27, <https://ncas.anrows.org.au/wp-content/uploads/2019/05/2017NCAS-Youth-SubReport.pdf>

12 Davey, Melissa, 'One in seven young Australians say rape justified if women change their mind, study finds', *The Guardian*, 22 May 2019,

<https://www.theguardian.com/australia-news/2019/may/22/one-in-seven-young-australians-say-justified-if-women-change-their-mind-study-finds>; Australia's National Resource Organisation for Women's Safety Limited, *Young Australians' attitudes to violence against women and gender equality: Findings from the 2017 National Community Attitudes towards Violence Against Women Survey (NCAS)*, ANROWS Insights, Issue 01, 2019, p 31, <https://ncas.anrows.org.au/wp-content/uploads/2019/05/2017NCAS-Youth-SubReport.pdf>

13 White Ribbon Canada, 'Boys Don't Cry: White Ribbon PSA', YouTube, 26 February 2019, <https://www.youtube.com/watch?v=fjo-hwAKcas>

14 Biddulph, Stephen, *Raising Boys in the 21st Century*, Finch Publishing, Sydney, 2018, p 15.

15 Biddulph, Stephen, *Raising Boys in the 21st Century*, Finch Publishing, Sydney, 2018, pp 40–45.

16 Box Office Mojo, 'Marvel Cinematic Universe', *Box Office Mojo*, 2019, <https://www.boxofficemojo.com/franchises/chart/?id=avengers.htm>

17 Biddulph, Stephen, *Raising Boys in the 21st Century*, Finch Publishing, Sydney, 2018, pp 60–61.

18 Klein, Ezra, 'Alison Gopnik changed how I think about love', *Vox*, 13 June 2019, <https://www.vox.com/podcasts/2019/6/13/18677595/alison-gopnik-changed-how-i-think-about-love>

19 Biddulph, Stephen, 'The trouble with men', *Sydney Morning Herald*, 4 April 2018, <https://www.smh.com.au/lifestyle/life-and-relationships/the-trouble-with-men-20180404-p4z7pa.html>

20 Molloy, Shannon, 'The men's mental health crisis Australia can no longer ignore—six male suicides a day', *News.com.au*, 10 October 2018, <https://www.news.com.au/lifestyle/health/mind/the-mens-mental-health-crisis-australia-can-no-longer-ignore-six-male-suicides-a-day/news-story/cc77b01572676c8b140424777c3ff642>

21 Beyond Blue, 'Men', Beyond Blue, 2019, <https://www.beyondblue.org.au/who-does-it-affect/men>

22 Campanella, Nas, 'The number of boys using Kids Helpline is falling', *Hack*, Triple J, 17 April 2019, <https://www.abc.net.au/triplej/programs/hack/number-of-boys-using-kids-helpline-declining/11020030>

23 Kids Helpline, *Key Insights 2018*, yourtown, 2019, <https://www.yourtown.com.au/sites/default/files/document/KHL%20Insights%202018%20Infographic.pdf>

24 Kids Helpline, *Key Insights 2018*, yourtown, 2019, <https://www.yourtown.com.au/sites/default/files/document/KHL%20Insights%202018%20Infographic.pdf>

7 The love quotient and free will

1 Gopnik, Alison, *The Gardener and the Carpenter: What the New Science of Child Development Tells Us about the Relationship between Parents and Children*, The Bodley Head, London, 2016, p 18.

2 Locke, Judith, *The Bonsai Child: Why Modern Parenting Limits Children's Potential and Practical Strategies to Turn It Around*, Judith Locke, Brisbane, 2015; Marriner, Cosima, 'Bonsai parenting: Why so many children end up in therapy', *Sydney Morning Herald*, 8 August 2015, <https://www.smh.com.au/national/why-so-many-children-are-ending-up-in-therapy-20150807-giu0zv.html>

3 See also similar statements in O'Brien, Kerry, *Keating*, ABC, Episode 1, September 2015, <https://www.abc.net.au/tv/programs/keating/>

4 Wade, Catherine and Green, Julie, 'Children's well-being goes hand in hand with their dads' mental health', *The Conversation*, 31 August 2018, <https://theconversation.com/childrens-well-being-goes-hand-in-hand-with-their-dads-mental-health-102347>; Cabrera, Natasha J., 'Fathers Are Parents, Too! Widening the Lens on Parenting for Children's Development', 8 January 2018, *Child Development Perspectives*, Volume 12, Issue 3, pp 152–157, <https://onlinelibrary.wiley.com/doi/full/10.1111/cdep.12275>

5 Hosseini, Sarah, '"Give Him Something For Boys": Kid's Face-Painter Tells A Story That Will Wreck You', *Scary Mommy*, 13 August 2017, <https://www.scarymommy.com/twitter-face-paint-male-violence/>

6 Maglaty, Jeanne, 'When Did Girls Start Wearing Pink?', *Smithsonian Magazine*, 7 April 2011, <https://www.smithsonianmag.com/arts-culture/when-did-girls-start-wearing-pink-1370097/?c=y&page=1>

7 Maglaty, Jeanne, 'When Did Girls Start Wearing Pink?', *Smithsonian Magazine*, 7 April 2011, <https://www.smithsonianmag.com/arts-culture/when-did-girls-start-wearing-pink-1370097/?c=y&page=1>

8 CKNW Kids' Fund, 'Pink Shirt Day', Pink Shirt Day Canada, 2019, <https://www.pinkshirtday.ca/about>

9 The Scone Advocate, 'Upper Hunter Shire Council hosting Pink Shirt Day this month to send anti-bullying message', *The Scone Advocate*, 8 March 2019, <https://www.sconeadvocate.com.au/story/5944279/time-to-stand-up-against-bullying/>

10 Fury, Alexander, 'Men's Grooming is Now a Multi-Billion Pound Worldwide Industry', *The Independent*, 14 January 2016, <https://www.independent.co.uk/life-style/fashion/features/mens-grooming-is-now-a-multi-billion-pound-worldwide-industry-a6813196.html>

11 Urbane Man, 'Australia's Metro Men—Grooming Trends', *Urbane Men*, 24 January 2019, <https://urbaneman.com.au/australias-metro-mens-grooming-trends/>

12 See the website for more information—War Paint. For Men, <https://warpaintformen.com/>

13 Marks, Lucy, 'Boys are born to prefer dolls over masculine toys like cars', *Sydney Morning Herald*, 5 January 2014, <https://www.smh.com.au/national/boys-are-born-to-prefer-dolls-over-masculine-toys-like-cars-20140104-30aq0.html>; Escudero, Paola et al, 'Sex Related preferences for real and doll faces versus real and toy objects in young infants and adults', *Journal of Experimental Child Psychology*, Volume 116, Issue 2, October 2013, pp 367–379, <https://www.sciencedirect.com/science/article/abs/pii/S0022096513001367?via%3Dihub>

14 Smith, Michelle, 'Barbie for boys? The gendered tyranny of the toy store', *The Conversation*, 4 December 2014, <https://theconversation.com/barbie-for-boys-the-gendered-tyranny-of-the-toy-store-34979>

15 Oksman, Olga, 'Are gendered toys harming childhood development?', *The Guardian*, 29 May 2016, <https://www.theguardian.com/lifeandstyle/2016/may/28/toys-kids-girls-boys-childhood-development-gender-research>

16 Associated Foreign Press, 'Girls with guns in 'gender neutral' toy catalogue', *ABC News*, 24 November 2012, <https://www.abc.net.au/news/2012-11-24/girls-with-guns-in-27gender-nuetral27-toy-catalogue/4390080>

17 Crouch, David, 'Toys R Us's Stockholm superstore goes gender neutral', *The Guardian*, 24 December 2013, <https://www.theguardian.com/world/2013/dec/23/toys-r-us-stockholm-gender-neutral>

18 Let Toys Be Toys, 'Why it Matters', Let Toys Be Toys, 2019, <http://lettoysbetoys.org.uk/why-it-matters/>

19 See also thread by Let Toys Be Toys on Twitter outlining their campaign, 2 May 2019, <https://twitter.com/LetToysBeToys/status/1123832128356147200>

20 Let Toys Be Toys, 'Progress from toy retailers, time for manufacturers to catch up', Let Toys Be Toys, 15 December 2016, <http://lettoysbetoys.org.uk/retailers-progress-toy-manufacturers-catch-up/>

21 Bainbridge, Jason, 'Beyond pink and blue: the quiet rise of gender-neutral toys', *The Conversation*, 6 June 2018, <https://theconversation.com/beyond-pink-and-blue-the-quiet-rise-of-gender-neutral-toys-95147>

22 Bainbridge, Jason, 'Beyond pink and blue: the quiet rise of gender-neutral toys', *The Conversation*, 6 June 2018, <https://theconversation.com/beyond-pink-and-blue-the-quiet-rise-of-gender-neutral-toys-95147>

23 The Daily Buzz, 'Dad dances with son to Frozen theme', YouTube, 25 January 2019, <https://www.youtube.com/watch?v=Jn47eRpqz4A>

24 Khalil, Shireen, 'Video of father and son dancing around as Elsa from Frozen has gone viral', *News.com.au*, 28 January 2019, <https://www.news.com.au/lifestyle/parenting/kids/video-of-father-and-son-dancing-around-as-elsa-from-frozen-has-gone-viral/news-story/40b773bfde1be0ff894e172ad4418451>

25 Good Morning Britain, 'Video of Father and Son Dancing as Elsa From Frozen Goes Viral', YouTube, 28 January 2019, <https://www.youtube.com/watch?v=BI7X8C-sLsw>

26 Roy Morgan, 'Wonder Woman top superhero for Young Australians', Roy Morgan, 24 September 2018, <http://www.roymorgan.com/findings/7737-young-australians-survey-june-2018-201809210904>

27 Staemer, Kimberly, 'What Is the Typical Career of a Ballet Dancer?', *Career Trend*, 30 December 2018, <https://careertrend.com/typical-career-ballet-dancer-15045.html>

28 Lawson, Valerie, 'Danseur documentary takes on stigma and bullying of boys in ballet', *Sydney Morning Herald*, 1 October 2018, <https://www.smh.com.au/entertainment/dance/youre-not-alone-documentary-takes-on-stigma-and-bullying-of-boys-in-ballet-20181001-h1630g.html>; See also the website for *Danseur*, produced and directed by Scott K. Gormley, 2018, <http://danseurmovie.com/>

29 Struthers, Karen, 'Getting in early to avoid gender stereotyping careers', *The Conversation*, 16 August 2015, <https://theconversation.com/getting-in-early-to-avoid-gender-stereotyping-careers-39867>

30 Baker, Jordan, 'Love letter to Bandit: How Bluey's brilliant dad upped my game at playtime', *Sydney Morning Herald*, 7 April 2019, <https://www.smh.com.au/education/love-letter-to-bandit-how-bluey-s-brilliant-dad-upped-my-game-at-playtime-20190406-p51bgi.html>

31 Public Schools NSW, 'The Case for Career-Related Learning in Primary Schools', Education & Communities NSW, 2014, p 2, <https://www.det.nsw.edu.au/vetinschools/documents/schooltowork/Career-Related_Learning_in_Primary_Schools_2014%20.pdf>

32 MullenLowe Group, 'Inspiring The Future—Redraw The Balance', YouTube, 15 March 2016, <https://www.youtube.com/watch?v=qv8VZVP5csA>

33 Workplace Gender Equality Agency, 'International Women's Day 2019: key facts about women and work', WGEA, 8 March 2019, <https://www.wgea.gov.au/newsroom/latest-news/international-womens-day-2019-key-facts-about-women-and-work>

34 Workplace Gender Equality Agency, 'Gender Segregation in Australia's Workforce', WGEA, 17 April 2019, <https://www.wgea.gov.au/data/fact-sheets/gender-segregation-in-australias-workforce>

35 Foundation for Young Australians, *The New Work Order: Ensuring young Australians have skills and experience for the jobs of the future, not the past,* FYA, August 2015, p 12, <https://www.fya.org.au/wp-content/uploads/2015/08/fya-future-of-work-report-final-lr.pdf>

36 Flanagan, Frances, 'A consensus for care', *Inside Story*, 15 May 2017, <https://insidestory.org.au/a-consensus-for-care/>

37 Vedantam, Shankar, 'Why More Men Don't Get Into The Field of Nursing', *National Public Radio*, United States, 2 October 2018, <https://www.npr.org/2018/10/02/653570048/why-more-men-dont-get-into-the-field-of-nursing>

38 Vedantam, Shankar, '"Man Up": How A Fear Of Appearing Feminine Restricts Men, And Affects Us All', *National Public Radio*, United States, 1 October 2018, <https://www.npr.org/2018/10/01/653339162/-man-up-how-a-fear-of-appearing-feminine-restricts-men-and-affects-us-all>

39 Vedantam, Shankar, '"Man Up": How A Fear Of Appearing Feminine Restricts Men, And Affects Us All', *National Public Radio*, United States, 1 October 2018, <https://www.npr.org/2018/10/01/653339162/-man-up-how-a-fear-of-appearing-feminine-restricts-men-and-affects-us-all>; see also Bosson, Jennifer and Vandello, Joseph, 'Hard Won and Easily Lost: A Review and Synthesis of Theory and Research on Precarious Manhood', *Psychology of Men & Masculinity*, Volume 14, Number 2, 2013, pp 101–113, <https://www.apa.org/pubs/journals/features/men-a0029826.pdf>

40 Ford, Clementine, 'Clementine Ford: For Pete's Sake, Let Your Boys Drink Pink Milk', *10Daily*, 3 July 2019, <https://10daily.com.au/views/a190703odayk/clementine-ford-for-petes-sake-let-your-boys-drink-pink-milk-20190703>

41 Pascoe, Bruce, *Dark Emu, Black Seeds: Agriculture or Accident?*, Magabala Books, Broome, 2014.

42 Pascoe, Bruce, 'Teach your children to rebel. Teach your children to doubt', *The Guardian*, 1 June 2019, <https://www.theguardian.com/books/2019/jun/01/bruce-pascoe-teach-your-children-to-rebel-teach-your-children-to-doubt>

43 Guardian News, 'Heartbreaking video of schoolboy Keaton Jones recounting being bullied', YouTube, 11 December 2017, <https://www.youtube.com/watch?v=kz1xzBYppW8>

44 Lang, Cady, '*Captain America* Star Chris Evans Invites Bullied Student to the *Avengers* Premiere', *Time*, 11 December 2017, <https://time.com/5058967/chris-evans-invites-bullied-student-keaton-jones-to-avengers-infinity-war-premiere/>

8   Having the wolf by the ear: tech and the internet

1   Thomas Jefferson Foundation, 'Famous Jefferson Quotes', citing Ford, Paul Leicester (editor), *The Works of Thomas Jefferson, Volume 12*, G. P. Putnam's Sons, New York, 1905, p 159, <https://www.monticello.org/site/research-and-collections/famous-jefferson-quotes>

2   Angus, Chris, 'Cyberbullying of children', New South Wales Parliamentary Research Service', March 2016, pp 5–6, <https://www.parliament. nsw.gov.au/researchpapers/Documents/cyberbullying-of-children/ Cyberbullying%20of%20Children.pdf>; Australian Institute of Family Studies, 'Children who bully at school: Child Family Community Australia (CFCA) Paper No. 27', AIFS, July 2014, <https://aifs.gov.au/cfca/ publications/children-who-bully-school/understanding-school-bullying>; Victoria University, 'Bullying & cyberbullying', Victoria University, Melbourne, <https://www.vu.edu.au/about-vu/facilities-services/safer-community/concerning-threatening-or-inappropriate-behaviour/bullying-cyberbullying>; Safe and Supportive School Communities Working Group, 'Facts and figures: Bullying', *Bullying. No Way!*, <https://bullyingnoway.gov. au/WhatIsBullying/FactsAndFigures>

3   Angus, Chris, 'Cyberbullying of children', New South Wales Parliamentary Research Service', March 2016, pp 6–7, <https://www.parliament. nsw.gov.au/researchpapers/Documents/cyberbullying-of-children/ Cyberbullying%20of%20Children.pdf>; Katz, Ilan et al, *Research on youth exposure to, and management of, cyberbullying incidents in Australia: Synthesis report*, University of New South Wales, June 2014, pp 3, 5, <https://www. arts.unsw.edu.au/sites/default/files/documents/Youth_exposure_to_and_ management_of_cyberbullying_in_Australia__Synthesis_report.pdf>

4   Victoria University, 'Bullying & cyberbullying', Victoria University, Melbourne, <https://www.vu.edu.au/about-vu/facilities-services/safer-community/concerning-threatening-or-inappropriate-behaviour/bullying-cyberbullying>

5   Safe and Supportive School Communities Working Group, 'Facts and figures: Bullying', *Bullying. No Way!*, <https://bullyingnoway.gov.au/ WhatIsBullying/FactsAndFigures>

6   Safe and Supportive School Communities Working Group, 'Facts and figures: Bullying', *Bullying. No Way!*, <https://bullyingnoway.gov.au/ WhatIsBullying/FactsAndFigures>

7   Angus, Chris, 'Cyberbullying of children', New South Wales Parliamentary Research Service', March 2016, pp 2–3, <https://www.parliament. nsw.gov.au/researchpapers/Documents/cyberbullying-of-children/ Cyberbullying%20of%20Children.pdf>

8   Kontominas, Bellinda, 'Online trolls and cyberbullies in NSW face up to five years in jail under law change', *ABC News*, 7 October 2018, <https://www.abc.net.au/news/2018-10-07/online-trolls-and-cyberbullies-in-nsw-face-tougher-new-laws/10348246>

9   Katz, Ilan et al, *Research on youth exposure to, and management of, cyberbullying incidents in Australia: Synthesis report*, University of New South Wales, June 2014, p 3, <https://www.arts.unsw.edu.au/sites/default/files/documents/Youth_exposure_to_and_management_of_cyberbullying_in_Australia__Synthesis_report.pdf>

10 Australian Women Against Violence Alliance, 'Gender lens to cyberbullying', AWAVA, 15 March 2018, <https://awava.org.au/2018/03/15/blog/gender-lens-cyberbullying?doing_wp_cron=1570575234.1205151081085205078125>

11 Katz, Ilan et al, *Research on youth exposure to, and management of, cyberbullying incidents in Australia: Synthesis report*, University of New South Wales, June 2014, p 5, <https://www.arts.unsw.edu.au/sites/default/files/documents/Youth_exposure_to_and_management_of_cyberbullying_in_Australia__Synthesis_report.pdf>

12 Rigby, Ken and Johnson, Kaye, *The Prevalence and Effectiveness of Anti-Bullying Strategies Employed in Australian Schools*, University of South Australia, 2016, p 63, <https://www.unisa.edu.au/siteassets/episerver-6-files/global/eass/eds/184856-anti-bullying-report-final-3large.pdf>

13 Gannon, Genevieve, 'Sticks and stones and mobile phones: The horrible truth about cyber bullying and its victims', *The Australian Women's Weekly*, 2 May 2018, <https://www.nowtolove.com.au/lifestyle/daily-life/cyberbullying-victims-australia-48007>

14 Abi, Jo, 'Father of dead teen urges action over cyberbullying', *9Honey*, February 2019, <https://honey.nine.com.au/latest/cyberbullying-melbourne-teenager-suicide/d583f188-ddf0-40b1-87e2-f4a883c5c76d>

15 Bully Zero, 'Our Vision', Bully Zero, <https://bullyzero.org.au/aboutus/our-story/>; Abi, Jo, 'Father of dead teen urges action over cyberbullying', *9Honey*, February 2019, <https://honey.nine.com.au/latest/cyberbullying-melbourne-teenager-suicide/d583f188-ddf0-40b1-87e2-f4a883c5c76d>

16 Precel, Nicole, 'Ursula didn't know what cyber flashing was until the day at the museum', *Sydney Morning Herald*, 20 June 2019, <https://www.smh.com.au/national/ursula-didn-t-know-what-cyber-flashing-was-until-the-day-at-the-museum-20190512-p51mm6.html>

17 Plan International, *"Don't Send Me That Pic": Australian young women and girls report online abuse and harassment are endemic*, Plan International,

March 2016, p 2, <https://www.plan.org.au/-/media/plan/documents/reports/dont-send-me-that-pic.pdf>

18   Plan International, *"Don't Send Me That Pic": Australian young women and girls report online abuse and harassment are endemic*, Plan International, March 2016, p 2, <https://www.plan.org.au/-/media/plan/documents/reports/dont-send-me-that-pic.pdf>

19   Australian Institute of Health and Welfare, *Family, domestic and sexual violence in Australia*, AIHW, 2018, p 17, <https://www.aihw.gov.au/getmedia/d1a8d479-a39a-48c1-bbe2-4b27c7a321e0/aihw-fdv-02.pdf.aspx?inline=true>

20   Foo, Kimberly, '2-year-old girl in China with smartphone addiction develops severe myopia of 900 degrees', *Asia One*, 11 June 2019, <https://www.asiaone.com/china/2-year-old-girl-china-smartphone-addiction-develops-severe-myopia-900-degrees>

21   Molloy, Shannon, 'Nomophobia: The word of the year has been crowned but chances are you've never heard of it', *News.com.au*, 31 December 2018, <https://www.news.com.au/lifestyle/health/nomophobia-the-word-of-the-year-has-been-crowned-but-chances-are-youve-never-heard-it/news-story/3f791f5d32e0379f71cc6ea654dbfda7>

22   Elmore, Tim, 'Nomophobia: A Rising Trend in Students', *Psychology Today*, 18 September 2014, <https://www.psychologytoday.com/us/blog/artificial-maturity/201409/nomophobia-rising-trend-in-students>

23   Roy Morgan, '9 in 10 Aussie teens now have a mobile (and most are already on to their second or subsequent handset)', Roy Morgan, 22 August 2016, <http://www.roymorgan.com/findings/6929-australian-teenagers-and-their-mobile-phones-june-2016-201608220922>

24   Stoneham, Bray, 'This is How Long the Average Australian Spends Using Their Phone Every Year', *Men's Health*, 7 February 2017, <https://www.menshealth.com.au/time-aussies-spend-on-phone>

25   Bragazzi, Nicola and Del Puente, Giovanni, 'A proposal for including nomophobia in the new DSM-V', *Psychology Research and Behaviour Management*, Volume 7, 2014, pp 155–160, <https://www.dovepress.com/a-proposal-for-including-nomophobia-in-the-new-dsm-v-peer-reviewed-article-PRBM>

26   Han, Seunghee and Kim, Ki Joon, 'Understanding Nomophobia: Structural Equation Modeling and Semantic Network Analysis of Smartphone Separation Anxiety', *Cyberpsychology, Behaviour, and Social Networking*, Volume 20, Number 7, July 2017, <https://www.liebertpub.com/doi/abs/10.1089/cyber.2017.0113?journalCode=cyber#>

27 Oviedo-Trespalacios, Oscar et al, 'Problematic Use of Mobile Phones in Australia … Is It Getting Worse?', *Frontiers in Psychiatry*, 12 March 2019, <https://www.frontiersin.org/articles/10.3389/fpsyt.2019.00105/full>

28 Oviedo-Trespalacios, Oscar et al, 'Problematic Use of Mobile Phones in Australia … Is It Getting Worse?', *Frontiers in Psychiatry*, 12 March 2019, <https://www.frontiersin.org/articles/10.3389/fpsyt.2019.00105/full>

29 Items 6 and Items 18 on the survey respectively as cited in Oviedo-Trespalacios, Oscar et al, 'Problematic Use of Mobile Phones in Australia … Is It Getting Worse?', *Frontiers in Psychiatry*, 12 March 2019, <https://www.frontiersin.org/articles/10.3389/fpsyt.2019.00105/full>

30 Haynes, Trevor, 'Dopamine, Smartphones & You: A battle for your time', Harvard University, 1 May 2018, <http://sitn.hms.harvard.edu/flash/2018/dopamine-smartphones-battle-time/>

31 Cooper, Anderson, 'What is "Brain Hacking"? Tech Insiders on Why You Should Care', *CBS News*, 9 April 2017, <https://www.cbsnews.com/news/brain-hacking-tech-insiders-60-minutes/>

32 Liebert, Mary Ann, 'Understanding smartphone separation anxiety and what smartphones meant to people', Phys.Org, 14 August 2017, <https://phys.org/news/2017-08-smartphone-anxiety-smartphones-people.html>

33 Australian Psychological Society, *Stress & wellbeing: How Australians are Coping with Life*, APS, November 2015, <https://www.headsup.org.au/docs/default-source/default-document-library/stress-and-wellbeing-in-australia-report.pdf?sfvrsn=7f08274d_4>

34 Australian Psychological Society, *Stress & wellbeing: How Australians are Coping with Life*, APS, November 2015, p 6, <https://www.headsup.org.au/docs/default-source/default-document-library/stress-and-wellbeing-in-australia-report.pdf?sfvrsn=7f08274d_4>

35 Australian Psychological Society, *Stress & wellbeing: How Australians are Coping with Life*, APS, November 2015, pp 31–32, <https://www.headsup.org.au/docs/default-source/default-document-library/stress-and-wellbeing-in-australia-report.pdf?sfvrsn=7f08274d_4>

36 Australian Psychological Society, *Stress & wellbeing: How Australians are Coping with Life*, APS, November 2015, p 34, <https://www.headsup.org.au/docs/default-source/default-document-library/stress-and-wellbeing-in-australia-report.pdf?sfvrsn=7f08274d_4>

37 Australian Psychological Society, *Stress & wellbeing: How Australians are Coping with Life*, APS, November 2015, p 32, <https://www.headsup.org.au/docs/default-source/default-document-library/stress-and-wellbeing-in-australia-report.pdf?sfvrsn=7f08274d_4>

38 Australian Psychological Society, *Stress & wellbeing: How Australians are Coping with Life*, APS, November 2015, p 33, <https://www.headsup.org.au/docs/default-source/default-document-library/stress-and-wellbeing-in-australia-report.pdf?sfvrsn=7f08274d_4>

39 Damjanovic, Dijana and Dayman, Isabel, '#FOMO leading to higher levels of depression, anxiety for heavy social media users', *ABC News*, 8 November 2015, <https://www.abc.net.au/news/2015-11-08/wellbeing-survey-finds-teens-feeling-left-out-on-social-media/6921780>

40 Jenkinson, Rebecca et al, 'Weighing up the odds: Sports betting and young men—Research Summary', Australian Institute of Family Studies, April 2019, <https://aifs.gov.au/agrc/publications/weighing-odds-sports-betting-and-young-men?utm_source=AIFS+Mailing+List&utm_campaign=8475343f7b-EMAIL_CAMPAIGN_2019_04_29_02_16&utm_medium=email&utm_term=0_3ad49f5cbc-8475343f7b-211280309

41 Evershed, Nick, 'Problem gambling affects almost 200,000 Australians, survey shows', *The Guardian*, 2 August 2017, <https://www.theguardian.com/australia-news/2017/aug/02/problem-gambling-affects-200000-australians-survey-shows>

42 Australian Gambling Research Centre, 'The impact of gambling problems on families', Discussion Paper No 1, Australian Institute of Family Studies, November 2014, <https://aifs.gov.au/agrc/publications/impact-gambling-problems-families/what-are-impacts-gambling-problems-families>; Dowling, N.A. et al, 'Problem gambling and family violence: Findings from a population-representative study', *Journal of Behavioural Addictions*, Volume 7, Issue 3, September 2018, pp 806–813, <https://www.ncbi.nlm.nih.gov/pubmed/30238783>

43 Gibson, Caitlin, 'The next level', *The Washington Post*, 7 December 2016, <https://www.washingtonpost.com/sf/style/2016/12/07/video-games-are-more-addictive-than-ever-this-is-what-happens-when-kids-cant-turn-them-off/?noredirect=on&utm_term=.60b8d67a57ba>

44 eSafety Commissioner, *State of Play—Youth and Online Gaming in Australia*, Office of the eSafety Commissioner, 2017, <https://www.esafety.gov.au/about-the-office/research-library/youth-online-gaming>

45 eSafety Commissioner, *State of Play—Youth and Online Gaming in Australia*, Office of the eSafety Commissioner, 5 March 2018, pp 6, 8, <https://www.esafety.gov.au/-/media/cesc/documents/corporate-office/youth_and_gaming_doc.docx p 4>

46 Clarke, Alice, 'The state of Australian gamers in 2019', *Sydney Morning Herald*, 4 August 2019, <https://www.smh.com.au/technology/video-games/the-state-of-australian-gamers-in-2019-20190801-p52cuk.html>

47 Shontell, Alyson, 'Twitch CEO: Here's Why We Sold to Amazon for $US970 Million', *Business Insider*, 26 August 2014, <https://www.businessinsider.com.au/twitch-ceo-heres-why-we-sold-to-amazon-for-970-million-2014-8?r=US&IR=T>

48 Iqbal, Mansoor, 'Twitch Revenue and Usage Statistics (2019)', Business of Apps, 27 February 2019, <https://www.businessofapps.com/data/twitch-statistics/>

49 Gibson, Caitlin, 'The next level', *The Washington Post*, 7 December 2016, <https://www.washingtonpost.com/sf/style/2016/12/07/video-games-are-more-addictive-than-ever-this-is-what-happens-when-kids-cant-turn-them-off/?noredirect=on&utm_term=.60b8d67a57ba>; Illinois Institute for Addiction Recovery, 'What is Video-game addiction?', IIAR, <http://www.addictionrecov.org/Addictions/?AID=45>; Radiological Society of North America, 'Online gaming addiction in men affects brain's impulse control', *ScienceDaily*, 28 November 2018, <https://www.sciencedaily.com/releases/2018/11/181128082640.htm>

50 Lindmeier, Christian, 'WHO releases new International Classification of Diseases (ICD 11)', World Health Organization, 18 June 2018, <https://www.who.int/news-room/detail/18-06-2018-who-releases-new-international-classification-of-diseases-(icd-11)>

51 Gibson, Caitlin, 'The next level', *The Washington Post*, 7 December 2016, <https://www.washingtonpost.com/sf/style/2016/12/07/video-games-are-more-addictive-than-ever-this-is-what-happens-when-kids-cant-turn-them-off/?noredirect=on&utm_term=.60b8d67a57ba>

52 reSTART, 'Screentime. Gaming. Smartphones: Helping teens and families connect with life and each other', reSTART, <https://www.netaddictionrecovery.com/services/program-for-teens/>; reSTART, 'We founded the first ever internet gaming addiction treatment center in the nation', reSTART, <https://www.netaddictionrecovery.com/about-restart-tech-treatment/>

53 Dudley-Nicholson, Jennifer, 'Fortnite addiction is destroying a new generation of underage Aussie kids', *Kidspot*, 27 May 2019, <https://www.kidspot.com.au/news/fortnite-addiction-is-destroying-a-new-generation-of-underage-aussie-kids/news-story/1e71f19ce22f15ebde9a1a446c0f6c5c>

54 50/50 by 2030 Foundation, *From Girls to Men: Social Attitudes to Gender Equality in Australia*, University of Canberra, September 2018, p 13, <https://www.5050foundation.edu.au/assets/reports/documents/From-Girls-to-Men.pdf>

55 50/50 by 2030 Foundation, *From Girls to Men: Social Attitudes to Gender Equality in Australia*, University of Canberra, September 2018, p 31,

<https://www.5050foundation.edu.au/assets/reports/documents/From-Girls-to-Men.pdf>

56 FeministFrequency, 'Damsel in Distress: Part 1—Tropes vs Women in Video Games', YouTube, 7 March 2013, <https://www.youtube.com/watch?v=X6p5AZp7r_Q&feature=youtu.be>

57 FeministFrequency, 'Ms. Male Character—Tropes vs Women in Video Games', YouTube, 18 November 2013, <https://www.youtube.com/watch?v=eYqYLfm1rWA&feature=youtu.be>

58 FeministFrequency, 'Women as Background Decoration: Part 2—Tropes vs Women in Video Games', YouTube, 25 August 2014, <https://youtu.be/5i_RPr9DwMA>

59 FeministFrequency, 'Women as Background Decoration: Part 2—Tropes vs Women in Video Games', YouTube, 25 August 2014, <https://youtu.be/5i_RPr9DwMA>

60 Shen, Cuihua and Ratan, Rabindra, 'Debunking one of the biggest stereotypes about women in the gaming community', *The Conversation*, 7 July 2016, <https://theconversation.com/debunking-one-of-the-biggest-stereotypes-about-women-in-the-gaming-community-60033>

61 Shen, Cuihua and Ratan, Rabindra, 'Debunking one of the biggest stereotypes about women in the gaming community', *The Conversation*, 7 July 2016, <https://theconversation.com/debunking-one-of-the-biggest-stereotypes-about-women-in-the-gaming-community-60033>

62 Wong, Julia Carrie, 'Women considered better coders—but only if they hide their gender', *The Guardian*, 12 February 2016, <https://www.theguardian.com/technology/2016/feb/12/women-considered-better-coders-hide-gender-github>

63 Parkin, Simon, 'Zoë Quinn's Depression Quest', *The New Yorker*, 9 September 2014, <https://www.newyorker.com/tech/annals-of-technology/zoe-quinns-depression-quest>

64 Parkin, Simon, 'Zoe Quinn's Depression Quest', *The New Yorker*, 9 September 2014, <https://www.newyorker.com/tech/annals-of-technology/zoe-quinns-depression-quest>

65 Parkin, Simon, 'Zoe Quinn's Depression Quest', *The New Yorker*, 9 September 2014, <https://www.newyorker.com/tech/annals-of-technology/zoe-quinns-depression-quest>

66 Hathaway, Jay, 'What Is Gamergate, and Why? An Explainer for Non-Geeks', *Gawker*, 10 October 2014, <https://gawker.com/what-is-gamergate-and-why-an-explainer-for-non-geeks-1642909080>

67 Cox, Carolyn, 'Female Game Journalists Quit Over Harassment, #GamerGate Harms Women', *The Mary Sue*, 4 September 2014, <https://www.themarysue.com/gamergate-harms-women/>

68 McDonald, Soraya Nadia, '"Gamergate": Feminist video game critic Anita Sarkeesian cancels Utah lecture after threat', *The Washington Post*, 15 October 2014, <https://www.washingtonpost.com/news/morning-mix/wp/2014/10/15/gamergate-feminist-video-game-critic-anita-sarkeesian-cancels-utah-lecture-after-threat-citing-police-inability-to-prevent-concealed-weapons-at-event/?utm_term=.df9bb8b280d0>

69 McDonald, Soraya Nadia, 'Gaming vlogger Anita Sarkeesian is forced from home after receiving harrowing death threats', *The Washington Post*, 29 August 2014, <https://www.washingtonpost.com/news/morning-mix/wp/2014/08/29/gaming-vlogger-anita-sarkeesian-is-forced-from-home-after-receiving-harrowing-death-threats/?utm_term=.ee27565e9cd7>

70 Beauchamp, Zack, 'Our incel problem', *Vox*, 23 April 2019, <https://www.vox.com/the-highlight/2019/4/16/18287446/incel-definition-reddit>

71 Jane, Emma, 'Stacys, Brads and "reverse rape": inside the terrifying world of "incels"', *ABC News*, 27 April 2018, <https://www.abc.net.au/news/2018-04-27/incels-inside-their-terrifying-online-world/9700932>

72 Beauchamp, Zack, 'Our incel problem', *Vox*, 23 April 2019, <https://www.vox.com/the-highlight/2019/4/16/18287446/incel-definition-reddit>

73 Jane, Emma, 'Stacys, Brads and "reverse rape": inside the terrifying world of "incels"', *ABC News*, 27 April 2018, <https://www.abc.net.au/news/2018-04-27/incels-inside-their-terrifying-online-world/9700932>

74 Beauchamp, Zack, 'Our incel problem', *Vox*, 23 April 2019, <https://www.vox.com/the-highlight/2019/4/16/18287446/incel-definition-reddit>

75 Subedar, Anisa and Yates, Will, 'The disturbing YouTube videos that are tricking children', *BBC News*, 27 March 2017, <https://www.bbc.com/news/blogs-trending-39381889>

76 Scarr, Lanai, 'Parents warned of Peppa Pig YouTube horror show', *Sunshine Coast Daily*, 18 August 2018, <https://www.sunshinecoastdaily.com.au/news/parents-warned-of-distorted-peppa-pig-youtube-kids/3496354/>

77 Bridle, James, 'Something is wrong on the internet', *Medium*, 7 November 2017, <https://medium.com/@jamesbridle/something-is-wrong-on-the-internet-c39c471271d2>

78 Roose, Kevin and Conger, Kate, 'YouTube to Remove Thousands of Videos Oushing Extreme Views', *The New York Times*, 5 June 2019, <https://www.nytimes.com/2019/06/05/business/youtube-remove-extremist-videos.html>

79 Roose, Kevin, 'The Making of a YouTube Radical', *The New York Times*, 8 June 2019, <https://www.nytimes.com/interactive/2019/06/08/technology/youtube-radical.html>

80 Fisher, Max and Taub, Amanda, 'How YouTube Radicalized Brazil', *The New York Times*, 11 August 2019, <https://www.nytimes.com/2019/08/11/world/americas/youtube-brazil.html>; see also Max Fisher's thread on Twitter from 12 August 2019, <https://twitter.com/Max_Fisher/status/1160955826233913347>

81 Internet Live Stats, 'Total number of websites', Internet Live Stats, July 2019, <https://www.internetlivestats.com/total-number-of-websites/>

82 Moye, David, 'Fake Photos of Trump Rescuing Flood Victims Goes Viral', *The Huffington Post*, 25 September 2018, <https://www.huffingtonpost.in/entry/fake-news-trump-flood-victims_n_5ba9419fe4b0375f8f9fa5f2>; Fernando, Gavin, 'Trump supporters are sharing these photos of his Hurricane Florence efforts. There's just one problem', *News.com.au*, 25 September 2018, <https://www.news.com.au/technology/online/social/trump-supporters-are-sharing-these-photos-of-his-hurricane-florence-efforts-theres-just-one-problem/news-story/6671825ad4ccb1d49a2833a746703d2d>

83 Leslie, Tim et al, 'Can you tell a fake video from a real one?', *ABC News*, 3 October 2018, <https://www.abc.net.au/news/2018-09-27/fake-news-part-one/10308638>

84 Park, Sora et al, *Digital News Report: Australia 2018*, University of Canberra, June 2018, p 28, <https://apo.org.au/sites/default/files/resource-files/2018/06/apo-nid174861-1241946.pdf>

85 Notley, Tanya and Dezuanni, Michael, 'Most young Australians can't identify fake news online', *The Conversation*, 20 November 2017, <https://theconversation.com/most-young-australians-cant-identify-fake-news-online-87100>; Notley, Tanya et al, *News and Australian Children: How Young People Access, Perceive and are Affected by the News*, Western Sydney University, Queensland University of Technology and Crinkling News, 2017, p 7, <https://www.westernsydney.edu.au/__data/assets/pdf_file/0009/1331847/EMBARGOED_to_Monday,_November_20,_2017._News_and_Australian_Children,_How_Young_People_Access,_Perceive_and_are_Affected_by_the_News-small1.pdf>

86 Oaten, James, 'Catching a catfish', *ABC News*, 6 June 2019, <https://mobile.abc.net.au/news/2019-04-09/lincoln-lewis-fake-catfish-internet-stalker-court-trial/10919538?pfmredir=sm>

87 Oaten, James, 'Catching a catfish', *ABC News*, 6 June 2019, <https://mobile.abc.net.au/news/2019-04-09/lincoln-lewis-fake-catfish-internet-stalker-court-trial/10919538?pfmredir=sm>

88   Marr, Bernard, 'How Much Data Do We Create Every Day? The Mind-Blowing Stats Everyone Should Read', *Forbes*, 21 May 2018, <https://www.forbes.com/sites/bernardmarr/2018/05/21/how-much-data-do-we-create-every-day-the-mind-blowing-stats-everyone-should-read/#18717aa660ba>; DOMO, 'Data Never Sleeps 5.0', DOMO, 2017, <https://www.domo.com/learn/data-never-sleeps-5?aid=ogsm072517_1&sf100871281=1>

89   Leetaru, Kalev, 'Social Media Companies Collect So Much Data Even They Can't Remember All The Ways They Surveil Us', *Forbes*, 25 October 2018, <https://www.forbes.com/sites/kalevleetaru/2018/10/25/social-media-companies-collect-so-much-data-even-they-cant-remember-all-the-ways-they-surveil-us/#45e2f6337d0b>

90   The Economist, 'The World's most valuable resource is no longer oil, but data', *The Economist*, 6 May 2017, <https://www.economist.com/leaders/2017/05/06/the-worlds-most-valuable-resource-is-no-longer-oil-but-data>

91   OnAudience, *Global Data Market Size: 2017–2019*, August 2018, *OnAudience.com*, p 4, <https://www.onaudience.com/resources/wp-content/uploads/2018/09/OnAudience.com_Global_Data_Market_Size_2017-2019-1.pdf>; Goldhill, Olivia, 'How big data got so powerful', *Quartz*, 8 July 2019, <https://qz.com/1656462/how-companies-use-big-data-to-profit-from-your-personal-info/>; Parietti, Melissa, 'The Top 10 Technology Companies', *Investopedia*, 29 September 2019, <https://www.investopedia.com/articles/markets/030816/worlds-top-10-technology-companies-aapl-googl.asp>

92   Leetaru, Kalev, 'Social Media Companies Collect So Much Data Even They Can't Remember All The Ways They Surveil Us', *Forbes*, 25 October 2018, <https://www.forbes.com/sites/kalevleetaru/2018/10/25/social-media-companies-collect-so-much-data-even-they-cant-remember-all-the-ways-they-surveil-us/#45e2f6337d0b>

93   Tiku, Nitasha, 'Get Ready for the Next Big Privacy Backlash Against Facebook', *Wired*, 21 May 2017, <https://www.wired.com/2017/05/welcome-next-phase-facebook-backlash/>; The Australian, 'Facebook targets 'insecure' kids, *The Australian*, 1 May 2017, http://www.theaustralian.com.au/business/media/digital/facebook-targets-insecure-young-people-to-sell-ads/news-story/a89949ad016eee7d7a61c3c30c909fa6; Levin, Sam, 'Facebook told advertisers it can identify teens feeling "insecure" and "worthless"', *The Guardian*, 2 May 2017, <https://www.theguardian.com/technology/2017/may/01/facebook-advertising-data-insecure-teens>

94 Leetaru, Kalev, 'Social Media Companies Collect So Much Data Even They Can't Remember All The Ways They Surveil Us', *Forbes*, 25 October 2018, <https://www.forbes.com/sites/kalevleetaru/2018/10/25/social-media-companies-collect-so-much-data-even-they-cant-remember-all-the-ways-they-surveil-us/#45e2f6337d0b>; Hill, Kashmir, 'Facebook Is Giving Advertisers Access To Your Shadow Contact Information', *Gizmodo*, 27 September 2018, <https://www.gizmodo.com.au/2018/09/facebook-is-giving-advertisers-access-to-your-shadow-contact-information/>

95 Kramer, Adam et al, 'Experimental evidence of massive-scale emotional contagion through social networks', *Proceedings of the National Academy of Sciences of the United States of America*, Volume 111, Issue 24, June 2014, pp 8788–8790, <https://www.ncbi.nlm.nih.gov/pmc/articles/PMC4066473/>;Meyer, Michelle, 'Everything You Need to Know About Facebook's Controversial Emotion Experiment', *Wired*, 30 June 2014, <https://www.wired.com/2014/06/everything-you-need-to-know-about-facebooks-manipulative-experiment/>

96 Marr, Bernard, 'How Much Data Do We Create Every Day? The Mind-Blowing Stats Everyone Should Read', *Forbes*, 21 May 2018, <https://www.forbes.com/sites/bernardmarr/2018/05/21/how-much-data-do-we-create-every-day-the-mind-blowing-stats-everyone-should-read/#18717aa660ba>

97 *Download This Show*, 'How much do you value your privacy?', ABC Radio National, 5 July 2019, <https://www.abc.net.au/radionational/programs/downloadthisshow/how-much-do-you-value-your-privacy/11234280>

98 Macaulay, Tom, 'What is the right to be forgotten, how is it enforced under GDPR and what do businesses need to do?', Computerworld, 14 September 2017, <https://www.computerworld.com/article/3427492/what-is-the-right-to-be-forgotten--how-is-it-enforced-under-gdpr-and-what-do-businesses-need-to-do-.html>; See also, General Data Protection Regulation, European Union, 'Key Issues: GDPR—Right to be Forgotten', <https://gdpr-info.eu/issues/right-to-be-forgotten/>

99 Wylie, Brooke, 'Instagramming tweens "brand-managing" themselves with multiple accounts', *ABC News*, 18 March 2018, <https://www.abc.net.au/news/2018-03-18/instagramming-tweens-brand-managing-themselves/9557170>

100 Marr, Bernard, 'How Much Data Do We Create Every Day? The Mind-Blowing Stats Everyone Should Read', *Forbes*, 21 May 2018, <https://www.forbes.com/sites/bernardmarr/2018/05/21/how-much-data-do-we-create-every-day-the-mind-blowing-stats-everyone-should-read/#18717aa660ba>

101 Johnston, Matt, 'Sydney Uni researchers uncover 2000 fake apps on Google Play store', IT News, 24 June 2019, <https://www.itnews.com.au/news/sydney-uni-researchers-uncover-2000-fake-apps-on-google-play-store-527194>

102 Gibbs, Samuel, 'Apple's Tim Cook: "I don't want my nephew on a social network"', The Guardian, 20 January 2018, <https://www.theguardian.com/technology/2018/jan/19/tim-cook-i-dont-want-my-nephew-on-a-social-network>

103 Bilton, Nick, 'Steve Jobs Was a Low-Tech Parent', The New York Times, 10 September 2014, <https://www.nytimes.com/2014/09/11/fashion/steve-jobs-apple-was-a-low-tech-parent.html?module=inline>

104 Gates, Melinda, 'Melinda Gates: I spent my career in technology. I wasn't prepared for its effect on my kids', The Washington Post, 24 August 2017, <https://www.washingtonpost.com/news/parenting/wp/2017/08/24/melinda-gates-i-spent-my-career-in-technology-i-wasnt-prepared-for-its-effect-on-my-kids/>

105 Henriques-Gomes, Luke, 'Victoria to ban mobile phones in all state primary and secondary schools', The Guardian, 25 June 2019, <https://www.theguardian.com/australia-news/2019/jun/25/victoria-to-ban-mobile-phones-in-all-state-primary-and-secondary-schools>

106 eSafety Commissioner, 'eSafety parents and carers', Office of the eSafety Commissioner, <https://www.esafety.gov.au/parents/skills-advice/are-they-old-enough>

107 Calixto, Julia, 'Primary schools across the Australia [sic] have begun teaching students how to computer code', SBS News, 10 March 2015, <https://www.sbs.com.au/news/computer-coding-classes-in-aussie-primary-schools>

108 Kamenetz, Anya, 'Can Screens Help Your Child's Brain? 4 Tips To Get the Most From Kids' Media', National Public Radio, United States, 24 June 2019, <https://www.npr.org/2019/06/20/734494867/the-brighter-side-of-screen-time

109 Kamenetz, Anya, 'Can Screens Help Your Child's Brain? 4 Tips To Get the Most From Kids' Media', National Public Radio, United States, 24 June 2019, <https://www.npr.org/2019/06/20/734494867/the-brighter-side-of-screen-time>

Mastering the trapeze

1 ABC News, 'MasterChef smashes ratings record', ABC News, 26 July 2010, <https://www.abc.net.au/news/2010-07-26/masterchef-smashes-ratings-record/918950>

2   Liaw, Adam, 'Adam Liaw: How fatherhood has changed me for the better', *Sydney Morning Herald*, 2 September 2018, <https://www.smh.com.au/lifestyle/life-and-relationships/adam-liaw-how-fatherhood-has-changed-me-for-the-better-20180829-p500fv.html>

9   Being with women

1   Jenkins, Kate, 'National Press Club: Everyone's Business: 2018 Sexual Harassment Survey', Australian Human Rights Commission, 12 September 2018, <https://www.humanrights.gov.au/about/news/speeches/national-press-club-everyones-business-2018-sexual-harassment-survey>; Jenkins, Kate, '#MeToo momentum on sexual harassment a powerful catalyst for change', *Sydney Morning Herald*, 4 October 2018, <https://www.smh.com.au/lifestyle/life-and-relationships/metoo-momentum-on-sexual-harassment-a-powerful-catalyst-for-change-20181004-p507pj.html>

2   North, Anna et al, 'Kevin Spacey is one of 263 celebrities, politicians, CEOs, and others who have been accused of sexual misconduct since April 2017', *Vox*, 9 January 2019, <https://www.vox.com/a/sexual-harassment-assault-allegations-list/kevin-spacey>

3   Mumford, Gwilym, 'Actor Terry Crews: I was sexually assaulted by Hollywood Executive', *The Guardian*, 12 October 2017, <https://www.theguardian.com/film/2017/oct/11/actor-terry-crews-sexually-assaulted-by-hollywood-executive>

4   Australian Institute of Health and Welfare, *Family, domestic and sexual violence in Australia*, AIHW, 2018, p ix, <https://www.aihw.gov.au/getmedia/d1a8d479-a39a-48c1-bbe2-4b27c7a321e0/aihw-fdv-02.pdf.aspx?inline=true>

5   Younger, Emma, 'When police misjudge domestic violence, victims are slapped with intervention order applications', *ABC News*, 15 August 2018, <https://www.abc.net.au/news/2018-08-15/domestic-violence-victims-mistaken-for-perpetrators/10120240>

6   Beres, Derek, 'Women fear violence. Men? Ridicule', *Big Think*, 3 April 2019, <https://bigthink.com/personal-growth/amy-schumer?rebelltitem=3#rebelltitem3>

7   Baker, Nick, '"Enough is Enough": Courtney Herron is the 20th woman to be killed in Australia this year', *SBS News*, 27 May 2019, <https://www.sbs.com.au/news/enough-is-enough-courtney-herron-is-the-20th-woman-to-be-killed-in-australia-this-year>

8   Australia's National Resource Organisation for Women's Safety Limited, *Young Australians' attitudes to violence against women and*

gender equality: Findings from the 2017 National Community Attitudes towards Violence Against Women Survey (NCAS), ANROWS Insights, Issue 01, 2019, pp 26–27, <https://ncas.anrows.org.au/wp-content/uploads/2019/05/2017NCAS-Youth-SubReport.pdf>; Voloder, Dubravka, 'One in three young Australian men believe "rape victims; led men on and regretted it"', *SBS News*, 22 May 2019, <https://www.sbs.com.au/news/one-in-three-australian-men-believe-rape-victims-just-regretted-consensual-sex>; Oppenheim, Maya, 'One in three young men believe rape victims actually just regret consensual sex, study in Australia says', *The Independent*, 22 May 2019, <https://www.independent.co.uk/news/world/australasia/rape-australia-sex-violence-women-consent-relationships-survey-a8925251.html>

9   Baidawi, Adam, 'Henry Cavill On His Life Lessons: "Your Head Can be Messed With, But It's Down to Me to Deal With That"', *GQ*, 10 July 2018, <https://www.gq.com.au/entertainment/celebrity/henry-cavill/image-gallery/faed7f272f09bdf899c92b63a7149cba?pos=14>

10 BBC Entertainment, 'Henry Cavill: Actor apologises after #MeToo rape backlash', *BBC News*, 13 July 2018, <https://www.bbc.com/news/entertainment-arts-44819116>

11 SimilarWeb, 'Pornhub.com: September 2019 Overview', SimilarWeb, 2019, <https://www.similarweb.com/website/pornhub.com#overview>

12 Megan, S.C. Lim et al, 'Young Australians' use of pornography and associations with sexual risk behaviours', *Australian and New Zealand Journal of Public* Health, 2017, p 3, <https://www.burnet.edu.au/system/asset/file/2649/Pornography_ANZJPH_paper.pdf>

13 Megan, S.C. Lim et al, 'Young Australians' use of pornography and associations with sexual risk behaviours', *Australian and New Zealand Journal of Public* Health, 2017, p 4, <https://www.burnet.edu.au/system/asset/file/2649/Pornography_ANZJPH_paper.pdf>

14 Quadara, Antonia et al, 'The effects of pornography in children and young people—Research Summary', Australian Institute of Family Studies, December 2017, <https://aifs.gov.au/publications/effects-pornography-children-and-young-people-snapshot>

15 Blum, Steven, 'This Guy Gets Paid to Study Gay Porn', *VICE*, 29 September 2017, <https://www.vice.com/en_ca/article/wjxpjx/this-guy-gets-paid-to-study-gay-porn>; Whitfield, T.H.F. et al, 'Viewing Sexually Explicit Media and Its Association with Mental Health Among Gay and Bisexual Men Across the U.S.', *Archives of Sexual Behavior*, Volume 47, Issue 4, May 2018, pp 1163–1172, <https://www.ncbi.nlm.nih.gov/pubmed/28884272>

16 Chatel, Amanda, '8 Places to Watch Ethical Porn That Focuses On Female Pleasure, According To A Feminist Pornographer', *Bustle*, 19 May 2018, <https://www.bustle.com/p/8-places-to-watch-ethical-porn-that-focuses-on-female-pleasure-according-to-a-feminist-pornographer-9108930>

17 Landripet, I. and Štulhofer, A., 'Is Pornography Use Associated with Sexual Difficulties and Dysfunctions among Younger Heterosexual Men?', *The Journal of Sexual Medicine*, Volume 12, Issue 5, May 2015, pp 1136–1139, <https://www.ncbi.nlm.nih.gov/pubmed/25816904>

18 Taylor, Kris, 'A Few Hard Truths about Porn and Erectile Dysfunction', *VICE*, 24 April 2017, <https://www.vice.com/en_nz/article/mgy9pp/a-few-hard-truths-about-porn-and-erectile-dysfunction>; Prause, Nicole and Pfaus, James, 'Viewing Sexual Stimuli Associated with Greater Sexual Responsiveness, Not Erectile Dysfunction', *Sexual Medicine,* Volume 3, Issue 2, June 2015, pp 90–98, <https://onlinelibrary.wiley.com/doi/full/10.1002/sm2.58>; Landripet, I. and Štulhofer, A., 'Is Pornography Use Associated with Sexual Difficulties and Dysfunctions among Younger Heterosexual Men?', *The Journal of Sexual Medicine*, Volume 12, Issue 5, May 2015, pp 1136–1139, <https://www.ncbi.nlm.nih.gov/pubmed/25816904>

19 Ciarrochi, Joseph, 'Nice guys finish first: empathetic boys attract more close female friends', *The Conversation*, 16 June 2016, <https://theconversation.com/nice-guys-finish-first-empathetic-boys-attract-more-close-female-friends-60783>

20 Lee, Murray et al, *Sexting among young people: Perceptions and practices*, Australian Institute of Criminology, 9 December 2015, <https://aic.gov.au/publications/tandi/tandi508>; Agnew, Elizabeth, 'Teenage sexting: we're letting young people down by not talking about it', *The Conversation*, 12 December 2018, <https://theconversation.com/teenage-sexting-were-letting-young-people-down-by-not-talking-about-it-107054>

21 Schetzer, Alana, 'Revenge porn: what to do if you're a victim', *SBS News*, 14 September 2018, <https://www.sbs.com.au/topics/life/culture/article/2017/08/01/revenge-porn-what-do-if-youre-victim>

22 Australian Associated Press, 'New revenge porn laws boost jail time to seven years', *Sydney Morning Herald*, 15 August 2018, <https://www.smh.com.au/politics/federal/new-revenge-porn-laws-boost-jail-time-to-seven-years-20180815-p4zxpv.html>

10 A final ride in the DeLorean

1 Petre, Daniel, *Father Time*, Ventura Press, Sydney, 2016.

INDEX

INDEX

Perpetual Guardian 87
Petre, Daniel 242–3
Pink Shirt Day 161, 174
Plooij, Frans 53
Polynesia 101
porn 225–8, 232, 238
postnatal depression 9, 43
puberty 113, 116–18

Quinn, Zoe 192, 196

rape 128, 227
Rees, Jimmy 65
Roosevelt, Franklin Delano 160–1
Roy Morgan 166

same-sex marriage 215
same-sex parents 13, 41
Samoa 101
Sarkeesian, Anita 192–3
schizophrenia, early onset 105–6
school 111–13, 205
sex *see also* gender
  biological 99
  casual 234–5
  consent 232–3
  healthy attitude towards 226
  respectful view 223–4
sexism 127, 128, 235–6
sexting 232
sexual harassment 182, 219, 220
sexuality 215
Shakeshift, Bernie 150–2
sharing 139–40
Sheldon, Tony 30–2
single parents 13
social media 185–6, 199–202
  see also internet and technology
Spacey, Kevin 220
sport 166–9

suicide 9, 145, 176, 182
Sweden 68, 102, 164

teenagers *see* adolescence
testosterone 105, 116–17
  see also hormones
toys 163–6
transgender 99, 100, 101
trauma, intergenerational 25, 105
Trump, Donald 197
Twitch 189–90

United Kingdom 165, 169–70
United States 190, 192
University of California 163–4
University of New South Wales
  Social Policy Research Centre
  182
University of Sydney 203
University of Western Sydney
  163–4

van de Rijt, Hetty 53
Vaughn, Robert 171
video gaming 187–93

White Ribbon Canada 128–9
Wight, Clark 96, 130, 131
women
  breadwinner role 41, 69
  consensual behavior towards 221
  incel community and 193–4
  men and, power imbalance
    between 219
  online gaming and 191–2
  rejection by 219, 220, 231
  relationships with 214
    casual 234–5
    platonic 229–230
    romantic 230–3